A National Repertoire

Britische und Irische Studien
zur deutschen Sprache und Literatur

British and Irish Studies
in German Language and Literature

Etudes britanniques et irlandaises
sur la langue et la littérature allemandes

Edited by H.S. Reiss and W.E. Yates

Band 42

PETER LANG

Oxford · Bern · Berlin · Bruxelles · Frankfurt/M. · New York · Wien

A National Repertoire

Schiller, Iffland and
the German Stage

Lesley Sharpe

PETER LANG

Oxford · Bern · Berlin · Bruxelles · Frankfurt/M. · New York · Wien

Bibliographic information published by Die Deutsche Bibliothek
Die Deutsche Bibliothek lists this publication in the Deutsche
Nationalbibliografie; detailed bibliographic data is available on the
Internet at ‹http://dnb.ddb.de›.

British Library and Library of Congress Cataloguing-in-Publication Data:
A catalogue record for this book is available from *The British Library,*
Great Britain, and from *The Library of Congress,* USA

ISSN 0171-6662
ISBN 978-3-03910-714-8

© Peter Lang AG, International Academic Publishers, Bern 2007
Hochfeldstrasse 32, Postfach 746, CH-3000 Bern 9, Switzerland
info@peterlang.com, www.peterlang.com, www.peterlang.net

Printed in Germany

Contents

List of illustrations

1. The Mannheim National Theatre as designed by Lorenzo Quaglio, from an engraving by Ignaz Klauber, reproduced from E.L. Stahl, *Das Europäische Mannheim. Die Wege zum deutschen Nationaltheater* (Mannheim: Hakenkreuzbanner-Verlag, 1940).
2. Title page of A.W. Iffland's *Dramatische Werke* (Leipzig: Göschen, 1798) with portrait.
3. Title page of *Die Räuber ein Trauerspiel von Friedrich Schiller* (Mannheim: Schwan, 1782).
4. 'Ich werde unsinnig, ich laufe davon!' (*Die Räuber. Ein Schauspiel*, Act 2, Scene 3). From a set of six etchings by Daniel Chodowiecki, reproduced from Jens Heiner Bauer, *Daniel Nikolaus Chodowiecki. Das druckgraphische Werk* (Hanover: Verlag Galeric Bauer, 1982).
5. The Weimar Court Theatre after its reconstruction by Thouret. Reproduced from Adolf Doebber, *Lauchstädt und Weimar. Eine theatergeschichtliche Studie* (Berlin: Mittler, 1908).
6. *Wallensteins Lager*: engraving by Christian Müller from the painting by Georg Melchior Kraus.
7. Iffland as Wallenstein, reproduced from Heinrich Härle, *Ifflands Schauspielkunst: ein Rekonstruktionsversuch auf Grund der etwa 500 Zeichnungen und Kupferstiche Wilhelm Henschels und seiner Brüder* (Berlin: Elsner, 1925).
8. Friederike Bethmann-Unzelmann as Maria Stuart, reproduced from A.W. Iffland (ed.) *Kostüme auf dem Königlichen National-Theater in Berlin*, vol. 2 (Berlin: Wittich, 1808).
9. 'Der Krönungszug, in dem Schauspiel: Die Jungfrau von Orléans. Sr. Wohlgebornen dem Herrn Direktor Iffland hochachtungsvoll zugeeignet von den Herausgebern': etching by Friedrich Jügel from a drawing by Heinrich Anton Dähling. Reproduced from Helmut Börsch-Supan, *Karl Friedrich Schinkel – Bühnenentwürfe* (Berlin: Ernst & Sohn, 1990).

10. *Die Braut von Messina*: etching by Christian Müller from a painting by Friedrich Matthäi.

Preface

In 1780 the German theatre repertoire contained almost no German plays more than twenty years old. In 1800 the situation was similar; few plays enjoyed more than ten years' life on the stage and were quickly replaced by others. By 1820, however, things were changing. The German theatre was acquiring what might be called a national repertoire, in other words a (still relatively small) stock of plays that, as part of a mixed repertoire, theatres could offer the more demanding sections of their public and which could stand alongside the classic dramas of other nations and thus have a representative function for an artistically ambitious theatre. The plays of Friedrich Schiller were the cornerstone of that emerging repertoire, for though only nine in number (counting *Wallenstein* as one) they were in the 1820s all being performed at one time or another at theatres across Germany. Indeed the frequency of performances increased in the course of the nineteenth century (see Appendix). Plays by Lessing and Goethe, though less frequently performed, also belonged to this emerging repertoire.

This study investigates how the constantly changing circumstances of the German stage in the later eighteenth and early nineteenth centuries gave rise to this repertoire. In particular it focuses on two key figures, Schiller himself and his now largely disregarded contemporary, the actor and dramatist August Wilhelm Iffland (1759–1814), and on the three theatres – in Mannheim, Weimar and Berlin – with which they were principally associated. As an actor Iffland was a rising star at the Mannheim National Theatre at the time (1783–84) when Schiller was its resident playwright. As a budding playwright himself, Iffland's keen sense of popular taste and readiness to continue the stage trend away from tragedy, particularly high tragedy, towards bourgeois drama in a contemporary setting marked him out for rapid success. In spite of the instant sensation of the première of *Die Räuber*, Schiller's struggle to establish himself at Mannheim as a stage writer was beset with difficulties, and his hopes there finally dashed by Iffland's rapid ascendancy. When he left Mannheim in 1785 he was turning his back not on drama but on the stage. Yet when he returned to writing plays in the later 1790s it was Iffland, now director of the Berlin National Theatre, who vigorously pursued a policy of giving his plays lavish productions. Many other theatres followed suit and in his last years Schiller enjoyed success as a stage writer to an extent he could never have anticipated, a success achieved in significant measure through the agency of his erstwhile rival. The lasting effects of that strange symbiosis are evident in the German repertoire to this day. It is, in short, one of the key relationships in German theatre history.

Critical writing on Schiller's dramas and on literary drama in general in the eighteenth century has often placed them within a literary narrative that stands apart from theatre trends and the cultural politics of particular theatres. The dramatic development that forms part of it often leaves out of account an evolving repertoire of largely forgotten, yet in their time very popular, plays. The dramas of the *Sturm und Drang* for instance, were rarely performed. Goethe's most popular stage work was his libretto *Erwin und Elmire*. The bulk of writing for the stage came not from literary but from theatre people, who produced above all comedies and librettos for *Singspiele*. Much of the repertoire was translated from French, English and Italian sources. By the 1770s and 1780s tragedy seemed to be in terminal decline. One of the aims of this study is to bridge this gap, at least as far as Schiller's dramas are concerned, between literary and theatre history.

Schiller is an unusual case in his time in being a dramatist with literary ambitions who made an instant and sustained impact as a stage writer. In the case of his early plays in particular, the stage context provides not merely anecdotal background to the production of dramatic texts but is a vital shaping force. Yet though he had an instinctive feel for the stage, Schiller had an uneasy relationship with the practical realm of theatre. In his early twenties his literary aspirations, an imaginative richness he found hard to control, a restless need to experiment (intensified by the impact of *Sturm und Drang* drama) and a tendency to bombast combined to make his plays simultaneously fascinating and problematic for the theatre. Though after *Don Karlos* he ceased writing plays for more than a decade, he was still a

10

regularly, if not frequently, performed dramatist. His early setbacks at Mannheim made him later at times unwilling to make concessions to the stage. While exploiting certain contemporary trends (particularly an increased demand for stage spectacle), his plays from *Wallenstein* to *Die Braut von Messina* also (for example by their tragic intensity and use of verse) defy the dominant taste for domestic drama with a happy ending. Yet his uncompromising belief in high art and contempt for popular stage works mellowed somewhat in his last years into a more pragmatic attitude to the staging of his own plays. *Wilhelm Tell*, one of his most popular works and one that avoids a tragic ending, would not have been written if he had not been alive to the debt he owed Iffland for the latter's commitment to his plays.

The story told here about Iffland is a largely unfamiliar one. His career falls into two main phases, the Mannheim period (1779–96) and the Berlin period (1796–1814). Skilfully judging the tastes and mood of contemporary theatre-goers, as well as the priorities of the Mannheim National Theatre, Iffland rapidly became the most popular and most performed dramatist from the late 1780s to the mid-1790s, thereafter sharing that honour with his even more prolific fellow dramatist August von Kotzebue. His family dramas, and the wave of imitations they brought forth, seemed to proclaim the end of high tragedy as a viable art form in performance, and their success emphasized the extent to which most of Schiller's plays ran counter to popular trends. Unlike him, Iffland had no pretensions to be a literary dramatist or to do more than write readily performable and entertaining plays with good dialogue, which gave him an opportunity to display his talents as a character actor. The didactic purpose he occasionally claimed for himself must be taken with a pinch of salt as catering for the penchant for moralizing among some sections of the public. His acting career is marked by a clear awareness of the need for professionalism as a means of securing success and also the social acceptance he craved. For him Goethe's and Schiller's distinction between literary drama as high art and merely transitory popular entertainment ignored the fact that acting itself was an art that could elevate and refine the play and its audience. His promotion of Schiller's dramas when he took over as director at the Berlin National Theatre sprang arguably less from any idealistic aim to make the stage more literary

11

than from a shrewd calculation of what the necessary ingredients were to secure the success of the theatre in a city such as Berlin. This study highlights Iffland's achievements as director, arguing that they, rather than his plays or his acting (the latter being for him the primary activity), constitute his lasting legacy to the German stage.

The theatres with which I am chiefly concerned, and others to which I allude, are mainly subsidized theatres. In the case of Mannheim, Weimar and Berlin that subsidy, which came from the ruler, varied from about 30% to as little as 10% of the running costs and so was by no means sufficient to free the theatres from commercial pressures. This continuing negotiation between commercial viability and artistic ambition, between popular success and literary value, is one of the recurring themes of this book. It does not therefore extend its range to cover the growth in this period of purely commercial theatre as entertainment, the great centre for which was the leading theatre city of the German-speaking world, namely Vienna. Austria's national theatre, the Burgtheater, was, however, an important example to the German theatre world and is mentioned at various points.

One of the prerequisites of a study such as this one is information regarding what was played at the various theatres it focuses on. It has been my aim to incorporate precise figures and statistics as much as possible, in order to demonstrate the impact of changing circumstances (for example, audience preferences, declining subventions, the upheavals of war, political sensitivities) on an environment as volatile as the theatre. Additional detail is contained in the Appendix. I have also included a glossary of frequently used German terms for which there is no satisfactory English equivalent.

Another prerequisite is that the reader should have a clear picture of the German theatre on which Schiller and Iffland made their first impact in the early 1780s. While some, indeed much, of the Introduction may be familiar to theatre specialists, for the sake of those approaching the book from a literary background I considered it important to begin with an account of the forces shaping the theatre world in the second half of the eighteenth century.

Acknowledgements

It is a pleasure to record my thanks to the many individuals and funding bodies that have supported the writing of this book. The Alexander von Humboldt-Stiftung generously allowed me take up my research fellowship for a final three months in 2003, which I spent at the Forschungsinstitut für Musiktheater, University of Bayreuth, and I am grateful to Professor Sieghart Döring and Professor Thomas Betzwieser for their help and advice during that time. The Arts and Humanities Research Council funded an extra semester's study leave in 2007 and the British Academy, through its Small Grants scheme, made possible a number of research visits to Germany in 2002, 2005 and 2006. The Department of Modern Languages at Exeter contributed to publication costs. I am also grateful to my former colleagues at the University of Bristol and to my present ones at Exeter for shouldering additional burdens when I was absent on study leave.

I should particularly like to thank the staff of the Deutsches Literaturarchiv, Marbach, for their unstinting help over the many years I have worked there. Professor Norbert Oellers very kindly gave me generous access to the remarkable Sammlung Oscar Fambach at the University of Bonn. I also benefited from the helpfulness and engagement of librarians and archivists at the Thüringisches Hauptstaatsarchiv, the Herzogin Anna Amalia Bibliothek and the Goethe- und Schiller-Archiv in Weimar, at the Preußisches Geheimes Staatsarchiv, the Stiftung Archiv der Akademie der Künste and at the Staatsbibliothek in Berlin, and at the theatre archive of the Reiss-Engelhorn Museums in Mannheim.

I owe a special debt to Dr James Baughan, whose interest in this project has been a constant support and inspiration. He read every chapter meticulously as it was written and then the entire manuscript, offering much detailed (and entertaining) comment, standing by with technical advice and helping to prepare the index. While on an administrative work placement at Exeter Jenny Fuchs expertly prepared a repertoire based on information drawn from the web 'Datenbank Berliner Nationaltheater', which was an invaluable resource. The editors of this series, Professor Hans Reiss and Professor W.E. Yates, took great pains over reading the manuscript and gave me numerous perceptive suggestions. Julie Crocker skilfully prepared the camera-ready copy. Finally, my husband, Jeremy Noakes, read all the chapters, helped prepare the bibliography and index, advised me on some historical matters and on occasions accompanied me on research visits (and also puzzled with me over Iffland's handwriting). I owe an immeasurable amount to his patience and encouragement.

Abbreviations

References to Schiller's and Goethe's works are inserted in the main text, using the abbreviations below followed by volume and page numbers. The primary Schiller edition used is the *Nationalausgabe* and the primary Goethe edition the *Münchner Ausgabe*, supplemented where appropriate by other standard editions.

NA   *Schillers Werke. Nationalausgabe*, ed. by Julius Petersen and others, 42 vols (Weimar: Hermann Böhlaus Nachfolger, 1943–)

FA   *Schiller, Werke und Briefe*, ed. by Otto Dann and others, 12 vols (Frankfurt am Main: Deutscher Klassiker Verlag, 1988–2004)

BA   *Schiller, Werke und Briefe. Berliner Ausgabe*, ed. by Jochen Golz and others (Berlin: Aufbau Verlag, 2005)

WA   *Goethes Werke. Herausgegeben im Auftrag der Großherzogin Sophie von Sachsen.* Four divisions, 143 vols (Weimar: Böhlau, 1887–1919)

GFA   *Johann Wolfgang Goethe. Sämtliche Werke. Briefe, Tagebücher und Gespräche*, ed. by Hendrik Birus and others, two divisions, 40 vols (Frankfurt am Main: Deutscher Klassiker Verlag, 1987–99)

MA   *Johann Wolfgang Goethe. Sämtliche Werke nach Epochen seines Schaffens. Münchner Ausgabe*, ed. by Karl Richter in collaboration with Herbert Göpfert and other. 21 vols in 30 (Munich: Hanser, 1985–99)

Introduction

The history of German theatre in the eighteenth and early nineteenth century can be summed up as the story of how court and commercial theatre moved towards a closer coexistence. In the first half of the eighteenth century the theatrical scene was diverse and, literally, mobile. There were almost no purpose-built commercial theatre buildings. The purpose-built theatres were almost exclusively court theatres and often located in royal palaces. This circumstance is indicative of the peculiar situation of German political and cultural life in this period. Nominally, the rulers of over three hundred separate states still owed allegiance to the Holy Roman Emperor in Vienna. Among these were large territories such as Austria and Prussia (both with possessions outside the Empire's boundaries as well), and the Electorates of Saxony, Bavaria and the Palatinate. At the other end of the spectrum were tiny states such as Hessen–Homburg (about 40 square miles) or Lichtenstein (about 60 square miles).[1] There were extensive ecclesiastical lands such as the archbishoprics of Cologne, Mainz, Trier and Salzburg and the bishoprics of Bamberg, Würzburg and Münster. There were fifty-one Free Imperial Cities, which were governed not by a prince but by their citizens, among them Frankfurt am Main, Hamburg, Lübeck and Nuremberg. There were Free Imperial Knights, who ruled their often very small territories by authority bestowed directly by the Emperor and resisted incorporation into any larger unit. In such a political landscape there was a huge proliferation of courts, from the modest to the magnificent.

In this court environment, theatre, opera and ballet were not only entertainment but also an indicator of power and prestige and some-

---

1   A survey of the states composing the Holy Roman Empire is given in Appendix 2 of W. II. Bruford, *Germany in the Eighteenth Century* (Cambridge: CUP, 1935), pp. 333–36.

times of political aspirations.[2] Few rulers were able to afford a standing opera – Dresden and Mannheim in the Electorates of Saxony and the Palatinate respectively were examples of capital cities with a standing opera – but elsewhere Italian companies were engaged, as were French ballet companies, to perform for a certain period of time for the court. What the Italian companies performed was *opera seria* and quite a number of rulers strained their states' finances in order to make their mark as patrons of opera on a grand scale. As French was the language spoken at many courts and France carried high cultural prestige, French-language drama was frequently performed there by French companies. Molière, Corneille, Racine, Voltaire and Marivaux were the dramatists prominent in the repertoire. Access to performances for those who were not members of the court aristocracy was restricted. Sometimes non-aristocratic court officials or army officers and members of court musicians' families were admitted.[3] As these opera houses and theatres were frequently integral parts of the ruler's palace (as was the case in Iffland's home city, Hanover) it was difficult to allow access to those outside the court on any regular basis. There was no ticketing system or charge for entry.

German-language theatre was provided by the travelling companies (*Wandertruppen* or *Wanderbühnen*), which, although they could not regularly enjoy the benefits of purpose-built theatres, nevertheless provided a varied repertoire in the towns and cities of the German states. At the head of the company was the so-called *Prinzi-*

---

2   This account draws principally on the following studies: Manfred Brauneck, *Die Welt als Bühne. Geschichte des europäischen Theaters* (Stuttgart, Weimar: Metzler, 1996), vol. 2, pp. 700–863; W. H. Bruford, *Theatre, Drama and Audience in Goethe's Germany* (London: Routledge and Kegan Paul, 1950); Erika Fischer-Lichte, *Kurze Geschichte des deutschen Theaters* (Tübingen and Basel: UTB, 1993), pp. 81–115; Heinz Kindermann, *Theatergeschichte Europas*, vols 4 and 5 (Salzburg: Otto Müller, 1961, 1962); Sibylle Maurer-Schmook, *Deutsches Theater im 18. Jahrhundert* (Tübingen: Niemeyer, 1982); Peter Schmitt, *Schauspieler und Theaterbetrieb. Studien zur Sozialgeschichte des Schauspielerstandes im deutschsprachigen Raum 1700–1900*, Theatron, 5 (Tübingen: Niemeyer, 1990).

3   Because their father was a low-ranking army officer, Schiller and his sister Christophine were as children able to attend Duke Carl Eugen's magnificent Ludwigsburg opera. See Chapter 1, p. 45.

pal, the actor–manager, who normally took most of the financial risk and hence the profits and losses of a very precarious existence. Having no permanent home, companies had to compete for the *Privilegium* or right to perform in a particular city, state or region. If they lost that right or if their audiences, and hence their income, declined they were forced to travel more frequently, with all the attendant expense, discomfort and loss of rehearsal time that travelling entailed. Loss of rehearsal time depressed the standard of performances and thus the esteem in which the companies and the acting profession in general were held. In the absence of purpose-built stages they used whatever public spaces were available: halls, markets, riding schools. From time to time they would be invited to play for a period at a court that had no standing theatre of its own. On three occasions, for example, renowned travelling companies were contracted by the ruler or regent to play at the palace theatre in Weimar: Carl Theophil Doebbelin's company played from 1756 to 1758, the contract ending when Duke Ernst August Constantin died suddenly; Gottfried Heinrich Koch's company then played in Weimar at the invitation of his widow, Duchess Anna Amalia, from 1768 to 1771, followed by the Seyler–Ekhof company from 1771 to 1774. When the ducal palace suffered a fire that destroyed the theatre, Anna Amalia found a home for the company at the nearby court of Gotha, and after a year, in 1775, the first court theatre that was the product of an alliance of the ruler and a travelling company playing in the German language was born.

Theatre buildings

Court theatres varied greatly in size, from the capacity of the Burgtheater in Vienna at about 1350 seats to that of the little Gotha court theatre at about 300. The larger theatres were constructed as *Logentheater*, which consisted of ascending tiers of boxes. Directly opposite the stage in an elevated position was usually the *Fürstenloge*, which was reserved for the ruler and his family. The seating arrangements generally were less the product of the need to see and hear the performance than to see and be seen by other significant members of the court. Typically, in a larger theatre the stalls were reserved for the nobility, with boxes set aside at higher levels for non-aristocratic spectators. As part of baroque court culture many theatres were thus constructed to reflect the highly stratified nature of German society and the absolutist concept of government that was the norm in states large and small.

The stage of a baroque court theatre was designed in the first instance with the needs of opera in mind and based on developments imported from Italy. Indeed several significant theatres and opera houses in German-speaking Europe were designed by members of the Galli-Bibiena family from Bologna, who were engaged in Prague, Potsdam, Vienna, Dresden and Bayreuth.[4] Baroque opera depended on illusion and spectacle. It was necessary to create stage machinery that allowed for rapid transformations and convincing stage effects: sudden appearances and disappearances, storms on land and at sea, rising and setting suns, *dei ex machina*, to name but the most obvious. The normal baroque stage presented first the proscenium arch, often elaborately decorated, to the audience. It depended for the transformations of sets on pairs of mobile wings (*Kulissen*) set at either side of the stage facing the audience and stretching to the back of the stage in such a way as to create a sense of depth and a realistic perspective. Most *Kulissen* stages had between five and seven pairs of wings. These ran on rollers that fitted into wooden grooves so that the wing could be slid on to the stage or withdrawn as necessary to effect a change of set. Usually this movement was made possible by machinery under the stage. *Kulissen* consisted usually of wooden frames over which painted canvas was stretched. Lamps were often fitted to the back of wings to increase the light supplied by the chandeliers that

---

4   On Bayreuth as an example of baroque theatre design, with a survey of comparable theatres in Europe, see Klaus-Dieter Reus (ed.), *Faszination der Bühne: Barockes Welttheater in Bayreuth, Barocke Bühnentechnik in Europa. Eine Dokumentation der Ausstellung des Grundkurses Theatergeschichte am Gymnasium Christian-Ernestinum, Bayreuth* (Bayreuth: Gymnasium Christian-Ernestinum, 1999).

would hang in front of the proscenium arch. The scene created by the wings was made into a totality by the back curtain, usually a curtain that could be rolled up and down, and by the soffits. These were canvases that hung down above the stage and could be raised and replaced by others. They completed the illusion by, for example, depicting the sky above a pastoral setting or the ceiling of a room, while at the same time concealing the upper stage machinery. It was usually possible to divide the stage by lowering an intermediate curtain so that more intimate scenes could be played at the front of the stage or more elaborate transformations could be prepared for during the performance. The stage itself often sloped upwards towards the back to improve visibility and also to enhance the impact of perspective. Thus wings, soffits and backdrop could be changed within seconds and the scene transformed. This was usually done within full view of the audience, for the main curtain was raised at the start of the performance and did not fall until the end. This emphasis on rapid transformation in opera carried over into stage practice for spoken theatre in so far as it meant that companies used few movable props and little furniture. Travelling companies could not in any case cope with the burdens of moving elaborate props. Nor could they carry with them many sets, which as a result tended to be fairly stereotyped – a landscape, a palace interior, a simple room being typical.

Up to the middle of the eighteenth century *Wandertruppen* based their costumes on contemporary French formal dress, worn regardless of the time-setting or type of play. In the course of the eighteenth century there was a gradual move towards more differentiated and appropriate costumes, which can loosely be grouped as contemporary, Roman/classical and oriental. Naturally, costumes at the court opera houses were more lavish and as the century progressed were sometimes specially designed for particularly prominent productions, as for example in the case of the Berlin National Theatre's productions of Schiller's later dramas under the directorship of Iffland.

Development of the repertoire

In the first half of the eighteenth century the repertoires of the travelling companies consisted of a broad spectrum of plays, many adapted from French, English and Italian sources. Debased versions of the standard English repertoire of the late sixteenth and early seventeenth centuries, including plays by Shakespeare and Marlowe, had their origins in performances by the so-called *englische Komö-dianten*, English companies who toured the German states in the late sixteenth and early seventeenth centuries and whose repertoires were gradually translated and adapted. There was a long tradition in the travelling companies of the use of a scenario as a basis for extemporization, which was a skill vital for actors whose rehearsal time was often minimal. Serious drama usually took the form of the *Haupt- und Staatsaktion,* in which the doings of kings and queens were represented with some pomp, while at intervals comic relief was provided by the traditional comic figure of Hanswurst, the German equivalent to the Italian Harlequin. Comedies, often translated from the French, were performed, as well as pastorals, short comic prologues and afterpieces, all often featuring songs and ballads. *Singspiele* were also given, though they seem to have become less frequent by the 1740s.[5] Thus the travelling companies maintained some tradition of drama with music in the vernacular, which, crude and rudimentary though it was, provided a basis out of which the *Singspiel,* reanimated by English and French influences, could begin to flourish again from the middle of the eighteenth century onwards.

A number of important developments came together in the second half of the eighteenth century to make the theatres with which Schiller and Iffland were associated – Mannheim, Weimar and Berlin – what they were. The first was the tendency for travelling companies to establish themselves in permanent homes and serve both a court and a wider non-aristocratic audience.[6] This tendency did not prevent

---

5   See the comments below on Schönemann's repertoire.
6   On the development of theatre building in the late eighteenth and early nine-teenth century, see Isabel Matthes, *'Der allgemeinen Vereinigung gewidmet':*

new travelling companies from springing up or the courts from engaging foreign performers, but it did mean that some of the most experienced companies had the opportunity to enjoy a more stable existence. This in turn led to the chance to establish a broader repertoire, raise the standard of performances, and with it the status of the acting profession, and thus overcome some of the prejudices against the theatre still prevalent in Protestant regions of Germany in particular. The interests of the travelling companies merged with those of some of the rulers. The Seven Years' War (1756–63) had emptied the coffers of many states and few princes could indulge in the conspicuous consumption that would allow them to keep permanent foreign theatre and opera companies. This circumstance gave a boost to German-language drama and opera, which could be offered on at least a semi-commercial basis.

A further factor was the impetus given by the national theatre movement. For decades playwrights, critics, *Prinzipale*, actors and the culturally engaged intelligentsia had been arguing for the importance of the theatre as an institution.[7] What was needed, it was felt, was a theatre that could draw together the best acting and best dramas of the time and where aesthetic considerations could be given weight as against the box office alone. Not only could such a theatre raise the prestige of German culture, still very much in the shadow of its powerful neighbour, France, but it could act as a channel for enlightened thinking and as a force for cultural cohesion in an Empire where the political system produced fragmentation and conflicts of interest among the many states. Such arguments were rehearsed many times in the course of the eighteenth century, and, gradually, circumstances and conviction came together to produce eventually a limited alliance of the nobility and the performers.

Öffentlicher Theaterbau in Deutschland zwischen Aufklärung und Vormärz (Tübingen: Niemeyer, 1995).

7   A useful collection of German documents translated into English on this subject is George W. Brandt (ed.), *German and Dutch Theatre 1600–1848*, compiled by George W. Brandt and Wiebke Hogendoorn (Cambridge: CUP, 1992). For an excellent overview of the national theatre debate see Roland Krebs, *L'Idée de 'Théâtre National' dans L'Allemagne des Lumières,* Wolfenbütteler Forschungen, 28 (Wiesbaden: Harrassowitz, 1985).

The first national theatre was created in Hamburg in 1767. Gott-hold Ephraim Lessing (1729–81) was its resident critic. But it was founded not on royal patronage (Hamburg was a Free Imperial City) but on the sponsorship of private individuals. The venture collapsed in only two years and one of the leading sponsors, Abel Seyler (1730–1800), a businessman, lost his fortune and was forced to form a travelling company made up of some of the leading Hamburg actors, among them the renowned Conrad Ekhof (1720–78), and embark on the precarious life of a *Prinzipal*. The Hamburg venture demonstrated how much a national theatre needed some kind of guaranteed income from subsidy in order to survive, and this became the pattern for a number of theatres that bore the name of *Nationaltheater* or *Hoftheater* and relied on a combination of box office takings and support from the ruler. In 1776 the Emperor Joseph II elevated one of the two court theatres in Vienna, the Burgtheater, to the status of 'National Theatre', setting a pattern that several significant theatres such as Mannheim and Berlin would follow. The national theatre movement grew from a conviction that German theatre could and should improve both in the quality of performances and in the quality of the material presented.

Spearheading the process of reform of the repertoires of travelling companies was the influential academic and critic Johann Christoph Gottsched (1700–66), who formed an alliance with the leading company of the 1720s and 30s, that of Johann and Caroline Neuber, the latter perhaps the most talented actress of her generation. Gottsched has been unjustly reviled in literary history because of his doctrinaire insistence on the need to imitate classical models in drama and hence his praise for the French neo-classical style. His narrow emphasis on *Regelmäßigkeit* (the strict adherence to classical form and conventions), and a restrictive idea of the natural meant that drama was being forced into an unproductive straightjacket. His influence was destroyed by his own rigidity, and his reputation was dealt a fatal blow by the attacks on him mounted by Lessing, the rising critic of the next generation, who recognized that German drama had to be allowed to experiment in order to flourish. Lessing directed his readers' attention towards English models and also, for example through his translation of Diderot, towards the emerging vogue for the *drame*, the serious play avoiding a tragic ending.[8] But in spite of his limitations, the Leipzig professor made a vital contribution to the development of theatre. His aim was to create a repertoire of German plays and translations that would preserve the legacy of the ancients and thus introduce works of undisputed literary merit to theatre audiences. If such a repertoire were established then the taste of audiences would be raised and the theatre could become the moral and cultural beacon Gottsched wished it to be. He collected the reformed repertoire and subsequently published it in six volumes under the title *Die Deutsche Schaubühne* (1740–45), in order to make it available to other companies and to educate a readership in the expectations they might bring to live theatre. The Neubers, who shared Gottsched's ambition to raise the standard of theatre and the status of the acting profession, collaborated with him in introducing elements of the new repertoire and style in practice. The staging of such plays required the abandonment of extemporization and not only the memorization of fixed texts but the speaking of verse, as the tragedies were all written in alexandrines. Gottsched aimed also at greater authenticity of costume, a practical effect of his concern with naturalness. In accordance with Gottsched's aims, the Neubers even banished Hanswurst ceremoniously from the stage in 1737, though he crept back under other guises, the Neubers needing to maintain their popularity, which by the late 1730s was entering a steady decline.[9]

Gottsched's own attempt at a classical tragedy in alexandrines, *Der sterbende Cato* (1732), was hardly a work to enthuse audiences for high art, and Gottsched himself admitted in the work's preface to cutting and pasting it from English and French sources, but the impulse to reform and improve and to create a German repertoire that

---

8   See *Das Theater des Herrn Diderot*, 2 vols (Leipzig: Voss, 1760).
9   See Lessing's comment in the *Hamburgische Dramaturgie*: 'Seitdem die Neuberin, sub Auspiciis Sr. Magnificenz des Herrn Prof. Gottscheds, den Harlekin öffentlich von ihrem Theater verbannte, haben alle deutsche Bühnen, denen daran gelegen war, regelmäßig zu heißen, dieser Verbannung beizutreten geschienen. Ich sage, geschicnen; denn im Grunde hatten sie nur das bunte Jäckchen und den Namen abgeschafft, aber den Narren behalten' (18. Stück) in *Gotthold Ephraim Lessings Werke und Briefe*, ed. by Wilfried Barner and others, 12 vols (Frankfurt am Main: Deutscher Klassiker Verlag, 1985–2003), vol. 6, p. 270.

would demand higher standards of actors and audiences caught the aspirations of his age and that of subsequent generations. Few German dramatists followed classical models, however, or wrote in alexandrines. The neo-classical drama that was performed was very substantially drawn from the French repertoire, from Corneille, Racine and Voltaire, the very occasional exceptions including the plays of Johann Elias Schlegel (1719–49) and *Panthea,* the sole tragedy written by Gottsched's wife, Luise Adelgunde Viktorie.

An examination of the repertoire of Schönemann's company in the 1740s and 50s gives a useful impression of the changes to actors' and the public's expectations.[10] Johann Friedrich Schönemann began his career with the Neubers in 1730, and in 1740, when they left the German states to travel to Russia, he formed his own company, touring mainly the northern part of Germany from Hamburg as far as Königsberg and with regular seasons in Rostock, Schwerin and Berlin. The publication of Gottsched's *Die Deutsche Schaubühne* made the reformed repertoire available for wider performance and Schönemann took advantage of this. His first performance was of a translation of Racine's *Mithridate.* In his first two years he also staged Gottsched's *Cato* and the latter's translation of Racine's *Iphigénie en Aulide,* Corneille's *Cinna* and *Le Cid,* Voltaire's *Zaïre,* Frau Gottsched's *Panthea* and Thomas Corneille's *Le Comte d' Essex.* Over the next twenty years the proportion of tragedies played declined and the bulk of the repertoire was composed of comedies (predominantly from the French) and prologues and afterpieces. The proportion of extemporized plays was fairly small, if plays listed without attribution to an author is indicative, and the majority of these are prologues and afterpieces. There is only one 'opera', namely the hugely popular and durable adaptation of Charles Coffey's ballad opera *The Devil to Pay* (1731), known in German as *Der Teufel ist los.* Shakespeare had not yet reappeared on the German stage after his original introduction some one hundred and fifty years previously by the *englische Komö-*

---

10   Schönemann's repertoire is printed in Hans Devrient, *Johann Friedrich Schöne-mann und seine Schauspielergesellschaft,* Theatergeschichtliche Forschungen, 11 (Leipzig and Hamburg: Voss, 1895).

dianten. It was not until the later 1770s that adapted versions of his plays were again in the repertoire.

From the 1760s onwards the performance of tragedy went into an even steeper decline than that indicated by the small number of Schönemann's productions in the previous two decades. This was to be the trend for the remainder of the century. One of the primary reasons for this was the rise of sentimental drama focusing on the private sphere. French dramatists such as Jean-François Marmontel, Pierre-Claude Nivelle de la Chaussée and, above all, Denis Diderot were a decisive influence in this development. In the late 1750s Diderot was advocating a turn from traditional classical subjects and manner to the presentation of contemporary social relationships. His own drama *Le Père de famille* (1758), translated as *Der Hausvater*, was a favourite for decades on the German stage, though his other notable play in that vein, *Le Fils naturel*, was not popular.[11] German dramatists had begun experimenting in the 1750s with domestic tragedy or *bürgerliches Trauerspiel* and with the *drame*, sometimes designated *Familiengemälde* or *Familiendrama*. The two earliest German examples of domestic tragedy are Johann Gottlob Benjamin Pfeil's *Lucie Woodvil* (1756) and Lessing's more famous *Miß Sara Sampson* (1755), both titles betraying the importance in this development of English models, particularly Lillo's *The London Merchant* (1731), itself often translated as *George Barnwell* and performed for several decades on the German stage. Although many examples of domestic tragedy were written during the century, few found their way into the repertoire, Lessing's *Emilia Galotti* (1772), Friedrich Wilhelm Gotter's *Mariane* (from La Harpe, 1776) and Schiller's *Kabale und Liebe* (1784) being the leading examples as far as stage popularity is concerned. Apart from *The London Merchant*, Edward Moore's domestic tragedy of

---

11   On the impact of Diderot in Germany see Roland Mortier, *Diderot en Allemagne (1750–1850)* (Paris: Presses Universitaires de France, 1954), translated into German as *Diderot in Deutschland* (Stuttgart: Metzler, 1972). On the rise of sentimental drama see Joseph Pinatel, *Le drame bourgeois en Allemagne au XIIIme siècle* (Lyon: Bosc et Riou, 1938,) and on its development into the nineteenth century see Birgit Pargner, *Zwischen Tränen und Kommerz. Das Rührtheater Charlotte Birch-Pfeiffers (1800–1868) in seiner künstlerischen und kommerziellen Verwertung* (Bielfeld: Aisthesis, 1999), esp. pp. 73–116.

1753, *The Gamester* (*Der Spieler*), had a long career. Many German domestic tragedies had a strongly didactic quality. Many indeed seem to have been conceived more as closet dramas, in which contemporary issues were aired and the punishment of vice served as a warning to the reader, than as stage vehicles.[12] Such plays were clearly less potentially appealing to audiences than the sentimental family dramas that increasingly came into the repertoire, in which good triumphs and a happy outcome is assured.

It might thus be said that the development of a non-aristocratic theatre-going public was encouraged by and in turn encouraged the production of a repertoire that reflected the sentimental spirit of the age, which, influenced by Rousseau, elevated country over town, the rustic over the courtly, natural feeling over sophisticated manners and convention. The sentimental moralizing found in much French and German drama of the later decades of the eighteenth century not only appealed to audiences' sensibilities, it also gave weight to the claim made by numerous advocates of theatre that the latter was not just a place of entertainment but a moral institution. Although strong prejudices against theatre and those who worked in it still prevailed in some German states, particularly where there was a strong Pietist tradition, as in the Prussian university town of Halle, this moral conviction joined with a belief in the cultural prestige of a developed theatrical life and crystallized, as we have seen, in the national theatre movement. By the last two decades of the eighteenth century that movement, supported by able and ambitious theatre people and by the economic conditions following the Seven Years' War, created the possibility of that growing together of court and non-aristocratic theatre that allowed theatrical life to begin to flourish.

---

12   For a detailed survey see Cornelia Mönch, *Abschrecken und Mitleiden. Das deutsche bürgerliche Trauerspiel im 18. Jahrhundert. Versuch einer Typologie* (Tübingen: Niemeyer, 1993).

The Rise of Opera

One of the most important features of the German stage in the second half of the eighteenth century is the rise of musical theatre (*Musiktheater*), a term that covers a wide range of works from the *durchkomponiert* opera to the *Schauspiel mit Gesang*, in which spoken dialogue takes clear precedence but musical numbers are included. German opera had flourished in the later seventeenth century, for example in Hamburg, and continued to be prominent up to the 1720s, but from the 1730s it was supplanted as a courtly entertainment by Italian *opera seria*. The travelling companies also offered musical theatre in German up to the first decades of the eighteenth century.[13] But a glance at Schönemann's repertoire of the early 1740s to mid-1750s suggests that musical theatre was no longer a regular feature, the only musical work listed being, as noted above, a version of Coffey's *The Devil to Pay*, though some prologues and afterpieces may well have involved songs and such music as untrained singers and at most a couple of instrumentalists could offer.

The revival and expansion of musical theatre in German occurred in the 1760s after the disruption caused by the Seven Years' War. It was two far-sighted *Prinzipale*, Gottfried Heinrich Koch and Abel Seyler, who did most to pioneer the creation of a distinctive musical theatre in the 1760s and 1770s in northern Germany.[14] Fruitful alli-

---

13 Gottsched's listing of printed German plays in *Die Deutsche Schaubühne* includes *Singspiele* such as *Berenice und Lucille, oder das tugendhafte Lieben, meistens aus dem italienischen genommen, und zu Darmstadt in einem Singspiel vorgestellt* (1712) and a more popular piece, *Des Harlequins Hochzeit und Kindertauffen-Schmauß in einem Sing-Spiele vorgestellt* (1735). See *Die Deutsche Schaubühne. Faksimiledruck der Ausgabe von 1741–1742*, ed. by Horst Steinmetz, 6 vols (Stuttgart: Metzler, 1972), vol. 3, pp. xxviii and xxx.

14 See Thomas Bauman's groundbreaking *North German Opera in the Age of Goethe* (Cambridge: CUP, 1985). On the development of *Musiktheater* see also Jörg Krämer, *Deutschsprachiges Musiktheater im späten 18. Jahrhundert. Typologie, Dramaturgie und Anthropologie einer populären Gattung*, 2 vols (Tübingen: Niemeyer, 1998) and Renate Schusky, *Das deutsche Singspiel im 18. Jahrhundert. Quellen und Zeugnisse zu Ästhetik und Rezeption* (Bonn:

ances with composers and librettists led to the production of works that, though often quickly superseded or part of a passing fashion, nevertheless established this type of theatre as an indispensable part of any company's repertoire. Every company had henceforth to find the means to extend its scope, but with the same resources as before. In the 1760s trained singers in the companies were still rare and those actors who could sing found themselves called on to do so. The Leipzig composer Johann Adam Hiller (1728–84) recalled: 'Das Theater hatte keine eigentlichen Sänger und Sängerinnen, sondern wer von Natur eine leidliche Stimme und ein bißchen Taktgefühl hatte, unternahm es in den Operetten zu singen.'[15]

In 1752 Koch began his pioneering reintroduction of musical theatre in his company in Leipzig. His alliance with the dramatist and librettist Christian Felix Weisse (1726–1804) led to a new translation of Coffey's *The Devil to Pay* with a new score by Johann Standfuss (dates uncertain). *Der Teufel ist los* proved a great success with Leipzig audiences, though the mere hint of an emergent opera in the city caused its influential citizen, Gottsched, an implacable enemy of opera as 'unnatural', to wage a campaign against Koch. After the Seven Years' War Koch renewed his collaboration with Weisse and brought him together with his friend the composer Hiller. Weisse's new version of his earlier libretto for *Der Teufel ist los* was entitled *Die verwandelten Weiber* and the première with Hiller's score was on 28 May 1766. Much less bawdy and violent than Coffey's original, the new libretto, though still firmly in the realm of farce, nevertheless reflects the time Weisse had spent in Paris, where he saw the latest in French drama and *opéra comique*, a form of opera featuring spoken dialogue and musical numbers. Librettos by Rousseau, Marmontel and Sedaine for composers such as Monsigny, Philidor and Grétry reflected the turn towards sentimental comedy and drama, often set in the country, where simple airs took on a pleasing naturalness. His next librettos for Hiller, *Lottchen am Hofe* (1767), *Die Liebe auf dem*

Bouvier, 1980). For a compact overview, see Hans-Albrecht Koch, *Das deutsche Singspiel*, Samlung Metzler, 133 (Stuttgart: Metzler, 1974), pp. 44–58.

15   Johann Adam Hiller, *Autobiographie, Briefe und Nekrologe,* ed. by Mark Lehmstedt (Leipzig: Lehmstedt, 2004), p. 23.

Lande (1768) and *Die Jagd* (1770), were all drawn from the French (Favart, Sedaine, Anseaume) and confirmed the influence of *opéra comique*.[16] The immensely successful *Die Jagd* was first performed in 1770 at Weimar, when Koch's company was engaged there at the invitation of Duchess Anna Amalia, to whom it is dedicated.

The Seyler–Ekhof company, another decisive influence on the development of north German opera, was formed in 1769 after the collapse of the Hamburg National Theatre project.[17] Opera had not formed part of the repertoire at the Hamburg National Theatre, but Seyler, who from 1769 was contracted to perform in the Hanoverian territories, introduced the popular Weisse–Hiller operas. He also engaged some talented singers and the composer Anton Schweitzer (1735–87) as musical director. From 1771 he was contracted to play at Weimar and during that period Schweitzer produced a number of successful operas, most notably *Alceste* (1773), the libretto for which was written by Christoph Martin Wieland (1733–1813). Normally there was no sung recitative in German opera but rather spoken dialogue, whereas *Alceste* was *durchkomponiert* and thus a departure from the light opera previously successful. At the Gotha court theatre (1775–79)[18] the court *Kapellmeister* Georg Benda (1722–95) collaborated with the actor and playwright Johann Christian Brandes (1735–99) and with the diplomatic official and theatre enthusiast Friedrich Wilhelm Gotter (1746–97) to produce more serious opera (for example *Walder* and *Romeo und Julie*) and to develop the German version of the melodrama, that is to say spoken drama in monologue or dualogue form, accompanied by music. The two notable examples are *Ariadne auf Naxos* and *Medea*.

In the south of Germany the Viennese tradition was dominant, the Emperor Joseph II having established a National *Singspiel* in 1777 as well as a National Theatre. The overwhelming success of Mozart's

---

16   See Marion Marquard, 'Zur Bedeutung der Singspiele von Weisse und Hiller für den französisch–sächsischen Kulturtransfer im 18. Jahrhundert', in *Cahiers d'Etudes Germaniques*, 28 (1995), 95–108.
17   For an extensive treatment of Seyler's introduction of opera, see Bauman, pp. 91–131.
18   After a year in Gotha (1774–75) the Seyler–Ekhof company split, Seyler moving on and Ekhof remaining with some company members in Gotha.

Die Entführung aus dem Serail (1782), which conquered all stages in Germany from south to north in the 1780s, opened the way for the flow of Viennese works (by, for example, Carl Ditters von Dittersdorf (1739–99) and Paul Wranitzky (1756–1808), as well as Mozart) in the 1780s and 1790s as rivals to the north German operatic tradition. But everywhere impulses came also from Italian *opera buffa*, and travelling buffists from the Italian states played extensively in Germany. As in the case of spoken theatre, tireless translation activity went on to produce German texts to put to existing scores. Foreign operas were invariably performed in German and not in the original language, and with a very few exceptions featured spoken dialogue, not recitative.

The development of *Musiktheater* came together with, indeed helped to produce, some of the vital changes in German theatrical life from about 1770 onwards. Ensembles and *Prinzipale* saw that this form of entertainment greatly enhanced their attractiveness to audiences and so strove to acquire at least a few singers and musicians to make performances possible. This enlargement of the ensemble meant that there was even more reason to attempt to settle for extended periods in one place. The increased costs of performances with music tended to be found at the expense of spoken theatre, the rehearsal time for which was frequently reduced. The decline in the number of performances of tragedy, although, as noted above, already a distinct trend by the 1760s and 70s, was hastened because tragic drama on the whole demanded more rehearsal time and was less popular with audiences. In addition, in order to recoup the outlay companies had to repeat operas more frequently than plays and thus opera commanded an increasingly large proportion of the programme, again particularly at the expense of serious spoken drama.[19]

In the final analysis, it was musical theatre that both kept commercial theatre alive and made it viable outside the court sphere. At the same time, it was a medium of such wide appeal that it helped draw court and non-aristocratic tastes and audiences together. For often the *Wandertruppen* were offering, though in the German language, the same French or Italian operas that were being performed at court. Krämer therefore modifies the accepted notion that the later eighteenth

---

19   See Krämer, pp. 18–19.

century produced a *Verbürgerlichung* of the theatre as a result of the impact of the rise of the middle classes, suggesting instead that such a concept obscures the importance of many members of the ruling class who promoted German-language opera and drama; the repertoire has thus to be seen as fluid and often common to courtly and bourgeois spheres, which can no longer be neatly segregated under the headings of *Hoftheater* and *Wanderbühne*.[20] In the larger theatres by the end of the eighteenth century the old-style arrangement that required most performers to move between musical and spoken theatre was giving way to specialization and to the development of entirely discrete groups of performers.[21] As a result, professional *Germanisten*, who came into being in the second half of the nineteenth century, tended to overlook the mutual influence of musical and spoken theatre in the last decades of the eighteenth century. A result of this tendency has been the over-emphasis of the literary influences on the development of performed drama in German theatres. In the case of Iffland's speciality, the sentimental family drama, certainly the French influence through Diderot must account in part for its emergence, but several French dramatists who mediated this kind of sentimental family piece to German audiences were also librettists, Marmontel and Sedaine in particular. Iffland began his acting career under Ekhof in Gotha in 1777, moving on to Mannheim in 1779 after the closure of the Gotha theatre. Although he did not usually perform in singing roles himself, he was familiar with the musical repertoire. Mannheim in 1779 was a city in which, by virtue of its proximity to France, *opéra comique* was much performed and very popular. The contrast of town and country, aristocratic pretension and bourgeois probity, the centrality of family love and family discipline – these recurring themes of *opéra comique* are given new dramatic expression by Iffland. Thus, ironically, opera, that distinctively non-naturalistic of art forms, gave a decisive boost to sentimental family drama, a type of drama associated with the growing tendency towards realism through the use of contemporary settings and in the style of acting and staging.

---

20   Krämer, pp. 119–20.
21   This was, not, for example, true of a small theatre such as the Weimar Court Theatre.

The scene is now set for the entrance of our two protagonists, Schiller and Iffland. Schiller was a dramatist who combined an instinct for stage effects with a predominantly literary approach to the writing of drama. His creative imagination leaned naturally towards the conflicts of drama but the primary influences on him were literary more than theatrical. For Iffland the theatre was his entire world and his dramatic writing was in the service of his acting career and the wider theatrical environment, rather than the fulfilment of any literary ambition. The following chapters are an examination of the circumstances that brought them together, created their rivalry and later their cooperation. Together they illuminate the relationship between literary drama and popular theatre and the forces that produced the beginnings of a national repertoire in Germany.

Chapter One
The Road to Mannheim

The careers of Schiller and Iffland were linked from 13 January 1782, when both men were only twenty-two years old, for that was the date of the première of *Die Räuber*, Schiller's first play, at the Mannheim National Theatre. That evening not only made Schiller famous, it gave a decisive boost to the career of Iffland, who played Franz Moor, a role he made his own and continued performing for many years. The two men had arrived in Mannheim by very different routes.

Iffland's early career

August Wilhelm Iffland was born on 19 April 1759 in Hanover, the son of the *Kanzleiregistrator* Johann Rudolf Iffland and Elisabeth Friedrerike Karoline (née Schröder).[1] He was therefore a little more

---

1 All biographical sketches of Iffland rely heavily on his own autobiography, *Über meine theatralische Laufbahn*, first published as volume 1 of Iffland's *Werke* in 1798 by the Leipzig publisher Göschen. For this present study I use the very helpfully annotated edition of the autobiography by Oscar Fambach: *Meine theatralische Laufbahn. Mit Anmerkungen und einer Zeittafel von Oscar Fambach* (Stuttgart: Reclam, 1976). Other useful works on Iffland's life up to his move to Berlin are Wilhelm Herrmann, *Thaliens liebster Sohn. Iffland und Mannheim* (Mannheim: Gesellschaft der Freunde des Mannheimer National-theater e. V., 1960) and, more substantially, Wilhelm K. Koffka, *Iffland und Dalberg. Geschichte der classischen Theaterzeit Mannheims* (Leipzig: Weber, 1865). For a compact survey see also Hermann Uhde, 'August Wilhelm Iffland' in *Westermanns Illustrierte Monatshefte*, 26 (1869), 586–99 and Sigrid Salehi, *August Wilhelm Ifflands dramatisches Werk. Versuch einer Neubewertung* (Frankfurt am Main and Berne: Lang, 1990) pp. 53–78. See also the intro-duction and annotations to Ludwig Geiger's two volumes of edited cor-

than six months older than Schiller. Hanover was regularly visited by Hamburg acting companies, and Iffland's first theatre experience was a performance by the famous Ackermann company of Molière's *Le Malade imaginaire* on 14 May 1764, when the young August Wilhelm (or Wilhelm August, as he was until his early twenties) was five years old.[2] He dates his irrepressible urge to be an actor from a visit by the Hamburg National Theatre company, led by Abel Seyler, in 1767.[3] He records how his brother read Lessing's *Hamburgische Dramaturgie* as the instalments appeared and discussed the performances with his schoolfriends; thus the younger boy's curiosity was first aroused.[4] Then Iffland's father came home moved by the sufferings of Lessing's heroine Sara Sampson: 'Es ist lehrreich anzusehen, sprach er, wie die Tochter in das Unglück gerät, und Kinder können da einsehen, was ein armer Vater durch ihren Leichtsinn leidet. Ich will alle meine Kinder hineinschicken, wenn dieses Schauspiel wiederholt wird.'[5] It is ironical that Iffland's father should have understood the play as a warning to children to obey their fathers, as his son's determination to become an actor led to a rift that was still not fully healed at the father's death in 1780. The actor, whose reminiscences are frequently unreliable and present circumstances in a manner that favours his courses of action, may of course be putting these words in his father's mouth to anticipate his own commitment to writing drama containing a moral lesson; or the words may simply reflect the common and growing sense among the bourgeoisie that the theatre could be seen as

---

respondence: *A. W. Ifflands Briefe an seine Schwester Louise und andere Verwandte 1772–1814*, Schriften der Gesellschaft für Theatergeschichte, 5 (Berlin: Gesellschaft für Theatergeschichte, 1904) and *A. W. Ifflands Briefe, meist an seine Schwester, nebst andern Aktenstücken und einem ungedruckten Drama*, Schriften der Gesellschaft für Theatergeschichte, 6 (Berlin: Gesellschaft für Theatergeschichte, 1905). Henceforth these volumes will be referred to as Geiger 1 and Geiger 2.

2   *Meine theatralische Laufbahn*, p. 7.

3   The company played in Hanover from December that year to May 1768 and returned at the end of 1768 until March 1769.

4   *Meine theatralische Laufbahn*, p. 9.

5   *Meine theatralische Laufbahn*, p. 10.

a school for morals and as such deserving of a respectable position in society.

The performances took place in the small electoral palace theatre, a reflection of the paucity of commercial theatre buildings in the German states at the time. The Elector of Hanover was also the British monarch, George III, and Iffland stresses the dignity of the theatre and those who worked in it by association with the dignity of the monarch. In the performance of *Miß Sara Sampson* he saw two of the stars of the Hamburg company, Conrad Ekhof as Mellefont and Sophie Hensel (1738–90), who was later to marry Abel Seyler, as Sara. Then, in 1773, he again saw the Ackermann company, which was now led by the great *Prinzipal*, Friedrich Ludwig Schröder (1744–1816), and included the actor Franz Karl Hieronymus Brockmann, later to become famous for playing Hamlet in Schröder's widely performed adaptation of Shakespeare's play. In 1776 he records seeing the Ackermann company play Goethe's *Clavigo* (1774) and *Stella* (1775) as well as Shakespeare's *Othello* (adapted by Schröder), and also *Graf Essex*[6] and Friedrich Justin Bertuch's adaptation of William Mason's *Elfrida*, both of which, though now forgotten, had a long life in the repertoire.[7] *Stella*, Goethe's controversial play, featuring a *ménage à trois*, had been banned in Hamburg after two performances and was played in Hanover on this one occasion only.[8] *Clavigo* was just beginning its long run as a staple of the repertoire.

Torn between his parents' hopes of his becoming a Protestant clergyman and his own of being an actor, Iffland left home without permission from his parents on 15 February 1777, about two months before his eighteenth birthday.[9] His first attempt to be taken on as an actor was with the mainly Frankfurt-based company of Theobald Marchand, which specialized in *Musiktheater*. His second was at the Gotha Court Theatre, set up by the ruler, Duke Ernst II, in 1775, where Ekhof was now joint director with Heinrich August Ottokar

---

6   Adapted from *The Unhappy Favourite or The Earl of Essex* by John Banks (1650–1706).
7   *Meine theatralische Laufbahn*, pp. 24–31.
8   *Meine theatralische Laufbahn*, p. 139.
9   On the dating see *Meine theatralische Laufbahn*, p. 140.

Reichard, editor of the *Gothaer Theaterkalender* (1775–1800) and of the *Theaterjournal für Deutschland* (1777–1784), the former one of the few durable theatre periodicals of its day. An influential and energetic figure at the Gotha court was the diplomatic official Friedrich Wilhelm Gotter, a playwright, translator and librettist who was much performed in the final decades of the eighteenth century.[10] Together with Seyler's resident composer Anton Schweitzer and the Gotha court composer Georg Benda he produced some of the most popular examples of *Musiktheater* of the 1770s, such as *Die Dorfgala* (with Schweitzer) and *Romeo und Julia* (with Benda), based on Christian Felix Weisse's version of Shakespeare's play.

Ekhof was acquainted with Iffland's family and so felt a particular responsibility towards the young actor's father, writing immediately after Iffland's arrival to a Hanover friend:

> Der junge Iffland, des Registrators unsers Freundes Sohn ist am Sonnabend hier angekommen [...] Der Freundschaft habe ich geglaubt schuldig zu seyn, wenigstens vors erste zu verhindern, daß dieser junge Mensch nicht weiter in der Irre herumgehe, und da mir das Schicksal ihn in die Hände geliefert, daß er nicht in schlimmere gerathen möge.[11]

Ekhof was anxious not to exacerbate the situation by seeming to collude in Iffland's defiance, though concerned to give him a chance by asking the Duke to engage him on a probationary basis. Iffland's father might then be approached again to give his consent to his son's chosen path:

---

10   His setting up of an amateur theatre group in Gotha in 1773 was important in preparing the way for the court theatre; see Erich Nippold, 'Vom höfischen Theater zum Hoftheater. Zur Geschichte des Gothaer Schloßtheaters 1745–74', *Abhandlungen und Berichte des Heimatmuseums Gotha* (1968), pp. 3–20 (p. 11).

11   See 'Ungedruckte Briefe Conrad Ekhofs. Aus der Handschrift veröffentlicht und erläutert von Professor Ludwig Geiger', *Bühne und Welt*, 7 (1905), 657–64 (p. 657). Kurt Binneberg uses these letters to expose discrepancies with Iffland's own account of his Gotha period; see 'A. W. Ifflands Gothaer Jahre. Kritische Anmerkungen zu seiner Autobiographie', in *Sammeln und Sichten. Festschrift für Oscar Fambach zum 80. Geburtstag*, ed. by Joachim Krause, Norbert Oellers and Karl Konrad Polheim (Bonn: Bouvier, 1982), pp. 158–82.

Ist dieser es zufrieden, daß er sich dem Theater widme, und der junge Mensch läßt sich so an, daß ihn der Herzog behalten will, so soll er unter meiner Aufsicht so gut als seines Vaters aufgehoben sein. Kann er aber die Einwilligung nicht erhalten, so weiß sein Vater doch, wo er ihn wieder haben kann.[12]

Ekhof was soon impressed with Iffland's talent, when he made his debut as the Jew in Johann Jakob Engel's afterpiece *Der Diamant* (1773): 'Er scheint viele Anlage und Bestimmung fürs Theater zu haben, und aus solchem Sujet ist etwas zu machen.'[13] But Iffland's account of his reception by Ekhof ('Er reichte mir treuherzig die Hand – Durch alle Glieder fuhr mir die Weihe. Seine Fürsorge entschied meine Anstellung. Ich verdanke es ihm ewig!)[14] obscures the fact that Ekhof as a family friend felt obliged to help the young runaway.[15]

Iffland did indeed have much to thank Ekhof for, in addition to that first opportunity to prove himself. For Ekhof's professionalism made a deep impression on the young actor. Ekhof began his career with the Schönemann company in 1740 and made his reputation in the 1740s.[16] Schönemann, who, as noted in the Introduction, had begun as a member of the Neuber company, was an important figure in the move to a more literary repertoire based on written texts and was supported in his efforts by the patronage of Duke Christian Ludwig II of Mecklenburg–Schwerin, who supplied an early example of how royal subsidy could raise standards by making an artistically ambitious company viable. In 1753 Ekhof founded his famous acting academy, which existed for just over a year. Its purpose was to provide a forum in which new plays could be considered, individual performances discussed and improved, and general questions concerning acting debated. Attendance was strictly regulated, with fines for absences and other infringements. Shortlived though it was, its articles convey a

---

12   'Ungedruckte Briefe', p. 658.
13   'Ungedruckte Briefe', p. 659.
14   *Meine theatralische Laufbahn*, p. 33.
15   As Binneberg comments, p. 161.
16   For a compact and informative account of Ekhof's career see Hugo Fetting, *Conrad Ekhof. Ein Schauspieler des achtzehnten Jahrhunderts* (Berlin: Henschelverlag, 1954).

clear sense of Ekhof's ambition to raise the professional standing of the actor as well as of the theatre by engendering professional pride and shared responsibility in the company.[17] The same thoroughness remained with Ekhof to the end of his career. Iffland later recorded a reminiscence from his Gotha years. Two young actors, who had no speaking part in a production of Bertuch's tragedy *Ines de Castro* (from La Motte) but in the roles of two grandees had to cross the stage and bow to the King of Spain, decided that on a spring morning they need not put in an appearance until the rehearsal was drawing to a close. They were roundly chastised by Ekhof, who demonstrated to them in front of the entire company not only that they had no idea how to cross the stage and bow to a Spanish king but also that they owed it to the other members of the company to rehearse thoroughly. Iffland's verdict on the incident was: 'Er hatte ihnen einen praktischen Begriff von Schauspielerproben gegeben und eine Achtsamkeit für das, was ihnen Kleinigkeit geschienen, welche nachher nicht ohne Nutzen geblieben ist'.[18] It is tempting to conclude that Iffland was one of the two young actors.

Even in that first Gotha period two striking characteristics of Iffland's future career quickly became visible: ambition and the tendency to live beyond his means. The two became inextricably linked. Ambition prompted him after only eight months in Gotha to seek an engagement with the Hamburg theatre and the admired Schröder. This move was envisaged for Easter 1778. However, the young actor, who was used by his upbringing to a comfortable existence, had already accumulated debts, which would have had to be cleared by an advance from Hamburg. Schröder also required the consent of Iffland's parents.[19] A further obstacle to the move was that the Hamburg company played in Hanover and Iffland's family was not at all prepared to see him or, more particularly, have him seen on stage in his home town. Ekhof had tried to help Iffland financially by having his wage increased from the autumn of 1777 and by writing to his family to

---

17   These are printed in Fetting, *Conrad Ekhof*, pp. 135–41.
18   'Anecdoten und Characterzüge aus der Theaterwelt' in *Almanach für Theater und Theaterfreunde* (Berlin: Oehmigke jun., 1807), pp. 256–63 (p. 263).
19   Geiger 1, p. 234.

clear his debts. The young actor seems to have incurred Ekhof's wrath at least once by concealing the extent of his indebtedness and being obliged to write the latter an exculpatory letter:

> Ich bitte Sie nur zu erwegen, daß nichts in der Welt mich dazu hätte bewegen können, als der Kummer, durch angehäufte theils unnöthige Schulden mir Ihre Unzufriedenheit zuzuziehen und daß ich ferner nicht wuste, daß eben dieser Zettel Ihnen bey meinem Vater eine Unwahrheit kosten sollte.[20]

Though his family did finally agree to his move to Hamburg, it did not in fact take place. Binneberg convincingly attributes the change of plan to the even larger debts that had accumulated by the time his family gave their consent, such that Hamburg no longer saw its way clear to advancing the necessary sum.[21]

As far as roles were concerned, Iffland's scope was restricted by existing members of the company. Michael Böck was more suited to young romantic leads and Iffland commented: 'Ich kann wegen Böc nie gute *junge* Rollen haben.'[22] In letters to his family he tells us little about the roles he did play but we can see from the repertoire at Gotha that he must have been introduced to the wide range of stage offerings current at the time. The Gotha repertoire was dominated by comedies.[23] During its existence from 1775 to 1779 only fourteen tragedies and eight *Dramen* or *Schauspiele* were performed. Thirty-three operas, *Singspiele* or melodramas were given. The rest of the repertoire, about 120 plays, was made up of comedies. These were, like the repertoire as a whole, a mixture of original German plays and translations. Goldoni, Sheridan, Garrick and Colman, Marivaux, Beaumarchais, Favart, Goldsmith and Molière were performed, as well as Lessing, J. E. Schlegel and Brandes. The most popular of the serious plays were Goethe's *Clavigo*, Gotter's *Mariane*, Beaumar-

---

20   Draft of letter, 23 October 1777, Geiger 1, p. 9.
21   Binneberg, pp. 174–75.
22   Geiger 2, p. 5.
23   Details of the Gotha repertoire are given in Rudolf Schlösser's *Vom Hamburger Nationaltheater zur Gothaer Hofbühne 1767–1779*, Theatergeschichtliche Forschungen, 13 (Hamburg and Leipzig: Voss, 1895), pp. 75–80.

chais's *Eugénie* (1767) and Shakespeare's *Hamlet*, most probably in Schröder's adaptation.

One accolade that suggests that from modest beginnings Iffland was nevertheless making his mark is contained in a letter to his sister of May 1779, written therefore at the end of his Gotha years. The popular Dresden writer August Gottlieb Meissner had honoured his performance as Lord Ogleby in Garrick's and Colman's *The Clandestine Marriage* (*Die heimliche Heirat*, first performed 1776) with the following lines:

> Als Eckhofs Schüler, Gotters Günstling,
> Thaliens liebster Sohn,
> bist Du glücklicher als je in Albion
> Einer Deiner Brüder war;
> Wenn man Deinen Staub auch nie bey
> Fürsten begräbt,
> Bist Du dennoch sicher, daß Dein Name
> Manchen Fürsten überlebt!

Iffland is connected flatteringly with Ekhof and Gotter, and in quoting the lines to his sister Iffland hoped this testimonial might be a further small step towards reconciliation with his family.[24] His first return to Hanover, mediated by his advocate Gotter, came in August that summer, when he was received back by his father, who up to this point had steadfastly refused to communicate with him directly, though he had sent his wayward son money and clothing via third parties. This partial reconciliation was of great importance to Iffland, particularly as both his parents died in the following months, his mother on 11 September 1779 and his father on 11 March 1780. Henceforth he was to return regularly, at least once a year, to Hanover. He was particularly attached to his older married sister Louise Eisendecher, with whom he maintained a regular correspondence throughout his life and whose husband Wilhelm he clearly thought of as a useful go-between at this stage with his family.

On 16 June 1778 Ekhof died. The following year Duke Ernst decided to dissolve the theatre. Again Iffland entertained hopes of a

---

24   Geiger 1, pp. 26–27.

move to Hamburg and again he was disappointed. The discontinuation of the Gotha theatre coincided with the search by the *Intendant* of the Mannheim National Theatre, Wolfgang Heribert von Dalberg (1750–1806), for actors to make up a standing company there.[25] Several Gotha actors signed up to move to Mannheim and remained there for the rest of their career. These included David Beil and Heinrich Beck as well as Wilhelm Christian Dietrich Meyer and Michael Böck. In Meyer's compilation of the Gotha actors Iffland is described thus:

> Herr Iffland, ein junger Mann von 19 Jahren, hat bei dem Gothaischen Theater angefangen, und seit ein paar Jahren große Fortschritte in der Kunst gemacht. Sein Spiel ist einsichtsvoll und richtig, und verräth allemal den denkenden Künstler. Er spielt komische Alte und Carrikaturen, doch ist er auch in jungen Rollen nicht schlecht. Seine Gage ist 6 Thlr. und 4 Klafter Holz.[26]

In the list of the members of the new Mannheim company with their wages and *Rollenfach* he is noted as specializing in 'Komische Alte und Caricatur-Rollen, auch Juden'.[27] He is not designated as a singer as well as an actor (those who sang had to have a contract specifically for musical and spoken theatre).[28] Iffland was slow to commit himself to Mannheim, but he eventually set out on the journey with Böck on 29 September 1779. Thus began a period of seventeen years during which Iffland rose to be the most prominent actor at the theatre, later *Regisseur*, and the most popular playwright on the German stage.

Schiller and theatre in Württemberg

Schiller began his first play, *Die Räuber*, while still a pupil at the military academy in Stuttgart, established by Württemberg's autocratic ruler Duke Carl Eugen to supply him with army officers and state

---

25 He remained *Intendant* until 1803.
26 Koffka, pp. 26–27.
27 Koffka, p. 46.
28 Friedrich Walter, *Archiv und Bibliothek des Großh. Hof- und Nationaltheaters in Mannheim 1779–1839*, 2 vols (Leipzig: Hirzel, 1899), vol. 1, p. 55.

servants of every kind. A pupil from the age of fourteen against his own and his parents' wishes, Schiller graduated at the end of 1780 and published the play at his own expense in Stuttgart in 1781. The academy functioned as a kind of school and university in one. The pupils were individually selected from the aristocratic and non-aristocratic families of Württemberg, educated at the Duke's expense and thereafter entirely dependent on him for their future prosperity. They had no holidays or home visits and thus led something of a sequestered existence.[29] The writing of a play so experimental in form and so offensive to contemporary ideas of good taste by a young man at such an institution, where individual expression and the reading of contemporary literature were not encouraged, makes one wonder what the author's early experience of drama and theatre was. For Schiller's first play – unwieldy, absurd in plot, vulgar and elevated by turns – shows nevertheless an instinctive feeling for theatrical effectiveness. In style it is a late flowering of the *Sturm und Drang*, with its flouting of the rules of dramatic composition, use of vigorous prose and elements of contemporary realism. It could not have been written without some knowledge of the works of the *Sturm und Drang*, the exciting forbidden reading at the academy, or of Shakespeare, to whom Schiller was introduced by his most influential teacher Johann Friedrich Abel. But though they lent him some themes (the brothers at enmity, criticism of corrupt administrations, the defiant central character who comes to grief) the writers of the *Sturm und Drang* – the young Goethe, Jakob Michael Reinhold Lenz (1751–92), Friedrich Maximilian Klinger (1752–1831), Heinrich Leopold Wagner (1747–79) – tended to disregard the practical

---

29 A detailed but concise account of the academy's origins, development and curriculum during Schiller's time there can be found in Kenneth Dewhurst and Nigel Reeves, *Friedrich Schiller. Medicine, Psychology and Literature* (Oxford: Sandford, 1978). Also informative is the first-person account of Schiller's schoolfriend Friedrich Wilhelm von Hoven, later a doctor in Stuttgart: *Biographie des Doktor Friedrich Willhelm von Hoven, Königl. Bayer'schen Obermedizinrats* (Nuremberg: Schrag, 1840), reprinted under the title *Lebenserinnerungen,* ed. by Hans-Günter Thalheim and Evelyn Laufer (Berlin: Rütten & Loeng, 1984). See also Robert Uhland, *Geschichte der Hohen Karlsschule in Stuttgart* (Stuttgart: Kohlhammer, 1953).

demands of the stage, whereas *Die Räuber*, though requiring a large cast, is eminently stageworthy. What therefore was Schiller's experience of actual performance?

Christophine Reinwald, the playwright's sister, recorded how as children they occasionally had the opportunity to attend the opera in Ludwigsburg and how dazzled they were by the spectacle.[30] Duke Carl Eugen maintained a huge palace at Ludwigsburg, and though court opera performances were closed to the general public Schiller's father as an army officer was now and then allowed to attend. The operas were Italian and performed in Italian and put on with considerable splendour. Indeed Carl Eugen made his state for a time one of the grand opera centres of Europe.[31] Michelsen has argued that Schiller's early experience of grand opera and court ballet left a decisive imprint on his dramatic imagination and that the lack of concern for verisimilitude, for example, and that the emphasis on the impact of grand gestures derive less from the *Sturm und Drang* than from the tradition of *opera seria* and of ballet.[32] While there is no ultimate proof of such influence, the concrete evidence being slight, it is easy to accept the possibility that the natural expansiveness of Schiller's imagination found an inspiration in those spectacles.

In the earlier part of his reign the Duke, like many comparable German princes, had wanted to enjoy the benefits and prestige of Italian opera, French theatre and ballet. These entertainments were costly

---

30 'Schillers Jugendjahre. Eine Skizze von Christophine Reinwald, geb. Schiller. Mitgetheilt von Robert Boxberger', *Archiv für Litteraturgeschichte*, vol. 1 (Leipzig: Teubner, 1870), pp. 452–60: 'Ganz natürlich mußten diese Vorstellungen auf das junge lebendige Gemüth des jungen Schiller, der aus ländlichen Einfachheit sich hier wie in eine Feenwelt versetzt glaubte, einen grossen Eindruck machen' (p. 457).

31 See *Das Ludwigsburger Schloßtheater. Kultur und Geschichte eines Hoftheaters*, ed. by the Ludwigsburger Schlossfestspiele (Stuttgart: DRW-Verlag, 1998). Also Joseph Sittard, *Zur Geschichte der Musik und des Theaters am Württembergischen Hof*, 2 vols (Stuttgart: Kohlhammer, 1890) and Rudolph Krauss, *Das Stuttgarter Hoftheater von den ältesten Zeiten bis zur Gegenwart* (Stuttgart: Metzler, 1908), esp. pp. 39–98.

32 Peter Michelsen, 'Die große Bühne' in Michelsen, *Der Bruch mit der Vaterwelt. Studien zu Schillers 'Räubern'*, Beihefte zum *Euphorion*, 16 (Heidelberg: Winter, 1979), pp. 9–63.

and the Duke placed heavy tax burdens on his subjects. Finally they complained to the Emperor that their long-established rights to consultation in matters of taxation had been infringed and the Duke was forced to moderate his spending. It was less expensive to train up young performers at home than to engage foreign nationals, and so for a time, in the mid-1770s, he used his military academy and newly founded *Ecole des demoiselles* as a source of performers.[33] In doing so he may also have been sensitive to a climate of change in which German performers were gaining a reputation for being able to hold their own against foreign competition. Carl Eugen treated his young talents with his customary high-handedness, obliging their parents to sign them over to him unconditionally and attempting to keep them (particularly the young women) as unpaid performers by not releasing them from their institutions when it was time for them to leave. At first the new home-grown talents took over the repertoires of foreign companies but by the late 1770s the growing interest in German drama and opera also made itself felt in Württemberg. Schiller and the other pupils at the military academy had therefore ample opportunity to see performances, particularly of opera. The court *Kapellmeister* and opera composer taught at the military academy and the pupils were involved regularly in elaborate operatic entertainments to celebrate the birthday of the Duke or his mistress Franziska von Hohenheim.[34]

A decisive event for the development of Württemberg theatre, which by comparison with musical life was underdeveloped, was the arrival in 1778 in Stuttgart for a season of the young Emanuel Schikaneder (1751–1812), later to make his name in Vienna. He had formed his own company that same year and it would go on to be particularly popular for its musical theatre. Schikaneder wrote his first libretto, *Die Lyranten oder das lustige Elend*, in 1776. He played in Stuttgart from May to early September 1778. His repertoire, consisting of nearly

---

33   For an account of this see Sittard, pp. 144–60.
34   In his first poetry collection, *Anthologie auf das Jahr 1782*, Schiller published *Semele. Eine lyrische Operette von zwo Scenen*, which the editors of the Nationalausgabe convincingly argue was a satire on the librettos written for such occasions in praise of the ruler and his mistress; see NA 5N, 499–522.

sixty works, included spoken drama, opera and ballet. The standard, according to the report in Reichard's *Theaterjournal*, was high enough to send away an audience reasonably satisfied.[35] The punishing schedule, exhausting by modern standards, was necessary in a situation where populations were small and the theatre-going public restricted in size. Schikaneder's repertoire was striking for its breadth and range. Shakespeare's *Macbeth* and *Hamlet* were played in adapted versions and Schikaneder, an imposing presence, was particularly praised for his playing of the Prince of Denmark. Voltaire's *Mérope* was given, as well as Christian Felix Weisse's versions of *Richard III* (1765) and *Romeo und Juliet* (1768). Other non-German playwrights performed were Goldoni, Sheridan, Cumberland, Lillo and Beaumarchais. Lessing's *Minna von Barnhelm* (1767), *Emilia Galotti* (1772) and the earlier *Miß Sara Sampson* (1755) were played. Popular German playwrights such as Brandes and Stephanie der Jüngere, and Johann Jakob Engel, later a director of the Berlin National Theatre, were represented mainly by comedies. Goethe's *Clavigo*, much more frequently played in general than the sprawling *Götz von Berlichingen,* was also given. Schikaneder showed his own predilection for musical theatre by the large number of operas, almost all German (as opposed to French). These included Goethe's and André's *Erwin und Elmire* (published 1775, first performed 1777), as well as Brandes's and Benda's melodrama *Ariadne auf Naxos*, a product of the Gotha Court Theatre. Buchwald's view is that Schiller and his fellow pupils were not allowed to attend these performances but that he would have heard about them from his teacher, Abel.[36]

It may have been the range and success of this season that prompted Carl Eugen in 1779 to found a national theatre. The relative proximity of Mannheim may also have spurred him on. The young

---

35 'Schreiben an Herrn Bibliothekar Reichard in Gotha über die Schikanederische Schauspielergesellschaft und ihren Aufenthalt in Stuttgart', in *Theaterjournal auf das Jahr 1779*, Heft 10, pp. 43–62, gives the repertoire. Not everything went well, 'doch der größte Theil so, daß billige Zuschauer nicht mißvergnügt nach Hauße gingen' (p. 49).

36 Reinhard Buchwald, 'Herzog Carl Eugen gründet ein Nationaltheater' in *Gestaltung Umgestaltung. Festschrift Hermann August Korff*, ed. by Joachim Müller (Leipzig: Koehler & Amelang, 1957), pp. 76–91 (p. 82).

performers, trained in French and Italian, were suddenly required to perform in German, though sadly for the standard of performance the actors were still rehearsed by an old French actor, Joseph Uriot, whose style and experience were entirely at odds with the requirements of the new repertoire, which had almost abandoned tragedy and was moving towards drama requiring greater naturalness in the acting style.[37] Unfortunately, the achievements of the newly established German theatre in Stuttgart did not match the standard set by Schikaneder. The actors were poorly trained and equipment and resources were scarce. The pupils at the military academy were often given the opportunity to attend performances but it is unlikely that Schiller would have seen much on a level or in a style to inspire him. In a later letter to Dalberg at Mannheim, he talks of the Stuttgart theatre being in a 'Stand der Minderjährigkeit' (NA 23, 18).[38] Its deficiencies may well be reflected in his first essay on theatre, 'Ueber das gegenwärtige teutsche Theater', which dates from his final months in Stuttgart.[39] Schiller complains of poor audience taste, lack of vision on the part of dramatists and vanity and immoral behaviour on the part of actors.[40] As an actor himself Schiller seems not to have been talented; at the military academy, where the pupils were allowed to put on amateur productions, he appeared in Goethe's *Clavigo*. Andreas Streicher, the friend of Schiller's Stuttgart years and companion in his flight from Württemberg, reports that in spite of boundless enthusiasm he was not very good, being inclined to exaggeration:

> Schiller konnte dem Drange nicht widerstehen, sich auch als Schauspieler zu versuchen, und übernahm im *Clavigo* eine Rolle, die er aber so darstellte, daß

---

37   Buchwald, p. 80.
38   This immaturity continued until in 1787. Daniel Christian Schubart (1734–91), a writer imprisoned for ten years by Carl Eugen for his satirical attacks on the ruler and his regime, was finally released and, in one of those extraordinary reversals of fortune that can occur under absolute monarchy, was appointed director of the theatre. He immediately set about training the actors.
39   It appeared in March 1782 in the first number of the journal, *Wirtembergisches Repertorium der Litteratur*, which Schiller founded with two friends from the Carlsschule.
40   See NA 20, 79–86.

48

sein Spiel noch lange nachher, sowohl ihm als seinen Freunden, reichen Stoff zum Lachen und zur Satire verschaffte.[41]

The circumstances of the Stuttgart stage, as well as the inflammatory nature of the play itself, may well have contributed to Schiller's doubts about the theatrical viability of *Die Räuber*. In his first preface to the play as published in Stuttgart in 1781 he claims he has written a 'dramatischen Roman', which may reflect his realization that in Württemberg there was no hope of its being staged rather than suggesting it is undramatic, which is clearly not the case.[42] In order to recoup his publication costs, he approached a prominent Mannheim bookseller and publisher, Christian Friedrich Schwan, with the proposition that Schwan buy the remaining copies. Schwan was clearly impressed with the play but later likened it to a newborn baby,

> das noch nicht von dem von seinem bisherigen Aufenthalte noch anklebenden Schmutze gesäubert ist, und mitunter Scenen enthielt, die ich als Buchhändler dem ehrsamen und gesitteten Publicum verkäuflich anzubieten für unschicklich hielt.[43]

Instead he brought it to the attention of Dalberg and of several of the Mannheim actors (including Iffland), who supported his belief that the play could be successfully performed. Schwan himself was an active translator and librettist for the Mannheim stage, as was Dalberg, who, he was sure, would give the talented young playwright useful guidance in tempering the play's wildness if he were to commission a stage adaptation.

---

41   Andreas Streicher, *Schillers Flucht*. New edition by Paul Raabe (Stuttgart: Steinkopf, 1959), p. 62.

42   Streicher records of Schiller's willingness to embark on the stage adaptation: 'Schiller willigte um so lieber in diesen Vorschlag, je entfernter der Zeitpunkt war, in welchem eine seiner Dichtungen auf dem Theater in Stuttgart hätte aufgeführt werden können, indem die Leistungen desselben bloß als Versuche von Anfängern gelten konnten' (p. 69).

43   See Schwan's letter of 14 November 1811 to Christian Gottfried Körner quoted in FA 2, 941.

The Mannheim National Theatre

At the time of the founding of the National Theatre in the late 1770s Mannheim, capital city of the Palatinate, had about 24,000 inhabitants. The Elector of the Palatinate, Carl Theodor (1724–99), who had come to the throne in 1742, did much to boost the city's standing through planning, prestige building, the creation of collections and through cultural patronage. He was a ruler with wide interests in literature, the arts, architecture, history and the natural sciences. While his collections and libraries reflected a desire to enhance his prestige, they also, by the way he allowed some public access, reflected his receptivity to enlightenment ideas of rulership and of the ruler's responsibility for the education and improvement of his subjects.[44] Theatrical and operatic life in Mannheim was lively, the court being the main consumer. French plays were performed in French for the court at the Elector's expense. For the non-court audience, theatre consisted of French plays performed in German translation. These performances were patronized by Carl Theodor, who went so far in 1770 as to dismiss the French court players. Between 1775 and 1778 a new stage was created for the performance of German plays and named the Electoral Court Theatre. It is not entirely clear what prompted Carl Theodor to give this decisive boost to German-language drama, whether an ideological commitment to native German culture or a need, shared by many rulers in the aftermath of the Seven Years' War, to reduce his own costs by dispensing with the French troupe and moving to an at least partly commercial theatre.[45] In 1775 the architect

---

44 A wide-ranging and informative impression of Carl Theodor's various cultural activities is gained from the two-volume catalogue to an extensive exhibition: see Alfried Wieczorek (ed.), *Lebenslust und Frömmigkeit: Kurfürst Carl Theodor (1724–1799) zwischen Barock und Aufklärung*, 2 vols (Regensburg: Pustet, 1999). See also Stephan Pflicht, *Kurfürst Carl Theodor von der Pfalz und seine Bedeutung für die Entwicklung des deutschen Theaters* (Reichling, Obb.: Ehresmann, 1976).

45 For a very detailed discussion of the circumstances surrounding the creation of the theatre, see Ute Daniel, *Hoftheater: Zur Geschichte des Theaters und der Höfe im 18. und im 19. Jahrhundert* (Stuttgart: Klett-Cotta, 1995). See also

Lorenzo Quaglio, who also designed the Frankfurt playhouse and the interior of the Munich National Theatre, was given the task of creating a theatre in Mannheim comparable with the theatre in the electoral palace and at his country residence of Schwetzingen. The result was imposing. The auditorium was twenty metres long. In the stalls there were fourteen rows of seats. A four-tiered arrangement of boxes rose up around the auditorium and in all there were about 1200 seats. The stage was sixteen metres deep and had seven pairs of *Kulissen*. Behind the stage was an extensive space for storage of sets and stage machinery, above which was a concert hall.

From its inception the Mannheim Theatre had close links with the *Kurpfälzische Deutsche Gesellschaft*, which, founded in 1775, was committed to raising the esteem of the German language and, by extension, of its expression in literary works.[46] Dalberg (president from 1778), Schwan and influential members of the Elector's administration were among its members, and it is clear that, apart from any practical considerations guiding the creation of the theatre, there was also an aspiration to promote the cultural standing of the Palatinate. The memoirs of one member, Stephan von Stengel, a minor court official, contain numerous significant details about the Mannheim National Theatre's inception. A key figure in his account of the process is his fellow member, the minister Baron Franz Karl von Hompesch. According to Stengel, the impetus to make Mannheim a centre for the performance of plays in German arose from some successful comedies put on in German at Schwetzingen:

> Dieser unbedeutende Anfang gab Hompeschen Anlas zu der Idee, ein eignes deutsches Theater in Mannheim (welches Marschand nur von Zeit zu Zeit mit seiner herumziehenden Truppe besuchte) zu errichten. Um der Sache mehr Ansehen und Würde zu geben und besonders um die Gattung von Verachtung,

---

Wilhelm Herrmann, *Hoftheater – Volkstheater – Nationaltheater* (Frankfurt am Main, Berne: Lang, 1999). Correspondence relating to the setting up of the theatre is printed in Walter, vol. 1, pp. 37–50. On the national theatre movement in general see Roland Krebs, *L'Idée de 'Théâtre National' dans L'Allemagne des Lumières*, Wolfenbütteler Forschungen, 28 (Wiesbaden: Harrassowitz, 1984).

46 On these connections see, for example, Friedrich Walter, *Geschichte des Theaters und der Musik am Kurpfälzischen Hofe* (Leipzig: Breitkopf & Härtel, 1898), esp. 'Nationale Tendenzen und das deutsche Schauspiel', pp. 250–76.

welche damal noch grösten Theils die deutschen Schauspieler niederdrükte, bis auf die lezte Spur zu verwischen, suchte Hompesch die deutsche Gesellschaft damit in Verbindung zu bringen.[47]

As one of the founding members of the society Stengel was consulted by Hompesch about the theatre scheme:

> Die Idee, die Schaubühne zur Würde der Künste empor zu heben und sie gleichsam zum Mittelpunkte zu machen, von welchem aus die bildenden Künste und der gute Geschmack einen neuen Schwung erhalten sollten, der Gedanke, in meiner Vaterstadt die erste regelmäsige national Schaubühne im vollen Glanze eines diesem so vieles zu opfern gewöhnten Hofes zu sehen und endlich die Ansicht, daß die Bühne das würksamste Vehikel seyn würde, eine reinere und vollkommene Sprache und Mundart unter meinen Landsleuten zu verbreiten, auch selbst den Hof für die Schönheiten unserer Muttersprache empfänglich zu machen, all dieses ware mehr als hinreichend, mich für Hompeschens Plan in Feuer zu setzen.[48]

The circumstances surrounding the emergence of a standing theatre in Mannheim for the performance of plays in German are complex. It is clear that the initiative quite soon passed out of the hands of Hompesch, as Carl Theodor pursued the idea of financing the building of the theatre from the Karl-Borromäus-Spital, an institution for the infirm, orphans and offenders, which the theatre's profits would in turn help to finance.[49] What Stengel's memoirs point to is the fact that the plans for a standing theatre in Mannheim found resonance with an enlightened elite, composed of *Bürger* such as Schwan as well as members of the aristocracy, who were imbued with the cultural ideals of the national theatre movement and with ambitions for their own *Vaterland*, the Palatinate.

In 1776 it was Hompesch, according to Stengel, who made efforts to secure Lessing's services for the Palatinate and invited the revered figure, who was brought to Mannheim by Schwan, to visit

---

47 Stephan von Stengel, *Denkwürdigkeiten*, ed. by Günther Ebersold (Mannheim: Palatium Verlag, 1993), p. 80.
48 Stengel, pp. 80–81.
49 Daniel, esp. pp. 183–88.

from Wolfenbüttel with a view to an involvement with the theatre.[50] Lessing made it clear that he could envisage no more than an advisory role, as Stengel reports: 'Die Direktion der national Bühne zu übernehmen, schlug er rund ab. Nur dazu wollte er sich noch verstehen, von Zeit zu Zeit seine Meinung zu sagen, seinen Rath zu geben.'[51] After some unsatisfactory and protracted negotiations concerning how Lessing might be attached to the Palatinate, he withdrew completely from any association, clearly of the view that he had been badly treated, particularly by Hompesch.[52] When in the same year a company was sought to play at the theatre, Stengel suggested engaging another figure who was part of the history of the Hamburg National Theatre, Conrad Ekhof. Stengel was opposed to offering the contract to a travelling company and was impressed by the fact that Ekhof was at that time director at Gotha, a court theatre. Though Abel Seyler was also considered, the Strasbourg *Prinzipal* Theobald Marchand, who was already familiar to Mannheim audiences from his periodic visits, had enough influential friends at court to secure the position for his company.[53]

Marchand's repertoire in 1778 shows a mixture of drama, ballet and opera typical of the time.[54] Four of the five operas given between April and September were by the hugely popular French composers Monsigny, Philidor and Grétry. This suggests the very strong emphasis in the western states of Germany on French *opéra-comique*. The only play in the repertoire instantly familiar to modern readers is Lessing's much-performed *Minna von Barnhelm*. Several of the leading popular playwrights of the day – Brandes, Engel, Grossmann, Stephanie der Jüngere – are represented, as are French and English dramatists: Nivelle de la Chaussée, Chamfort, Cumberland and Col-

---

50 A full and compact appraisal of the negotiations with Lessing is in Herrmann, *Hoftheater – Volkstheater – Nationaltheater*, pp. 269–86.
51 Stengel, p. 83.
52 See Lessing's correspondence with Hompesch, Schwan and Friedrich (Maler) Müller in the spring of 1777 in *Lessings Werke und Briefe*, vol. 12 (*Briefe von und an Lessing 1776–1781*), pp. 31–74.
53 Stengel, p. 82.
54 For a chronological repertoire for the theatre from April 1778 to December 1803, see Walter, vol. 2, pp. 259–377. Marchand's repertoire is on pp. 259–60.

man. Shakespeare had yet to find his way into the repertoire and no work of the *Sturm und Drang* was played.

On 31 December 1777 the Elector of Bavaria, Maximilian III. Joseph, died and Carl Theodor of the Palatinate succeeded to the throne, a development that, according to the terms of the succession, required him to move his court to Munich, which he did in the autumn of the following year, taking Marchand's company with him. Many leading citizens were concerned about the future prosperity of the abandoned former *Residenzstadt*, now seemingly pushed to the cultural and political periphery of the Elector's domains. Dalberg, a passionate theatre lover, petitioned the Elector through Baron Hompesch to provide a subvention to allow the theatre to continue and help enliven the cultural life there, by, amongst other things, drawing the aristocracy into the city in the winter:

> ein noch anderes mittel, frembdes geld in die stadt zu bringen [...] mögte alenfallß seyn, adliche familien oder solche leute herzuziehen, die ihre einkünfte in freyheit und Vergnügen zu genießen suchen; [...] diese würden gewiß alle sich wenigstens zu winterzeit hierher begeben, in der Versicherung, angenehm und frey leben zu können; wollte in dieser rücksicht der Kurfürst alljährlich einen gewißen fond zu öffentlichen Vergnügungen worunter ein schauspiel bestimmen, so würde gewiß diese absicht um so eher erreicht werden; [...] bey errichtung eines solchen schauspiels könnten jene nicht in ausübung gekomme[nen] plane zur erhöhung der dramatischen Kunst in teütschland gebraucht und da manche hinterniße wegfielen, jetzt in ausübung kommen, plane welche Ew. Excelenz einst so sehnlichst ausgeführt zu sehen gewünscht haben.[55]

An additional suggestion was that of moving the university from Heidelberg to Mannheim, but the Elector understandably responded that his Heidelberg subjects would then suffer. Hompesch clearly managed to recommend the theatre initiative to Carl Theodor, and Dalberg found himself in the position of having to take on the role of *Intendant*. The Elector agreed to give financial support (about a quarter of the running costs)[56] and Dalberg was given authority to engage actors and a director. He again approached Seyler first to play a season in 1778/79, then as director (*Regisseur*) from October 1779.

---

55 For Dalberg's letter see Walter, vol. 1, pp. 47–49.
56 Koffka, p. 59.

In 1778/79 Seyler was based mainly in Mainz, later in Frankfurt, and travelled regularly to Mannheim to play once or more a week in the season. From the autumn of 1779 he moved fully to Mannheim, bringing with him part of his company from Frankfurt. These were supplemented by, among others, several members of the Gotha company. The theatre began its third season on Thursday 7 October 1779 (its first with a standing company) with a performance of Johann Christian Bock's adaptation of Goldoni's *Un accidente curioso*, entitled *Geschwind eh es jemand erfährt*.

After these somewhat turbulent beginnings the Mannheim National Theatre had to prove not only that it could keep itself afloat but that it could do so in the absence of the court aristocracy, the gradual departure of which took place between 1778 and 1781. In fact the citizens of Mannheim rose to the occasion, particularly prized their theatre and identified strongly with it as a symbol of the increased cultural freedom and self-sufficiency that was the positive aspect of the court's removal. Mannheim was a city, for example, in which the respect and importance accorded to the theatre as an institution also extended to the performers; Sophie La Roche, for example, in her *Briefe über Mannheim*, writes of 'diese Bühne, deren allgemeiner Charakter Sittlichkeit ist'.[57] Actors in Mannheim acquired unusual respectability in the city, as the election of Beck and Iffland to the *Kurpfälzische Deutsche Gesellschaft* in 1785 demonstrates. The removal of the court also gave Dalberg as *Intendant* unusual freedom from censorship and other kinds of court intervention. Responsibility for what was put on rested with him and he was expected to exercise his judgment (as indeed he did, for example when he put back the setting of *Die Räuber* from the eighteenth to the fifteenth century) to avoid unnecessary controversy.[58]

Seyler's repertoire in the early Mannheim years still shows the influence of his Hamburg period as well as the legacy of the Weimar/Gotha years of the 1770s. Like all repertoires of the period, it is

---

57   Sophie La Roche, *Briefe über Mannheim* (Zurich: Orell, Gessner & Füssli, 1791), p. 21.

58   On the significance of the theatre for the city see Lothar Gall, *Bürgertum in Deutschland* (Berlin: Seidler, 1989), pp. 199–214.

evidence of the sharp decline of tragedy by comparison with the middle decades of the century. Of the works of the French tragedians Voltaire's *Mérope* was still played, as was Corneille's *Rodogune*. Seyler also brought Shakespeare to the Mannheim stage in the form of Schröder's version of *Hamlet* and Heinrich Leopold Wagner's *Macbeth*.[59] Seyler, as one of the pioneers of North German opera, brought to Mannheim the hugely popular collaborations of Christian Felix Weisse and Johann Adam Hiller (*Die Jagd, Lottchen am Hofe* and *Die Liebe auf dem Lande*), also the Schweitzer/Wieland opera *Alceste*. Seyler also brought to Mannheim the melodramas *Ariadne auf Naxos* and *Medea*, which continued to be popular into the 1780s. Once in Mannheim, Seyler took over into his repertoire some of the popular *opéras-comiques* played by Marchand. Of the plays of the *Sturm und Drang* authors, few were performed; Lenz's *Der Hofmeister* (1774) was staged in 1780 and repeated occasionally for the next few years, and later in 1784 Dalberg's adaptation of Leisewitz's *Julius von Tarent* (1776).

The Hamburg tradition in style and aesthetics was strong at the theatre, not only as a result of the lasting influence of Lessing's plays and criticism but also through the influence on Dalberg of men who shared that tradition and outlook: Seyler, Gotter and the Hamburg actor and *Prinzipal* Friedrich Ludwig Schröder. The latter arrived for a *Gastspiel* in 1780, introducing the audience to *King Lear* and *Hamlet*, which he had adapted and in which he played the title role. Schröder's strong opposition to the French classical style may have influenced Dalberg's distanced view of that tradition.[60] Iffland recalls, however, that Schröder's masterly playing made the Mannheim audience dissatisfied afterwards with the efforts of the young company.[61] Lessing's *Miß Sara Sampson, Der Freygeist, Emilia Galotti* and *Minna von Barnhelm* were all played, the latter two in particular typifying the Hamburg emphasis on psychologically convincing character portrayal and some realism of language and style. The dramas,

---

59   See Walter, vol. 2, pp. 260–62.
60   See Fritz Alafberg, *Wolfgang Heribert von Dalberg als Bühnenleiter und als Dramatiker* (Berlin: Ebering, 1907), pp. 23–25.
61   *Meine theatralische Laufbahn*, p. 53.

translations and adaptations by Gotter and operas for which he was librettist were staples of the repertoire. His standing with Dalberg, Seyler and Schröder was high.[62]

Gotter was a staunch admirer of Lessing and a severe critic of the *Sturm und Drang* style in drama. While acknowledging Shakespeare's unique talent he deplored the imitators of the English playwright who threw aside dramatic form, unity and decorum and who thereby jeopardized all the progress Germany had made towards creating a stage with high artistic and literary standards. Writing in a preface to his works, he states:

> Shakespear und einige nach seinem Vorbilde mit Glück gemodelte väterländische Originale bezauberten das Publikum, und verdrehten dem Völkchen der Nachahmer die Köpfe. Es geschah, was Lessing selbst im prophetischen Geiste vorhergesehen hatte; wir prallten gegen den Rand eines andern Abgrunds zurück. Wir suchten den erstaunenden Beyfall, mit dem jene Stücke allgemein aufgenommen wurden, nicht in der Kunst, eine Reihe von Begebenheiten in ein großes Ganzes zusammen zu drängen und so zu ordnen, daß eine jede zur Erreichung eines gemeinschaftlichen Endzweckes das ihrige beytrage; nicht in der unnachahmlichen Gabe, durch Entwickelung der geheimsten Falten des Herzens, die ansprechenden Saiten des unsrigen zu treffen, die Sprache dem Charakter, das Kolorit der Situation anzupassen [...]; wir suchten ihn in der Umstossung aller Regeln, in der Ueberladung an Personen und Vorfällen, Machinerie und Gepränge, in der geschmacklosesten Mischung des Schrecklichen und Lächerlichen, des Schwulstigen und Pöbelhaften, in der Kühnheit, ungesehene Dinge in einer unerhörten Sprache vorzutragen. Die Kraftgenies entstanden, und machten zum wenigsten ein ephemeres Glück.
>
> Die Schauspieldirektoren fanden ihre Rechnung dabey, die Zuschauer durch die Lockspeise der Neuheit anzuklirren, und erniedrigten lieber das Theater zur Marktschreyerbude, um Logen und Parterre anzufüllen, als daß sie sich

---

62   See Rudolf Schlösser, *Friedrich Wilhelm Gotter. Sein Leben und seine Werke. Ein Beitrag zur Geschichte der Bühne und Bühnendichtung im 18. Jahrhundert*, Theatergeschichtliche Forschungen, 10 (Hamburg and Leipzig: Voss, 1894), esp. pp. 121–40. In fact Schröder tried at one point to tempt him away from Gotha to be attached to the Hamburg theatre but Gotter declined; see their correspondence as collected in *Schröder und Gotter. Eine Episode aus der deutschen Theatergeschichte*, ed. and with an introduction by Berthold Litzmann, (Hamburg and Leipzig: Voss, 1887).

der Gefahr aussetzten, bei leeren Wänden den Musen ein ihrer Gottheit würdiges Opfer zu bringen.[63]

These comments provide a clear insight into the disquiet aroused by the *avant-garde* drama of the 1770s among many theatre lovers and practical theatre people, who were anxious to preserve the slow but perceptible progress being made towards a cultivated theatre acceptable and accessible to the bourgeoisie as well as to the aristocracy.

Iffland's early Mannheim years

Iffland made his Mannheim debut on Thursday 7 October 1779, when the theatre opened with its own standing company. His letters to members of his family tell us little about his acting experiences or about the plays. His comments on performances are usually connected with an account of how lavishly he was praised or how heartily he was applauded. This is understandable, given the recipients of the letters, who are meant not only to be impressed with their relative's success (and Iffland usually comments on the plaudits he receives from those of elevated rank) but also to understand that he is being honoured as an artist who holds a respectable position in society. Thus, explaining why he may not be able to travel to Hanover, he also assures his bother-in-law that the Elector Carl Theodor admires him: 'Außer daß ich in fast allen Stücken zu thun habe, so ist es gewiß, daß ich einer seiner Lieblingsschauspieler bin. H. Schröder hat er daß gesagt.'[64] On the three evenings a week on which the theatre was open, the company gave thirty-seven performances by the end of 1779, thirty of which were of plays new to the repertoire.[65] This must have been a strenuous but useful schedule for the young actor, whose appetite for new and varied roles became legendary. During his *Gastspiel* in

---

63 *Gedichte* (Gotha: Ettinger, 1788), vol. 2, pp. xiii–xiv.
64 Letter to Eisendecher, 27 September 1780, Geiger 1, p. 61.
65 Koffka, p. 60

Weimar in 1796, for example, he performed thirteen roles in twenty-eight days. These latter were of course prominent roles, whereas he must have had many minor ones in these early Mannheim years, particularly as young romantic leads were outside his *Rollenfach*. Nevertheless, he clearly acquired immense versatility through his early training. In the first years up to his breakthrough role, Franz Moor in *Die Räuber*, he mentions few individual plays: *Der Galeerensklave* (Falbaire) and *Die heimliche Heirat* (Garrick and Colman). An early commendation came in December 1779 when the Duke of Sachsen–Weimar–Eisenach, Carl August, attended a performance of Goethe's *Clavigo* with the playwright himself. Iffland, who played the role of Carlos, writes to his elder brother Philipp that Goethe's words to him were: 'Mit so viel Wahrheit und Delikatesse sah ich seit Ekhoff [*sic*] nicht spielen.'[66] It was clearly an important success for him.

Seyler took a fatherly interest in the young actor, helping to create something of a familial atmosphere through his and his wife's hospitality. The involvement of Dalberg as a shaping force in the artistic development of the theatre becomes clear. Usually an *Intendant* was a member of the court aristocracy whose responsibility was merely to oversee administrative arrangements. Iffland tells his father shortly after his arrival in Mannheim:

> Die Direktion hat Hr. Dalberg und Hr. Seiler [...]. Aber alle vier Wochen ist eine Zusammenkunft, wo von neuen Stücken und deren Besetzung die Rede ist. Diese Zusammenkunft besteht aus Hn. von Dalberg, Hn. Seyler, Herrn Böck und mir. Alle Montag von 3 bis 5 Uhr ist die ganze Gesellschaft bei Hn. von Dalberg, wo jeder über sein Spiel in der ganzen Woche beurtheilt wird. Die Garderobe ist fürtrefflich, und die Kleider zu den Hauptrollen sind jedem angemessen worden.[67]

If Iffland is not exaggerating his role in the small circle of those scrutinizing the repertoire, we gain the impression that he quickly showed himself to be ambitious both for himself and for the theatre as an enterprise. Seyler proved a supportive friend in another respect. Iffland brought debts from his Gotha period with him to Mannheim.

---

66 See his letter of 24 December 1779, quoted in GFA I, 40/2, 231.
67 Letter of 31 October 1779, Geiger 1, p. 38.

On 11 March 1780 his father died. On 31 March Seyler wrote to Iffland's brother-in-law Wilhelm Eisendecher with his condolences. Amid assurances of the esteem in which the young actor was held, Seyler asked Eisendecher to relieve Iffland's debts, which, according to Seyler, had not increased in Mannheim.[68] These continuing money problems would be mere footnotes, if they did not become in time the motor for much of Iffland's career. Dalberg's fear of losing him gave the actor the power to gain ever better conditions in Mannheim and when that possibility was exhausted he was able to look elsewhere and in the King of Prussia find a ruler prepared to pay off his accumulated debts.

Though the court had begun its move to Munich about a year before, when Iffland arrived in Mannheim in the autumn of 1779, the impact of the move was not yet keenly felt. The change began to bite during his first two years, as he recalls in his autobiography:

> Die allgemeine Stimmung war nirgend fühlbarer als im Theater, und hier war sie sehr drückend. Diese Periode, so sehr im Widerspruch mit unserm fröhlichen Anfange, war beengend und ängstlich. Das Theater ging zwar seinen Weg damals fort, aber ohne Ermunterung, ohne Kraft, ohne Freude, in der gewohnheitsmäßigen, nicht geachteten Anstrengung alltäglicher Handwerker.[69]

His disappointment at having failed to impress Schröder may well have contributed to the gloom.[70] He writes of having decided at one point to leave Mannheim. Instead, he, Beil and Beck committed themselves to self-improvement. Iffland's narrative then focuses on an important event, the decision to try his hand at writing plays. He had tried writing some short pieces about acting for the *Rheinische Beiträge zur Gelehrsamkeit* in 1781 and 1782 but had not found the experience satisfying.[71] The determination to write plays came to him

---

68 See Seyler's unpublished letter to Wilhelm Eisendecher (GSA 48/IV, 11) in the Goethe- und Schiller-Archiv, Weimar. Eisendecher and Iffland's elder brother Philipp held the legacy from Iffland's father in trust for him until he reached the age of thirty.

69 *Meine theatralische Laufbahn*, p. 52.

70 *Meine theatralische Laufbahn*, pp. 52–53. During his visit Schröder engaged the Mannheim actor Franz Zuccarini for Hamburg.

71 For further details see p. 108 .

in 1781 as the result of a performance of *Alceste*, the opera by Anton Schweitzer with a libretto by Wieland.[72] Admittedly it was the overture that Iffland records as having moved him particularly, but it is nevertheless somehow fitting that the most successful playwright of his generation should be inspired by this particular work because of the opera's roots in the German theatrical and music-theatre tradition. Though it uses mythological content, the libretto's sentimental qualities are typical of much drama of the period and also of much opera and *Singspiel*.[73] The first result of this determination, *Liebe und Pflicht im Streit* (later published and more widely known as *Albert von Thurneisen*), was first performed in Mannheim on 27 May 1781, with incidental music by Franz Danzi, at about the time *Die Räuber* was being published in Stuttgart. It was moderately successful.[74] The friendly reception enjoyed by the play at its première made the actor decide to continue his playwriting: 'So entstand der Vorsatz, mehrere bürgerliche Verhältnisse nach und nach dramatisch zu behandeln.'[75] So at an early stage Iffland fixed on a limited range of milieux and subjects that would ensure a resonance with the public and be in harmony with the moralizing tendency of much of the contemporary German repertoire and with the ethos of the Mannheim Theatre.

In its first printed edition the play is called *Albert von Thurneisen. Ein bürgerliches Trauerspiel*.[76] This title hints at the strange mixture this play is, on the one hand a treatment of an archetypal conflict of the kind particularly exploited by French neo-classical tragedy, on the other an attempt to explore this theme among

---

72   *Meine theatralische Laufbahn*, p. 55.

73   Goethe famously objected to the reduction of the play's content to the level of the *drame bourgeois* in his satire of 1773, *Götter, Helden und Wieland*.

74   See *Meine theatralische Laufbahn*, p. 55 and the positive comment in the *Literatur- und Theaterzeitung*, ed. by Christoph August Bertram (reprinted Munich: Kraus, 1981), Jahrgang 4 (1781), p. 764: 'Liebe und Pflicht in Streit, ein Originaltrauerspiel von Iffland, machte großen Eindruck auf empfindsame Herzen.'

75   *Meine theatralische Laufbahn*, p. 55.

76   Published in Mannheim by Schwan, 1781. A revised version was performed at the Berlin National Theatre in 1798 and is the version mainly adopted in editions of Iffland's collected plays.

characters of less elevated status than those of high tragedy (though all the characters are members of the aristocracy). The action takes place within a besieged fortress, presumably during the Seven Years' War. Sophie, the daughter of General von Dolzig, is betrothed to Graf Hohenthal but has fallen in love with the dashing officer Thurneisen. Under pressure from her father to marry immediately because of the impending danger of attack, Sophie summons Thurneisen, who abandons his post defending one of the towers of the fortress, which is attacked by the enemy in his brief absence. A court martial finds him guilty and he is sentenced to death. General von Dolzig has to struggle with his duty and his concern for his daughter. All the characters demonstrate exemplary nobility of spirit as events take their inevitable course, so that, though sentimental, it is nevertheless a very sombre piece. An officer who, like Thurneisen, abandons his post at the crucial part of a siege is, however, bound to arouse mixed feelings in an audience. Iffland had found some of the elements of the family drama that would bring him success in the near future – conflicts between parent and child, the threat of unhappy marriage – but had set himself an impossible task in introducing questions of military discipline in combination with the family elements. It is a significant beginning as representing a direction Iffland abandoned in favour of the private sphere, in which the virtue of the bourgeoisie can prevail and meets with no effective challenge, and of the happy ending. As an actor he knew that, however high the standing of tragedy in the literary hierarchy, audiences liked to go home happy.

In choosing his theme Iffland may have wanted to take advantage of the popularity at the time of soldier plays. One possible influence is Heinrich Ferdinand Möller's *Der Graf von Walltron, oder die Subordination* (1776), which was played at the Gotha theatre and, like Iffland's play, deals with the effects of disobeying military orders. Iffland's subtitle *Ein bürgerliches Trauerspiel* points to the influence of Lessing's serious drama, but not only to his literary influence.[77] We

---

77   Alexander Košenina notes textual reminiscences of *Emilia Galotti* in his discussion of the characters' physical manifestations of emotion. See *Anthropologie und Schauspielkunst. Studien zur 'eloquentia corporis' im 18. Jahrhundert*, Theatron, 11 (Tübingen: Niemeyer, 1995), pp. 238 and 243.

may detect here Iffland's early appreciation of the importance of identifying himself with Lessing at Mannheim. The legacy of the revered playwright, who died that very year, was, as discussed above, the dominant aesthetic influence at the theatre. In the next chapter it will become clear how much Schiller recognized the need to present himself as Lessing's heir if he wanted to secure a lasting future at Mannheim. For the ambitious Iffland this tactic was already obvious.

By the time *Die Räuber* was premièred, the Mannheim Theatre had entered its second phase. Seyler, known for a certain fondness for the bottle, boxed the ears of one of the actresses at a rehearsal and had, to Dalberg's regret, to be dismissed as *Regisseur*. Though an existing member of the company thereafter took on the task of *Regisseur*, from that point onwards until the end of the decade Dalberg tried to exercise a direct influence over the development of the young theatre by allowing a certain experimentation in the repertoire (hence his staging of *Die Räuber*) and encouraging the members of the company to contribute to an aesthetic dialogue that scrutinized fundamental principles of acting and repertoire development. This change provided an opportunity for an ambitious and articulate, if still very junior, member such as Iffland to come to prominence. It also explains why Dalberg was at least partially open to the acquisition of a *Theaterdichter* in the form of the young Schiller.

The staging of *Die Räuber*

It is ironical that Mannheim is permanently associated with the *Sturm und Drang* through the première of *Die Räuber*, when in fact Schiller's play, although clearly inspired by the *Sturm und Drang*, was very much the exception to the trend of the repertoire. It was accepted for performance because Dalberg was persuaded that it would tap into audience taste for two kinds of play: the historical *Ritterstück* and the family drama. Graf August von Törring's *Agnes Bernauerin* (1780) and Jakob Meier's *Der Sturm von Boxberg* (1780) – both set in the late Middle Ages and both involving stage spectacle – had been two successful examples of the former. Already established with audiences was the *Familiendrama* as exemplified most recently at the theatre by Otto Freiherr von Gemmingen's reworking of Diderot's popular *Le Père de famille* in his play *Die Familie oder Der teutsche Hausvater* (1780). Gemmingen, a young court official, was also a member of the *Kurpfälzische Deutsche Gesellschaft* and of the Mannheim literary set and was a strong supporter of the theatre. *Die Räuber*, though with its catastrophic ending anything but a cosy family drama, does have family conflict at its heart and this circumstance may have led Dalberg to believe it would appeal to his public. The version that Schiller produced at Dalberg's request in the course of the autumn of 1781 was not the version that was performed, for even after Schiller had completed his adaptation Dalberg made further interventions. What was performed at the momentous première is preserved in the Mannheim prompt book, a version Schiller presumably only heard spoken but never read.[78] Shortly after the première he gave Schwan his own stage adaptation for publication, insisting that Schwan change not one line of it, an indication perhaps of his annoyance at the freedom Dalberg had allowed himself with Schiller's hard work.[79] The stage version appeared under the title *Die Räuber ein Trauerspiel von Friedrich Schiller. Neue für die Mannheimer Bühne verbesserte Auflage* (1782).

Dalberg's letters in the months preceding the première, in which he presumably outlined to the writer his requirements for the adaptation, are lost. Schiller's letters to Dalberg allow us to deduce a certain amount about the proposed changes and his response to them. The young writer was quickly to discover that in the world of theatre the playwright's wishes and intentions, his concerns about coherence or literary quality, carried little weight. One proposed change that appears to have come from Dalberg was to allude in the title of the

---

78 For the text used on the Mannheim stage see *Schillers Räuber. Urtext des Mannheimer Soufflierbuches* (henceforth *Soufflierbuch*), ed. by Herbert Stubenrauch and Günter Schulz (Mannheim: Bibliographisches Institut, 1959). On Dalberg's requirements see Otto Schmidt, 'Die Uraufführung der *Räuber* – ein theatergeschichtliches Ereignis', in *Soufflierbuch*, pp. 151–80 (pp. 153–56).

79 See his letter to Schwan of 2 February 1782 (NA 23, 31).

play to the Prodigal Son and thus stress its family aspect.[80] In sending his new version Schiller writes: 'Hier erscheint endlich der *Verlorne Sohn*, oder die umgeschmolzenen Räuber' (NA 23, 20). The 'family drama', however, was usually conservative in its stress on established hierarchies and on the efficacy of virtues such as loyalty, obedience and honesty in solving problems. Schiller's drama presents us with a family whose rifts cannot be healed, the parable of the Prodigal Son being used to provide a mythic representation of estrangement and dislocation expressed in opposing philosophies, Promethean idealism and radical materialism, of the later Enlightenment.

In the end the original title remained, but significant changes to the action also reflect the moralizing tendency characteristic of family drama and favoured by Dalberg. In the *Schauspiel* version Franz, overcome with terror at the certainty of retribution for his misdeeds and hearing the robbers approach, hangs himself. In the prompt book and in the *Trauerspiel*, Franz tries to escape the robbers by leaping into the fire engulfing the castle but is nevertheless captured and brought to Karl for judgment. Karl turns him over to a tribunal of robbers, who decree that he should be thrown into the dungeon of the tower from which his father has been released. This 'court' and judgement no doubt satisfied the audience but it puts Karl in a position of moral superiority to Franz that by the end of the play he cannot claim. In the *Schauspiel* version Schweitzer, Karl's most loyal follower, shoots himself when, sent to capture Franz, he finds the latter already dead. Because the Franz of the prompt book and *Trauerspiel* does not hang himself, Schweitzer too is still alive at the end of the play and Schiller uses him in the remodelled ending. Karl dismisses the robbers and then calls Schweitzer and Kosinsky, the noblest of the band, and tells them to become good citizens.[81] In the *Schauspiel* the robbers dismiss Karl's insight into his own moral degradation and his desire to atone as 'Gross-Mann-Sucht' (Act 5, 2) and turn from him. His final words, 'dem Mann kann geholfen werden', are a statement of the wish to perform a simple, good act, an indication that he is not thinking solely of himself. He does not, as in the *Trauerspiel*, tell

---

80 See Herbert Stubenrauch's commentary in NA 3, 313–15.
81 *Soufflierbuch*, p. 134; *Trauerspiel*, Act 5, 8.

the robbers to be good citizens, a wish hardly likely to be fulfilled, for Karl has no moral authority to tell anyone what to do. The prompt book adds these final words to the play: 'Er führe mich vor die Richter – ein Glüklicher mehr – Sonne – Untergang. Ich sterbe groß durch eine solche That!'[82] The reference to the setting sun is an echo of the scene (*Schauspiel* and *Trauerspiel* Act 3, 2) after the battle in the Bohemian Forests where Karl admires the setting sun and sees in its glory a metaphor for a dying hero. The words added to the prompt book ending underline the moral of Karl's repentance but turn his new and uncharacteristic humility into an expression of the 'Großmannssucht' the robbers of the *Schauspiel* have derided.[83]

Dalberg combined the sentimental, moralizing tendency with the romance of the *Ritterstück* by insisting that the action of the play be put back to the end of the fifteenth century. Schiller was unhappy about this change, for his characters belong to a modern age and speak accordingly.[84] Dalberg stood firm even when not only Schiller but also the actors raised objections.[85] These admittedly focused on the fact that the costumes would look too newly made and thus, one assumes, break the illusion. Dalberg's reply stressed the fact that the play must be seen in an 'idealistic' light. It showed events, he claimed, too remote from contemporary reality to convince of their plausibility and would thus alienate the audience.[86] But the distancing effect of the historical setting was undoubtedly more to do with the explosiveness of some of the contemporary criticism.

---

82   *Soufflierbuch*, p. 134.
83   The facsimile of the final page of the prompt book (facing page 112 of the *Soufflierbuch*) shows deletions and pencil markings that suggests that the words 'Er führe [...] mehr' may have been omitted and indeed that at the première or in subsequent performances all the additional words may have been cut again. They are, however, clearly there in the original version of the MS in the prompter's (Trinkle's) hand.
84   See his letters to Dalberg of 3 November and 12 December 1781, NA 23, 23–26.
85   See *Die Protokolle des Mannheimer Nationaltheaters unter Dalberg aus den Jahren 1781 bis 1789*, ed. by Max Martersteig (Mannheim: Bensheimer, 1890), pp. 45–46.
86   Martersteig, *Protokolle*, p. 46.

Amendments to the role of Franz also suggest an attempt to bring the play within more comfortable and reassuring limits. The *Trauerspiel* version makes him reject the temptation to kill Karl and he asserts some moral feeling (Act 4, 9, *Soufflierbuch*, p. 100), whereas in the *Schauspiel* Franz's only moral impulse is the terror and panic he feels at the approach of retribution. Iffland's playing of Franz supported this humanizing tendency. At the time of the Mannheim première he was, like Schiller, twenty-two, and was quite slightly built. He played Franz with the evidence of intelligence and polish befitting a nobleman. Recollecting the role in a later essay, he explained his approach as being to help the audience to understand how such a figure, neglected and disadvantaged by his family, could develop the kind of resentment that would account for his actions and overwhelming desire for revenge and dominance.[87] This psychological approach is typical of Iffland and worked very well for the kind of character role in family drama in which he specialized, but is not necessarily appropriate for a play that decidedly steps out of a realist framework. Thus the enormity of Franz is moderated. Goethe's much later comment on this interpretation in a review of the 1807 *Almanach für Theater und Theaterfreunde* is significant: 'So gewinnt man auch bei einer solchen Behandlung des Franz Moor nur das, daß endlich ein würdiger Hundsfott fertig wird, den ein ehrlicher Mann ohne Schande spielen kann.'[88] Goethe's comment suggests an intrusion of moral judgment on the part of the actor, who scales down the horror of Franz in order to make him a more palatable and morally worthy part to play and thus destroys the balance of the characters. Goethe, however, was writing when *Die Räuber* had been part of the repertoire for twenty-five years. In 1782 Schiller was very conscious of the difficulty of realising Franz on stage and clearly appreciated Iffland's nuanced and intelligent approach to the part: 'diese Rolle, die gar nicht für die

---

87   See Iffland's essay 'Über Darstellung boshafter und intriganter Charaktere auf der Bühne' in *Über Schauspieler und Schauspielkunst. Ausgewählte Abhandlungen von August Wilhelm Iffland und Johann Gottfried Seume* (Dresden: Verlag der Kunst, 1954), pp. 23–34. It was first published in *Almanach für Theater und Theaterfreunde 1807*, pp. 50–86.

88   See WA I/40, 173.

Bühne ist, hatt ich schon für verloren gehalten, und nie bin ich noch so angenehm betrogen worden. Iffland hat sich in den letztern Szenen als Meister gezeigt' (NA 22, 310).

The care and thought lavished on the production,[89] the fact that it was put on by an ensemble with a number of emerging young talents and by an *Intendant* who knew his public meant that it had a great chance of success. At the same time it was a different play from the one Schiller originally wrote and the ways in which it differed from the original tell us some of the reasons why Schiller's future at the Mannheim theatre would be limited. His style identified him with the *Sturm und Drang* and his content was a challenge to moralizing drama. Gotter's response to the news that Dalberg had staged *Die Räuber* demonstrates diplomatically controlled hostility: 'Die Räuber aufzuführen war ein kühnes Unternehmen, vielleicht nur in Mannheim möglich [...] das Stück [behält] in der Gattung des Schrecklichen den Preis. Aber der Himmel bewahre uns von mehr Stücken dieser Gattung.'[90] This kind of response may help to explain Dalberg's reluctance to commit himself to Schiller when the young playwright finally abandoned Württemberg, his family and his livelihood in order to pursue a career as a writer.

---

89   This is confirmed by Iffland in *Meine theatralische Laufbahn*, p. 56.
90   Letter to Dalberg, 24 March 1782, quoted by Schlösser, *Friedrich Wilhelm Gotter*, p. 123.

Chapter Two
Friends and Rivals

A new era in Mannheim

After the departure of Abel Seyler in March 1781 the theatre was without a *Regisseur*. Rather than engage a replacement from outside, Dalberg decided that a *Regisseur* should be elected from among the company. He was known as the *erster Ausschuss*. The *zweiter Ausschuss* was his assistant, nominated by Dalberg from among the actors for a three-month or six-month period. These two actors together with Dalberg and two or three further elected members of the company made up the theatre's committee (*Ausschuss*). Max Martersteig, who edited the collected minutes of the meetings up to the point they ceased in 1789, sees the move to this innovative form of governance thus:

> die Erscheinung, die nun in's Leben trat, ging zunächst von der Erkenntniß so vieler, frischer, jugendlicher Geister aus, daß das alte Prinzipalwesen sich überlebt habe, daß die Herrschaft eines einzelnen über den Theaterhaushalt dem strebsamen Drange einer Kunstgenossenschaft, die, wie gar nicht zu verkennen ist, eine starke Intelligenz in sich vereinigte, nicht mehr angemessen sei.[1]

This suggests a power on the part of the members of the company that they certainly did not possess (though Iffland may have possessed it later). What is true is that Dalberg was an *Intendant*, not an independent theatre entrepreneur but a court official entrusted with the running of the theatre (and with keeping it within a certain budget), and the members of the company were paid by the Elector. Dalberg had been a member of one of the many enthusiastic amateur acting groups that flourished at that time in aristocratic circles and was also a writer of

---

1   Martersteig, *Protokolle*, p. 412.

plays and librettos that were performed at Mannheim and elsewhere.[2] He was prepared to conduct an experiment in developing a company and repertoire that fulfilled, within the bounds of the financially possible, the aspirations of a national theatre. The collected minutes provide a fascinating insight into the practical and aesthetic considerations operating within the theatre and into Dalberg's fluctuating level of commitment to the enterprise. The committee was originally to meet fortnightly, though the frequency varied in practice, and its primary task was to plan the repertoire, review performances, consider possible new productions and deal with discipline.

Such an institution not only gave Dalberg a much larger role than he had had during Seyler's time in determining the artistic direction of the theatre, but also gave an ambitious young talent such as Iffland a unique opportunity to influence its development and to establish himself as a key figure. Dalberg encouraged discussion rather then simply decreeing what would be done. He was also absent quite frequently from Mannheim, particularly in the summer, when he usually spent some months at his family estate at Herrnsheim and needed to be kept informed of events. Iffland took full advantage of Dalberg's open ear and of his own indefatigability as a letter writer to express views that are a combination of actorly know-how, educated opinion and, to some extent at least, calculated self-interest. Disinterested judgement and ambition become particularly hard to disentangle in the case of his dealings with Schiller towards the end of the latter's association with Mannheim.

From October 1782 the *Ausschuss* was given extended responsibility for the quality and standard of productions and for assessing plays for possible staging, and there was increased involvement on the part of Dalberg.[3] He proposed significant aesthetic topics for written responses, the first being 'Was ist Natur, und welches sind die wahren

2   For example, *Walwais und Adelaide* (a drama, 1778), *Cora* (a libretto, 1780), *Die weibliche Ehescheue* (a comedy, 1787) and several translations and adaptations, a number of which will be mentioned in the course of this and the following chapter. Alafberg provides the fullest account of Dalberg's theatrical career.

3   Martersteig, *Protokolle*, pp. 63–69.

Grenzen derselben bei theatralischen Vorstellungen?'[4] Shortly after this, at the third meeting of the theatre year, probably around 21 November 1782, the minutes record that Iffland has been invited by 'Professor Strobel' (the Munich writer, translator and bookseller Johann Baptist Strobl) to contribute to the latter's new journal *Der dramatische Censor* and has promised to write on the history of the Mannheim theatre.[5] The journal was shortlived, lasting only from October 1782 to March 1783,[6] but a two-part article appeared in the first and third numbers[7] in which Iffland pays homage to Seyler and his imaginative leadership and highlights recent successes at Mannheim by pointing to three significant productions, namely *Agnes Bernauerin*, *Der Sturm von Boxberg* and *Die Räuber*: 'Jedes dieser Stücke hat Epoche veranlaßt; jedes war ein fürtreffliches Ganzes; sie sind alle dreye mit einem Aufwand gegeben worden, den man bey wenig deutschen Theatern machen kann.'[8]

The involvement with Strobl's journal is an example of Iffland's life-long assiduity as a writer. Alongside his dramatic writing, though more sporadically, he engaged in theatre journalism and writing on aspects of acting. Theatre journals were constantly springing up in the final decades of the eighteenth century and almost all, like *Der dramatische Censor*, were short-lived.[9] Iffland's topic shows he was keen to raise the profile and standing of his own theatre beyond the boundaries of the Palatinate and, one may assume, to continue to make a mark, however small, on the wider literary scene. After the moderate success of *Liebe und Pflicht im Streit* (1781), which was repeated four times at Mannheim after its première, his next two plays had not survived beyond a single performance. A drama, *Wilhelm von Schenk*,

---

4   Martersteig, *Protokolle*, p. 74.
5   Martersteig, *Protokolle*, p. 88.
6   Geiger 1, p. 258.
7   Geiger (1, p. 263) reproduces sections.
8   Geiger 1, p. 263.
9   See Wolfgang Bender, Siegfried Bushuven and Michael Huesmann, *Theaterperiodika des 18. Jahrhunderts. Bibliographie und inhaltliche Erschließung deutschsprachiger Theaterzeitschriften, Theaterkalender und Theatertaschenbücher*, Teil 1: 1750–1780, 2 vols, Teil 2: 1781–1790, 3 vols, (München, New Providence, London: Saur, 1994).

was premièred on 12 September 1781 and a comedy, *Wie man's treibt, so geht's*, on 3 November 1781.[10] He destroyed them both and was perhaps conscious that he was not finding the formula to appeal to popular taste and so turned to journalism as another means of reaching the reading public and boosting the prestige of acting.

Die Verschwörung des Fiesko zu Genua on stage

Die Verschwörung des Fiesko zu Genua was the play on which Schiller pinned his hopes of an escape from Württemberg. *Die Räuber* had brought him into conflict with Duke Carl Eugen. A notoriously profligate and self-indulgent ruler in his earlier years, whose ambition was to recreate the splendour of Versailles in his own capital, Stuttgart, Carl Eugen underwent something like a midlife crisis at the age of about forty and decided to take his responsibilities more seriously. One of his most cherished projects was the military academy Schiller was forced to attend, which was set up principally to train army officers and state bureaucrats. Having changed from law studies to medicine in the course of his time there, Schiller emerged eventually as an army surgeon, a post that in salary and prospects fell far behind what he and his parents might have hoped for.[11] According to his friend Andreas Streicher, Schiller was anything but troubled about his low pay, being instead delighted at the age of twenty-one at last to have his freedom to write.[12] This freedom was shortlived, however. Carl Eugen heard that in *Die Räuber* there was a deregatory comment about Les Grisons in Switzerland that had caused a native of Les Grisons to respond in

---

10   See Walter, vol. 2, pp. 275–76.
11   Christophine Schiller recorded that her brother was given 'statt dieser [guten Stelle] eine ganz untergeordnete für Geist und Wirken, als Regimentsmedikus […] über dieß alles trug die Stelle nicht so viel, daß er nur die nöthigsten Lebenbedürfnisse schaffen konnte: sein Vater mußte ihn immer unterstützen' (Boxberger, p. 460).
12   Streicher, p. 65.

print to this supposed insult. The unwelcome news that one of his subjects might be causing controversy abroad, however slight, led the Duke in August 1782 to forbid Schiller to publish anything in future but medical treatises or to have dealings with 'foreigners', that is with those from states beyond the borders of Württemberg.[13] Schiller had already incurred his displeasure by travelling again without leave to Mannheim in May. His absence was noted and reported to the Duke, who placed him under arrest for fourteen days, though this was not an excessive punishment according to the prevailing rules.

Thus, even before he was banned from writing, Schiller's view of his situation was growing increasingly bleak. Whereas in Mannheim he was fêted and treated as the rising star in the dramatic firmament, in Stuttgart he had no prospect of pursuing what to him was his true passion and vocation. The key figure was Dalberg. If he could be sure of Dalberg's support and a place to go for the immediate future he could risk trying to leave Württemberg. He had clearly received encouragement from Dalberg to believe he had prospects at the Mannheim theatre;[14] Dalberg had, for example, suggested to him that he adapt Goethe's *Götz von Berlichingen*.[15] A revealing letter in which Schiller appeals movingly to Dalberg for practical help also shows how astutely he had weighed up how to present the matter to the Duke. For example, if Dalberg were to ask for Schiller 'on loan' for a particular period of time with a specified end date the Duke might not see his departure as a potential desertion.[16] The 'borrowing' of Schiller would have been a simple expedient involving Dalberg in no long-term commitment. Once Schiller's despair at his ruler's *Schreibverbot* led him to flee and thus to be technically speaking an army deserter, it is easier to understand that Dalberg was reluctant to seem to have encouraged this step.

---

13   In his letter of 1 September 1782 to the Duke, Schiller refers to the command to him 'nichts litterarisches mehr zu schreiben, oder mit Ausländern zu communiciren' (NA 23, 39).

14   Christophine Schiller records: 'Hier [in Mannheim] wurden ihm die vorteilhaftesten Aussichten eröfnet, die er in der Folge auch annahm' (Boxberger, p. 460).

15   See Schiller's letter to Dalberg of 1 April 1782 (NA 23, 32).

16   See Schiller's letter to Dalberg of 2 June 1782 (NA 23, 35–37).

A draft of his new play *Die Verschwörung des Fiesko zu Genua* was in Schiller's luggage as he made his escape with his musician friend Streicher on 22 September 1782. He knew that *Fiesko* would be crucial as a means of convincing Dalberg of his productivity and suitability for a longer-term engagement. It is tempting to speculate whether Schiller's career would have been different if his second play, on which so much depended, had simply been better than it is and had immediately impressed Dalberg. The *Intendant* was absent when he arrived in Mannheim and Schiller's reading of the first two acts to the Mannheim actors at the house of the *erster Ausschuss* Meyer was not a success, partly, Streicher tells us, because of the author's exaggerated declamation and Swabian accent.[17] The reading took so long that when a break was suggested most of the actors drifted away, with the notable exception of Iffland. By the time Dalberg returned and responded to the offer of *Fiesko* to the theatre Schiller was living incognito at an inn at Oggersheim near Ludwigshafen to escape Carl Eugen's spies and was extremely low in funds. Dalberg wanted changes to the play, but when Schiller, despite his anxieties, managed to settle to make the changes, the new version still did not convince Dalberg and he would not take it on. As a result of his disappointment Schiller took his play directly to Schwan for publication in order to earn what he could from it. It appeared in April the following year and was premièred in Bonn by the notable Frankfurt *Prinzipal* Gustav Friedrich Wilhelm Grossmann on 20 July 1783.

At the same *Ausschuss* meeting at which Iffland's invitation to contribute to *Der dramatische Censor* was reported, Iffland delivered his assessment of the revised *Fiesko*, a 500-word analysis of the play's strengths and weaknesses from a theatrical point of view. The opening does not bode well: 'Der Verfasser der Räuber hat in seinem Fiesko mehr als jemals Shakespeares Fehler nachgeahmt.'[18] This indicates what a damning verdict it was to be regarded as an imitator of Shakespeare. Yet Iffland is keen to give Schiller credit where he believes it is due. He makes thoroughly justified criticisms of the play: for example, the characters analyse themselves too lengthily; Julia

---

17 Streicher, p. 125.
18 Martersteig, *Protokolle*, p. 88.

Imperiali is mean-spirited when she should be proud; Fiesco himself with his youth and all his advantages would be unlikely to follow the tortuous path of intricate subterfuge rather than that of open rebellion. Some comments are distinctly practical: there are too many roles for senators for a normal company to fill and there is not enough stage spectacle. And yet,

> aller dieser Fehler ohngeachtet, wie viel Stücke haben wir, welche solche Scenen enthalten, als diese sind, wo Verrina seine Tochter entehrt findet, wo das Volk zu Fiesko eindringt und dann Fieskos Monolog darauf folgt? Wo Doria mit seinem Neffen spricht, wo der Mohr den Fiesko erstechen will? Der ganze Mohr überhaupt![19]

Iffland does his professional best to estimate the play's value to the Mannheim theatre and, though doubtful, he is also conscious of Schiller's worth. He judges that the theatre has a debt of honour to him after his willingness to adapt the play and suggests paying him an honorarium at least comparable with what would be paid for a run-of-the-mill play or adaptation.[20] Iffland's report presumably confirmed Dalberg's original doubts: the fact that Schiller was continuing in the 'Shakespearian' style was clearly not in his favour. Dalberg did not pay him any money.

The disappointment of his hopes of at least a temporary home at the Mannheim theatre caused an even deeper crisis in Schiller's life. A fugitive, unable to return to Württemberg, with no money, family or means of earning a living, he was offered refuge at a small house on the estate at Bauerbach near Meiningen belonging to his Stuttgart friend Henriette von Wolzogen, whose son Wilhelm had also been a pupil at the military academy. There he worked on *Kabale und Liebe* and began the planning of *Don Karlos*. Finally, in the summer of 1783, he was offered a one-year contract with the Mannheim theatre with the requirement of delivering three plays, the first of which would be *Fiesko*. Much of Schiller's salary went immediately on clearing his debts and almost at once his work was hampered by his succumbing to the malaria epidemic that affected more than a quarter

---

19   Martersteig, *Protokolle*, p. 89.
20   Martersteig, *Protokolle*, pp. 89–90.

of Mannheim's population.[21] The Mannheim première of *Fiesko* did not therefore take place until 11 January 1784. Yet in spite of the practical theatrical problems of the kind Iffland identified, it is clear that Schiller conceived *Fiesko* from the first much more with stage performance in mind than was the case with *Die Räuber*. One of the striking features as soon as one opens the book version is that he gives exact descriptions of the *dramatis personae*, as though he were fitting them to the standard roles theatre companies expected to cover regularly (the *Rollenfach*). He had also tried from the outset to avoid some of the pitfalls of *Die Räuber* and to motivate the action and rein in the wildness and inconsistency of the play's language.[22]

Though it was given a lavish production, costly in money and in rehearsal time because of the large numbers of extras who were engaged, the play was not warmly received in Mannheim. Though repeated twice, as planned, it failed to establish itself in the repertoire and was not played again in Mannheim for some thirty years. *Fiesko* is in many ways Schiller's least appealing play and it is not difficult to imagine why it disappointed audiences hoping for something similar to *Die Räuber*. And part of its problem lies in Schiller's attempt to write something more consonant with the Mannheim style. The chief requirement for the Mannheim première was a version that avoided a tragic ending. In the new version Fiesko is challenged by Verrina publicly to renounce the Ducal purple. When he refuses, Verrina attempts to assassinate him but is disarmed. In a *coup de théâtre* Fiesko then voluntarily renounces power and pledges himself to become Genoa's 'glücklichster Bürger'. Leonore does not die. In his 'Erinnerung an das Publikum' Schiller gives a moral spin to the changed ending: 'Wenn jeder von uns zum Besten des Vaterlands *diejenige* Krone hinwegwerfen lernt, die *er* fähig ist zu erringen, so ist die Moral des Fiesko die größte des Lebens' (NA 22, 91). It is an argument in tune with Dalberg's thinking and with the ethos of the Mannheim Theatre. The new ending turns *Fiesko* into a *Schauspiel*. The audience's taste for tragedy was limited and Dalberg assumed they preferred to go home happy and in the knowledge that they had

---

21   It caused the death of the *erster Ausschuss*, Meyer, for example.
22   Iffland, however, criticizes the stylistic variety (Martersteig, *Protokolle*, p. 89).

been edified, and yet the lukewarm reception may have been not wholly because people were disappointed at the lack, by comparison with *Die Räuber*, of extreme events but also because they detected that the action is now something of a wild goose chase. The death of Fiesko is the only logical conclusion.

Fiesko provides evidence of another strategy on Schiller's part to show himself willing to mould himself to the Mannheim theatre, that of paying clear homage to Lessing in his work. He changes the circumstances of the rape of Bertha from those of his original version. It now follows an abduction planned by Gianettino, who is advised by his counsellor Lomellino. Bertha returns to her home in her father's absence and recounts that after her abduction she was led into a 'Kabinett'. These changes echo *Emilia Galotti*, in which the heroine is also betrothed to another but abducted and led away (Act 3, Scene 5) for a private conversation with the Prince, though Lessing's Hettore Gonzaga is much more appealing than Schiller's thuggish Gianettino. A similar strategy is evident again in *Kabale und Liebe*, the plot of which, possibly conceived as early as 1782, shows marked similarities to that of *Emilia Galotti*. It is evident in the history of the writing of *Don Karlos* too. While still in Bauerbach, Schiller produced a plan for the play (the 'Bauerbacher Entwurf') that Böckmann has convincingly argued was designed to impress the aesthetically conservative Gotter with its logical progression and clarity.[23] Schiller's famous assurance to Dalberg in 1784 that his new play would be 'nichts weniger [...] als ein politisches Stük – sondern eigentlich ein Familiengemählde in einem fürstlichen Hauße' (7 June 1784: NA 23, 144) is a clear indication that he is trying to combine the court setting with the emerging popularity of the *drame* as pioneered by Diderot and supported by Lessing, which was chiefly concerned with the private sphere.[24] In July 1784 Schiller sent Dalberg the outline of a *Mannheimer Dramaturgie*. It would take the form of a monthly journal, an agreed number of copies of which would be given to Dalberg for the use of the theatre

---

23   Paul Böckmann, *Schillers Don Karlos. Edition der ursprünglichen Fassung und entstehungsgeschichtlicher Kommentar* (Stuttgart: Klett, 1974), pp. 431–35.
24   Kluge casts plausible doubt on Schiller's intention to take up Diderot's dramatic ideas in practice; see FA 3, 1023–24.

committee. The purpose was to forge a link between the theatre and its public that would promote discussion, involvement and creativity. Again, the example of Lessing and the *Hamburgische Dramaturgie* is clear and Schiller's proposal also built on the fact that Dalberg himself, as already noted, was trying to encourage reflection, at least among the actors, on their art and on the aesthetics of the theatre. We can thus see Schiller trying, as soon as the success of *Die Räuber* opens up the possibility of further collaboration with Dalberg, to show he has recognized the dominant style and ethos of the theatre and is trying to respond to them.

Mannheim and family drama

Streicher reports of Schiller's early work on *Kabale und Liebe* in Oggersheim: 'Dieses Trauerspiel […] wollte er mehr als einen Versuch unternehmen, ob er sich auch in die bürgerliche Sphäre herablassen könne, als daß er sich öfters, oder gar für immer dieser Gattung hätte widmen wollen.'[25] The fact that after a few months in Bauerbach, in the spring of 1783, he was known in Mannheim to have written such a play and was ready to publish it was a source of great interest to the actors and to Dalberg. Either by Schiller's intention or not, it successfully provided the bait that *Fiesko* could not. This circumstance may explain why he did not publish the play at this point, in spite of being in negotiation with possible publishers. He recognized that it would need to be adapted for stage performance and, more importantly, that unpublished it was his exclusive property and not available to any theatre.

Kabale und Liebe certainly proved once and for all that Schiller could not only tune in to the taste of the mainstream theatre-going public but could also turn out a compact and carefully plotted play of performable length and with economy of means. To Grossmann, the

---

25   Streicher, p. 138.

Frankfurt *Prinzipal*, he wrote, implicitly responding to the problems of *Fiesko*:

> Ich darf hoffen, daß es der teutschen Bühne keine unwillkommene Acquisition seyn werde, weil es durch die Einfachheit der Vorstellung, den wenigen Aufwand von Maschinerei und Statisten, und durch leichte Faßlichkeit des Plans, für die Direction bequemer, und für das Publikum genießbarer ist als die Räuber und der Fiesko.[26]

The Mannheim première was on 15 April 1784, two days after the play's first performance in Frankfurt by Grossmann's company, for it had been published the month before by Schwan. This publication before the Mannheim première surely contravened the terms of Schiller's contract and the usual practice of *Theaterdichter* and may justifiably have angered Dalberg. It is probably explained by the writer's continued indebtedness and pressing need for income.

The adaptation of *Kabale und Liebe* Schiller prepared for the Mannheim première is about one eighth shorter than the book version and considerably toned down in terms of imagery, length of tirades and use of colloquialisms (for example in Miller's speeches). Though the exact extent of Schiller's involvement in the less drastic final version is not determinable now, the play still demonstrates his youthful prose style, to many of his contemporaries bombastic and tasteless but still powered by an immense creative energy. Whereas Grossmann had omitted the politically sensitive Kammerdiener scene with its condemnation of the sale of soldiers to fight in America, it was retained for the Mannheim premiere.[27] A noteworthy addition to the printed version in Act V, 1 is an account by Miller of his imprisonment and explanation of the absence of Frau Miller on the grounds of sickness contracted in prison.[28] This addition fills an obvious gap in the events as they stand in the printed version. The cast was:

---

26   Letter of 8 Feb. 1784 (NA 23, 131–32).
27   Walter (vol. 1, p. 52) explains the omission by the death of Grossmann's wife, which prevented Grossmann from appearing in the role, as had been intended.
28   See Herbert Stubenrauch, 'Musikus Miller im Turm. Schillers unbekannte Bühnenbearbeitung von *Kabale und Liebe*', *Weimarer Beiträge*, 1 (1955), 233–45, also NA 5N, 151–53 and 481.

Ferdinand: Beck
Luise: Karoline Beck
Miller: Beil
Präsident: Böck
Wurm: Iffland
Hofmarschall von Kalb: Rennschüb
Lady Milford: Frau Rennschüb
Frau Miller: Frau Wallenstein.

There was a tussle between Böck and Iffland for the role of the
Präsident, in which Iffland claimed to have generously given way.[29]
The performance was a considerable success but to Schiller's disappointment the play was not frequently repeated. One reason for this
may be that Dalberg was already moving towards the decision not to
retain Schiller and this decision would be harder to justify if a play
from his pen were being performed on a regular basis.

An indication that Dalberg was not well disposed to Schiller is
provided by his comments on a notable première that preceded that of
Kabale und Liebe. Iffland had taken up his pen again as a playwright
and for the first time, in his new play *Verbrechen aus Ehrsucht*, had
struck the right note with the public. Dedicated to Dalberg's wife and
designated in its subtitle *Ein ernsthaftes Familiengemälde in fünf Aufzügen*, the play was first performed on 9 March 1784 and was an instant and lasting success. Indeed Iffland went on to write two sequels,
Bewußtseyn (1786) and *Reue versöhnt* (1789), though neither repeated
the success of the first in the series. *Verbrechen aus Ehrsucht* is a
strongly didactic play with a simple plot. Eduard Ruhberg, the *bürgerlich* son of a marriage between an aristocratic mother and non-
aristocratic father, has his head turned by the foolish pursuit of an
aristocratic match, steals public money in his father's keeping in order
to pay his debts and is discovered. He is saved from disgrace when the

---

29   To his sister Louise: 'In Louise Millerin wollte der Dichter Boeck eine kleinere,
      mir eine grösere Rolle geben – Boeck wollte bereits seine Kabale wieder
      anheben, und das Stück hätte gebüßt. Ich gieng also zu Schiller (dem Verf.),
      entsagte freiwillig, spiele die kleinere und laße dem Elenden die größere. Aber
      das Spiel – dafür *bürge* ich – soll *mich* zum Größeren machen' (Geiger 1,
      pp. 146–47).

plain-speaking Ahlden, whose son hopes to marry Ruhberg's sister, steps in and repays the sum but he must leave home and family to seek employment far away. His conduct has also inflicted a fatal blow on his father, who will die after his departure. The play underlines the virtues of honesty, of living by work and within one's means and the folly of being dazzled by shows of wealth and motivated by social ambition. Whereas *Albert von Thurneisen*, like most examples of *bürgerliches Trauerspiel*, has at its centre a father–daughter relationship, *Verbrechen aus Ehrsucht* begins a long series of Iffland plays in which the father–son relationship is crucial.[30] Iffland's own natural and nuanced style of acting was ideally suited to this type of play. The anti-court and anti-aristocratic sentiment is not so pronounced as to give offence and panders to the self-image of the virtuous bourgeoisie. Dalberg's approving comments to the *Ausschuss* on Iffland's play read like an advance criticism of Schiller's and may even have been meant also as a signal to Schiller not to entertain hopes of being kept on at the theatre:

> Dieses Stück macht seinem Verfasser und unsrer Bühne viel Ehre. Als Stück ist es wahre, große Freskomalerei; herrlich gewählte Situationen; edle Simplicität im Plan; Wahrheit in Sprache und Ausdruck; reine Moral, fern von Lokal-Anspielungen, Satyre und bitterer Kritik. Ein fürtreffliches Schauspiel! Würden alle die vorzüglichsten Pflichten dem Menschen unter diesem Gesichtspunkt, und mit so lebhaften Bildern einzeln auf der Bühne dargestellt werden, so könnte die Bühne wahre Schule der Sitten werden; und das Theater, für welches solche Stücke geschrieben wären, würde eine neue Epoche machen.[31]

The mention of the absence of local allusions, satire and bitter criticism does sound like a not particularly thinly veiled reproach to Schiller. The *Kurpfälzische Deutsche Gesellschaft*, of which Dalberg was president, awarded Iffland a commemorative gold medal 'zum ehrenvollen Denkmal und Beweis ihres Beifalls, sonderlich in Rücksicht

---

30   See Michael Niehaus, 'Voreilige Reden, zurückgehaltene Worte. Familienkommunikation bei Iffland', in Johannes Birgfeld and Claude D. Conter (eds), *Das Unterhaltungsstück um 1800. Literaturhistorische Konfigurationen – Signaturen der Moderne* (Hanover: Wehrhahn, 2006), pp. 121–43 (p. 128). Niehaus analyses the process of negotiation between fathers and sons.

31   Martersteig, *Protokolle*, p. 246.

auf den moralischen Werth des Stücks und zur ferneren Aufmunterung im dramatischen Fache'.[32]

It was noted in Chapter 1 that Dalberg may have been moved to accept *Die Räuber* for performance because he saw in it the opportunity to emphasize the family conflict and so capitalize on the audience's taste for family dramas. Two fairly recent successful examples were Gemmingen's *Der teutsche Hausvater* and, in a lighter vein, Grossmann's *Nicht mehr als sechs Schüsseln* (written 1777, published 1780). Gemmingen's play concerns a young count, Karl, who has fallen in love with Lottchen, the daughter of a painter. Karl's sister Sophie impresses upon him the need to make an advantageous marriage within his own social sphere and he determines to abandon the pregnant Lottchen, who is in despair, in order to marry the spirited Countess Amaldi. Finally, the father of the play's title intervenes and obliges his son to marry Lottchen, though the play is not a plea for a loosening of social convention, for the young couple are sent off to a remote estate, where they will not provide a dangerous example to others. Gemmingen's sober didacticism did not prevent the play from being popular for four decades, its success perhaps boosted by the extolling of German virtues indicated by the title.[33] Schiller may have taken the idea of making Miller a musician from the fact that Lottchen's father is a painter and Countess Amaldi is sometimes identified as an inspiration for Lady Milford, who, like Amaldi, loves the play's hero but renounces him in the end. *Nicht mehr als sechs Schüsseln* may well have furnished Iffland with a few of his ideas for *Verbrechen aus Ehrsucht*, for both plays feature a married couple in which the husband is a bourgeois and the wife an aristocrat and in which the family, and in particular the children, almost come to grief

---

32   Martersteig, *Protokolle*, p. 440.

33   The play was performed 28 times at the Berlin National Theatre during Iffland's time there and in Mannheim 30 times up to 1818. See Hugo Fetting, *Das Repertoire des Berliner Königlichen Nationaltheaters unter der Leitung von August Wilhelm Iffland (1796–1814) bei Berücksichtigung der künstlerischen Prinzipien und kulturpolitischen Wirkungsfaktoren*, unpublished doctoral dissertation, University of Greifswald, 1977, Appendix, p. 71, and Oscar Fambach, *Das Repertorium des Hof- und Nationaltheaters in Mannheim 1804–1832* (Bonn: Bouvier, 1980), p. 314.

because of the corruption and unprincipled behaviour of those in court circles. As in the case of Gemmingen's play, lasting harm is avoided and the virtue of the bourgeoisie vindicated.

In his preface to the published version Iffland notes that a tragic style must be strenuously avoided, as it would destroy the play.[34] Schiller is neither able nor willing to do any such thing; *Kabale und Liebe* is utterly different in language from *Verbrechen aus Ehrsucht*, for even where Schiller is achieving some degree of realism of speech, for example when portraying the Millers or the Präsident, he employs a range of expression that gives his characters individuality and sometimes eloquence. The most difficult character to handle in the stage adaptation is Ferdinand, for his rhetoric and overblown imagery give the impression of exaggerated characterization and yet are vital in indicating an extreme psychology that is one of the mainsprings of the action. The stage version contains him to some extent but does not entirely solve the problem. In *Kabale und Liebe* a dramatist destined for high tragedy tries to confine himself to the domestic sphere. Yet no other example of domestic tragedy or *Familiengemälde* exposes so starkly the threatened existence of the subjects of princely absolutism, for in this world morality and virtue are powerless. Schiller somehow manages to convey a sense of the injustice done to the lovers, while displaying the frightening force of romantic love itself. He understands the potential destructiveness of Ferdinand's idealism just as he sees through the ineffectual self-righteousness of the bourgeoisie.

---

34   Iffland insists, 'daß bei der Vorstellung doch alles fein häuslich zugehen möge; Tragödienton würde dieses Stück umbringen.' See *Verbrechen aus Ehrsucht. Ein ernsthaftes Familiengemälde in fünf Aufzügen* (Mannheim: Schwan, 1784), p. viii.

A growing rivalry

The success of *Verbrechen aus Ehrsucht* made 1784 a landmark year for Iffland. He had found a way of appealing to audiences, of following the example of Gemmingen and Grossmann, of satisfying Dalberg's preference for dramas balancing naturalnesss with idealization and of creating a vehicle suitable for his own acting talent for nuanced characterization. It is no exaggeration to say that, from the moment *Verbrechen aus Ehrsucht* was performed, Schiller and Iffland were rivals, not because Schiller wished after *Kabale und Liebe* to continue writing dramas of the private sphere but because Iffland had shown he could supply the theatre with actable plays in this genre, whereas Schiller's productivity was in doubt and his inclination for tragedy made him an exponent of a type of drama more difficult to make successful on the stage. At the same time, his association with the *Sturm und Drang* style, which *Kabale und Liebe* again accentuated, put him at odds with the artistic ethos of the Mannheim theatre. Dalberg's comments on Iffland's play, cited above, may have boosted this perception and must have brought home to Schiller the precariousness of his position.

1784 was also momentous for Iffland because it saw the first of the frequent *Gastspiele* for which he was to become famous. He and David Beil were invited to play with Grossmann's company in Frankfurt. *Kabale und Liebe* was also to be performed again and Schiller travelled with the two actors at the end of April. *Verbrechen aus Ehrsucht* was played first, followed by *Die väterliche Rache* (Schröder's adaptation of Congreve's *Love for Love*[35]) and then *Kabale und Liebe*. Schiller wrote to Dalberg and to Rennschüb the *Regisseur* about how well received Iffland's play and the two actors had been.[36] His own play was performed with the *Kammerdiener* scene reintroduced but without any allusions to America. Iffland himself played the *Kammer-*

---

35   This play was very popular on the German stage and was played 14 times at Mannheim between 1783 and 1795; see Walter, vol. 2, p. 413.
36   See his letters of 1 May 1784 (NA 23, 133–35).

diener.[37] The *Frankfurter Staats-Ristretto* claimed it was as great a success as the première (NA 5, 354).

The period of Schiller's contract was by now more than two-thirds over and there was no sign of the third play he was contracted to write, although he had begun work on a plan for *Don Karlos* in Bauerbach in 1783. In the summer months of 1784 he bent his efforts to convincing Dalberg that he was a worthwhile investment, but he was doing so at a difficult time in the theatre's development. The flooding in the city early in 1784 had affected audience numbers. There had nevertheless been the full programme of premières, which ran at an average through the 1780s of about thirty a year. On 28 May Dalberg held an extraordinary meeting of the *Ausschuss*, at which Schiller was present, which was the occasion for a review of the season and of the theatre's policy for the repertoire in general. Dalberg begins by criticizing the actors for bad memorization, extemporization and poor discipline at rehearsals. He declares himself ready to resign but is prevented by the knowledge of disappointed hopes for a theatre that might have been able to achieve something of artistic merit.[38] Iffland makes a lengthy reply to Dalberg's complaints, claiming that the actors are aware of the problem but putting part of the blame on the choice of repertoire: 'Wo hinaus wollen wir, wenn [...] bloß Epochen- und Parade-Stücke uns zu der Darstellung eines Ganzen anfeuern sollen?'[39] By 'Epochen- und Parade-Stücke' Iffland is probably referring to expensive productions that cater to the audience's taste for novelty and spectacle. *Fiesko* would be one obvious example. His comments combine an understandable wish to defend the actors' professionalism with the suggestion that the repertoire places too much emphasis on fashion, a point he puts even more forcefully (see below, p. 93) before the start of the new season. This analysis was not calculated to boost Schiller's chances of retention.

---

37   'Ifland wird den Kammerdiener spielen, den ich, mit Wegwerfung aller ameri-kanischer Beziehungen, wieder ins Stük hineingeschoben habe' (Schiller to Dalberg, 1 May 1784, NA 23, 134).
38   Martersteig, *Protokolle*, pp. 260–62.
39   Martersteig, *Protokolle*, p. 264.

On 7 June Schiller wrote to Henriette von Wolzogen: 'Noch ligt eine undurchdringliche Deke vor meiner Zukunft. Ich kann nicht einen Augenblik sagen, wie lang mein hiesiger Aufenthalt dauren wird' (NA 23, 146). Dalberg left Mannheim for most of the summer to spend time on his estate at Herrnsheim. Schiller corresponded with him, and by virtue of that correspondence we can trace the efforts the playwright was making to secure some kind of future at the theatre. That future involved the *Kurpfälzische Deutsche Gesellschaft*. Schiller was proposed for membership in January 1784 by its secretary Anton von Klein[40] and was no doubt aware of the important link, above all through Dalberg, its president, Schwan and Klein, of the society with the theatre. He may too have been aware of its importance in bringing the theatre into being in the 1770s.[41] His idea was to gain valuable publicity for the theatre by publishing a periodical to be called the *Mannheimer Dramaturgie* and for Dalberg to set up a small committee of members of the society that would consider the theatre repertoire in particular and thus formalize the relationship.[42] Schiller's own role was to be that of a kind of secretary moving between the society and the theatre to ensure coordination. These proposals did not secure enough support among the members of the *Kurpfälzische Deutsche Gesellschaft* to be pursued. Many years later Schwan attributed this lack of support to the machinations of Anton von Klein:

> Bey dem Mannheimer Theater ist Schiller nie angestellt gewesen, wohl aber war man damals willens, ihn bei der deutschen Gesellschaft als beständigen Sekretär mit einer anständigen Besoldung anzustellen, welches auch geschehen wäre, wenn nicht der Ex-Jesuit, nachheriger Titulargeheimrath und sogenannter Ritter von Klein gegen ihn cabaliert hätte, welchem auszuweichen Schiller ihm aus dem Wege ging.[43]

---

40   See NA 41/IIA, 241–42.

41   On the role of *Kurpfälzische Deutsche Gesellschaft* in the creation of the Mannheim Theatre see chapter 1, pp. 51-52.

42   See his letter to Dalberg of 7 June 1784, NA 23, 142–43.

43   In 1811 Schiller's close friend Körner asked Schwan for details of Schiller's life in Mannheim to help him with a biographical sketch that was to preface a new edition of the writer's works. See Jakob Minor, *Aus dem Schiller-Archiv. Ungedrucktes und Unbekanntes zu Schillers Leben und Schriften* (Weimar: Böhlau, 1890), pp. 15–16.

Schwan was of course wrong in his claim that Schiller had never had a post at the theatre One has also to take into account his strongly anti-Jesuit feeling in this accusation. While not being able to confirm or deny Schwan's recollection, Klein's biographer, Karl Krükl, is of the opinion that Klein would have been unwilling to allow anyone to gain a foothold in the society whose activities might challenge his position.[44] Schings has also drawn attention to the tensions and rivalries caused during this period by the activities of the Illuminati in Mannheim, of whom Klein was one and to whom Dalberg, as a leading Freemason, was strongly opposed.[45] Such factors may have had a bearing, though there is no secure evidence, on the collapse of the scheme. Added to this is the likely unease felt by the actors at the prospect of such external intervention in the running of the theatre. With Dalberg's consent Schiller did put the idea for his *Mannheimer Dramaturgie* to him in writing (see NA 22, 313–14) but the undoubtedly wide-ranging and stimulating contents Schiller envisaged (history of the theatre, its governance, repertoire and actors, reviews, articles on acting, essay prizes) did not persuade the *Intendant* to risk the 50 Dukaten Schiller specified as the necessary financial outlay. Theatre journals at the time were numerous but almost invariably short-lived and Dalberg's financial sense would have told him that a journal, however welcome the publicity it might bring, would be unlikely to recoup its costs. Schiller pursued his idea after his contract with Mannheim came to an end in the form of his own journal, the *Rheinische Thalia*, the title of which points to its proposed focus on the theatre, though by the time the first number of the journal appeared Schiller's interests had already moved away from the practical realm of theatre to his own writing projects, chiefly *Don Karlos*.

It is in the context of Schiller's attempts to carve out a niche for himself somewhere within or between the theatre and the *Kurpfälzische Deutsche Gesellschaft* that his famous speech of 26 June to

---

44   Karl Krükl, *Leben und Werk des elsässischen Schriftstellers Anton von Klein. Ein Beitrag zur Geschichte der Aufklärung in der Pfalz* (Strassburg: Oleire, 1901), p. 60.

45   Hans-Jürgen Schings, *Die Brüder des Marquis Posa. Schiller und der Geheimbund der Illuminaten* (Tübingen: Niemeyer, 1996), p. 63 and pp. 74–100.

the society, published as 'Was kann eine gute stehende Schaubühne eigentlich wirken?', must be read.[46] It was calculated to support Dalberg's conception of the moral function of theatre, and indeed Schiller may have chosen the topic because at the *Ausschuss* meeting of 14 May 1784 Dalberg had proposed the following topic for responses from the members: 'Was ist National-Schaubühne im eigentlichsten Verstande? wodurch kann ein Theater National-Schaubühne werden? und giebt es wirklich schon ein deutsches Theater, welches Nationalbühne genannt zu werden verdient?'[47] The speech is an eloquent plea for the effectiveness of the theatre as an influence for good on the moral life of rulers and ruled, serving as a support to both law and religion in the way that it can act directly on the individual's moral sensibilities. It can also be a force of cultural integration. In 1768, in the final pages of the *Hamburgische Dramaturgie*, Lessing had reflected despondently on the imminent collapse of the Hamburg National Theatre, claiming that it was impossible for Germany to have a national theatre when it was not a nation.[48] Schiller deliberately turns this process on its head: 'Wenn wir es erlebten eine Nationalbühne zu haben, so würden wir auch eine Nation' (NA 20, 99). He sees the task of a national theatre as being to give expression to the characteristic traditions of thought and feeling in a nation, which he sees as a distillation also of its best moral and intellectual traditions. He supports this from the example of the Greeks, thereby giving his audience a prestigious forerunner and possibly flattering them with the glimmer of a hope that they might achieve it:

> Was *kettete* Griechenland so fest aneinander? Was zog das Volk so unwiderstehlich nach seiner Bühne? – Nichts anders als der väterländische Inhalt der Stücke, der griechische Geist, das große überwältigende Interesse des Staats, der besseren Menschheit, das in denselbigen athmete. (NA 20, 99)

---

46 The original title of the speech was 'Vom Wirken der Schaubühne auf das Volk'. It reached its final and most familiar form when Schiller revised his shorter prose works in 1802 and renamed it 'Die Schaubühne als eine moralische Anstalt betrachtet'.

47 Martersteig, *Protokolle*, p. 259.

48 'Über den gutherzigen Einfall, den Deutschen ein Nationaltheater zu verschaffen, da wir Deutsche keine Nation sind!' (Lessing, *Werke und Briefe*, vol. 6, p. 684).

Though this speech is frequently referred to in criticism as a statement of Schiller's conviction of the educative function of theatre, it is doubtful how far he himself believed its enthusiastic claims. For the short-lived *Wirtembergisches Repertorium* he had written the 1782 essay 'Über das gegenwärtige teutsche Theater', which is much more rooted than his Mannheim lecture in independent observation of the stage and casts doubt on any direct moral efficacy. Though he weaves into the 'Schaubühne' speech examples from his own *Räuber*, citing for example the awakening of Franz Moor's conscience as an example of how we cannot escape our own inner tribunal, that play and all his others strongly resist interpretation in terms of clear moral lessons. Generously, he slips in an approving reference to Iffland's Ruhberg from *Verbrechen aus Ehrsucht*, a play much more illustrative of his point. He is thus showing Dalberg that he can deploy all his eloquence in the cause of the theatre and its standing with the members of the *Kurpfälzische Deutsche Gesellschaft*, demonstrating that he is an asset as a polemicist as well as in his primary function as a dramatist.

The rivalry with Iffland sharpened at the very end of his time at the theatre. Dalberg himself had originally brought the Don Karlos theme to the poet's attention in 1782, though in the form of the Abbé de St Réal's *nouvelle historique*, which weaves a romantic tale around the invention of a frustrated love between Karlos and Elisabeth. Schiller had begun planning a drama in Bauerbach but little concrete progress seems to have been made. So towards the end of his year as *Theaterdichter* Schiller had still not produced the third of the three plays he was contracted to supply. Thus he was keen to make Dalberg believe a third play was on the way and suitable for the Mannheim repertoire. To return to his much quoted description of *Don Karlos* in his letter of 7 June 1784 as 'nichts weniger [...] als ein politisches Stük – sondern eigentlich ein Familiengemählde in einem fürstlichen Hauße' (NA 23, 144), not only do these words allude, as noted above, to the influence of Diderot and Lessing, their significance deepens when they are read in their precise theatrical context. *Don Karlos*, Schiller is reassuring Dalberg, will build on the success of the family drama with Mannheim audiences but be set in a more elevated sphere (implying dignity and restraint) and thus complement such plays as *Verbrechen aus Ehrsucht*. In that sense Schiller is avoiding direct rivalry with Iffland, emphasizing instead a distinctive contribution he can make to the repertoire. These words have acquired significance as part of one of the central critical debates on *Don Karlos*, namely the extent to which the private and political levels of the play's action originated together or whether the political superimposed itself on the private. Given that at this point Schiller had written not one word of *Don Karlos*, it seems safer to interpret his use of the term *Familiengemälde* as a tactic with Dalberg rather than as an expression of artistic intent.

By the time his contract came to an end he was writing to Dalberg of his Don Karlos project in terms of a new style. Of his reading of French literature, he writes:

> Fürs Erste erweitert es überhaupt meine dramatische Kenntniß und bereichert meine Phantasie, fürs andere hoffe ich dadurch zwischen zwei Extremen, Englischem und Französischem Geschmak in ein heilsames Gleichgewicht zu kommen. [...] Ich kann mir es jezt nicht vergeben, daß ich so eigensinnig, vielleicht so eitel war, um in einer entgegengesezten Sphäre zu glänzen, meine Phantasie in die Schranken des bürgerlichen Kothurns einzäunen zu wollen, da die hohe Tragödie ein so fruchtbares Feld, und für mich, möcht ich sagen, *da* ist [...]. Durch mich allein wird und muß unser Theater einen Zuwachs an vielen vortreflichen neuen Stücken bekommen, worunter *Makbeth* und *Timon*, und einige französische sind. Nach dem *Karlos* gehe ich an den 2ten Theil der Räuber, welcher eine völlige Apologie des Verfassers über den ersten Theil seyn soll, und worinn alle Immoralität in die erhabenste Moral sich auflösen muß. (24 August 1784: NA 23, 155)

These two letters show Schiller still trying to convince Dalberg of his productivity, his suitability, his distinctiveness and finally his moral reliability. Shakespeare adaptations, as will be shown in Chapter 3, were close to Dalberg's heart and Schiller presents himself as a willing helper in realising those ambitions. He was considering the possibility, urged by Dalberg himself, of returning to medicine, for which he would need a further year's training.[49] Thus

---

49 See his letter to Dalberg, probably dating from late June 1784, NA 23, 148–49. On the sequence of events and problem of dating this letter, see Herbert Stubenrauch, 'Schillers Fall – Mannheim 1784. Zur Chronologie eines undatier-

he was trying to persuade the *Intendant* to support this plan on the basis of what he could do for the theatre when he had completed his training and thus had a profession he could practise alongside his dramatic interests.

Dalberg's doubts about the longer-term value of the playwright were shared by at least some others at the theatre. On 3 August 1784 Gotter's two-act comedy *Der schwarze Mann*, an adaptation of Gernevalde's *L'Homme noir, ou: Le Spleen* and already successful at other German theatres, was performed. The play opens with a play-wright, the significantly named Flickwort, who is dressed in a blue coat with yellow lining, a costume, one assumes, meant to create an association with Goethe's Werther and thus with the *Sturm und Drang*. He complains extravagantly of his inability to finish his play. Iffland played the role of Flickwort with further details of clothing and in a manner that convinced the audience that they were seeing Schiller parodied (Iffland was known for the mischievous pleasure he took in impersonations and Schiller was a well-known figure in Mannhcim). It has been claimed that Gotter himself was taking his revenge on Schiller because he disapproved of the *Sturm und Drang* style of drama and its impact on the German theatre. While it is indeed true that Gotter disapproved of such dramas (see pp. 57–58), it is more likely that some of the actors, sensitive perhaps to the impression that Schiller did not always hold them in high regard, wcrc using the opporlunity of Dalberg's absence to pay him back, though Schiller too was absent from Mannheim.[50] Though denying any such intention, Iffland was later, in a letter of 19 September 1784, to express regret to Dalberg at the incident, which he claimed to be demeaning not only to Schiller but also to the theatre. Clearly he felt it necessary to admit some kind of responsibility to Dalberg, as the following frequently-quoted part of the letter confirms:

---

ten Schillerbriefes', *Jahrbuch der Deutschen Schillergesellschaft*, 1 (1957), 142–56.

50 Schlösser's account of *Der schwarze Mann* in his *Friedrich Wilhelm Gotter*, pp. 260–67, dismisses fairly convincingly the possibility that Gotter himself had any part in this attack on Schiller, whereas Herbert Meyer regards him as guilty; see 'Schiller und der Theaterdichter Flickwort. Betrachtungen zu cincm unbe-kannten Brief Gotters', *Mannheimer Hefte*, 1961/ Heft 1, 14–22.

Wir hätten dieses Stück niemals geben sollen. Aus Achtung für *Schiller* nicht. Wir selbst haben damit im Angesicht des Publikums (das ihn ohnehin nicht ganz fasset) den ersten Stein auf *Schiller* geworfen. Ich habe ängstlich jede Analogie vermieden, dennoch hat man gierig Schiller zu dem Gemälde sitzen lassen. Schon damit ist die Unfehlbarkeit von Schiller genommen, die Unverletzlichkeit des großen Mannes. Wie soll er nun mit seinen Werken auftreten?[51]

These words are part of a general discussion of the development of the repertoire, in which he gives Dalberg his view of the dangers involved in overloading the audience's capacity for serious drama:

Wollen Ihre Excellenz meiner Bemerkung einigen Fleiß und meiner Erfahrung einige Richtigkeit zutrauen, so sollen nicht die Räuber, noch Fiesko diesen Winter gegeben werden. – Das Publikum *erklärt gegen* diese Gattung, bekömmt sonst ihrer Fünfe zu einer Zeit zu sehen, wo *zwei so* zu stellen sind, daß sie gewinnen. Lear, Fiesko, Julius Cäsar, Göz[52] und die Räuber. Ich setze hinzu, daß die Räuber das Letztemal leer waren, daß Fiesko, vermöge nöthiger doppelter Statistenproben, schwerlich die Kosten tragen würde. Diese Bemerkungen sind unläugbar. Zugleich giebt uns *Schiller* einen fürtrefflichen *Karlos*. Ich erinnere daß, weil sonst, um ein plus von 250 fl. zu bewürken, die Laune des Publikums widerrechtlich geprüft, die Kräfte der Schauspieler unbillig erschöpft werden.[53]

Iffland goes on to stress how tragedies exhaust the actor and threaten his health as well as having a more powerful impact on the audience when they are performed infrequently. His primary objection to *Der schwarze Mann* is that it undermines the actors' ambition to be seen as performers of tragedy by making tragic drama itself seem ridiculous: 'Den "schwarzen Mann" könnten wir nicht geben, ohne uns zu parodiren, und zugleich mit dieser Parodie, ein stillschweigendes Versprechen zu geben, diese Bahn zu verlassen.'[54] This is quite a weighty argument against any further stagings of the play, and from Iffland's point of view an ingenious one, in so far as it gives him a

---

51   Koffka, p. 141.
52   Goethe's *Götz von Berlichingen* was not yet in the repertoire. It was premièred at Mannheim in 1786.
53   Koffka, p. 140.
54   Koffka, p. 141.

broader artistic reason for admitting the performance was ill-judged than that it made Schiller a figure of fun. From the context it is clear that by 'diese Bahn' he is not thinking solely of *Sturm und Drang* drama but also of Shakespeare, whose plays were still strongly associated with experimental drama and who was not yet established on the German stage as a world playwright adding lustre to the repertoire.

He closes the letter by identifying five questions he considers central to determining the artistic direction of the theatre:

1) Was hat die deutsche Bühne durch Vorstellung der Räuber gewonnen oder verloren?
2) Was verliert sie durch ungermanisirte Englische Lustspiele?
3) Ist Befriedigung der *Neuheitsgierde* oder Ernst auf Darstellung guter alter Stücke, der Bühne heilsamer?
4) Darf die Bühne *Moden* mitmachen oder muß sie einem Plane gemäß handeln, und ist sie
5) Im Stande, Retterin des gesunkenen Geschmacks zu sein?[55]

The raising of these questions is understandable for a serious and ambitious theatre practitioner such as Iffland. They do not necessarily indicate strong feelings of personal rivalry with Schiller, but they do call into question Dalberg's wish to make some concessions to more experimental trends in the theatre and suggest that that policy threatens the possibility of building up a sustainable repertoire. Iffland might have mentioned another recent production that was due to Dalberg's initiative, namely *Julius von Tarent*, one of the more readily performable works of the *Sturm und Drang*, which Dalberg himself adapted. The première, as reported at the *Ausschuss* on 2 April 1784, 'brachte im Ganzen die Wirkung nicht hervor, die man sich beim Lesen davon versprechen konnte',[56] though it did eventually gain in popularity and was repeated seventeen times up to 1795. There is not enough evidence, however, to conclude that Iffland was intending to boost his own dramas through these comments; *Verbrechen aus Ehrsucht* was, after all, his only real success

---

55   Koffka, pp. 142–43.
56   Martersteig, *Protokolle*, p. 242.

up to this point. But the ingredients he chooses for his plays are drawn from what he would call 'gute alte Stücke', in that the majority are formally compact and in content build on the established popularity of the contemporary family drama and by extension on the Diderot/Lessing legacy. Ironically, it would be Schiller's later plays, still experimental in their way and certainly out of step with popular theatre trends, that would help provide a bedrock for the repertoire.

Schiller leaves Mannheim

Dalberg's steadfast refusal to clarify Schiller's position continued up to the expiry of his contract. Finding himself once again without employment, he turned in the autumn of 1785 to his own enterprises to keep afloat. His idea for a theatre journal, the *Mannheimer Dramaturgie*, was transformed into the *Rheinische Thalia*. Announcing it in November 1784 Schiller prefaces his description of the envisaged content with a bravura short autobiography in which he styles himself a 'Weltbürger, der keinem Fürsten dient' (NA 22, 93), one who now places himself and his writing before the public. The scope of the journal has widened considerably since the plan for a *Mannheimer Dramaturgie* and embraces biography, philosophy and the arts, though German theatre is still to occupy a central position and within that the Mannheim theatre, which is distinctive through having 'ein gewisses Kunstsystem' (NA 22, 96). From his new position of independence he announces that '*Bewunderung* selten – gerechter *Tadel* immer verbessert' (NA 22, 97) and so gives the Mannheim actors some cause to fear that negative reviews may be on their way. Before publication of the one number of the journal[57] there was a controversy with the theatre that shows the extent of the tension between some of the actors and the former *Theaterdichter*. Schiller complained to Dalberg on 19 January 1785 about the per-

---

57   Schiller continued it under the title *Thalia* after he left Mannheim.

formance of *Kabale und Liebe* of the previous evening: 'Kabale und Liebe war durch das nachläßige Einstudieren der mehresten [Schauspieler] ganz in Lumpen zerrissen.' He complains that his plays are at the mercy of the whims of the actors, who are capable of playing mediocre plays well but neglect to learn their lines when performing his:

Mir selbst kann zwar an diesem Umstand sehr wenig liegen, denn ich glaube behaupten zu dürfen, daß biß jezt das Theater mehr durch meine Stüke gewonnen hat, als meine Stüke durch das Theater. Niemals werde ich mich in den Fall sezen, den Werth meiner Arbeit von diesem abhängig zu machen. Aber weil ich doch einmal von der hiesigen Bühne *öffentlich* sprechen soll, so konnte mir die Sache nicht gleichgültig bleiben. (NA 23, 173–74)

Schiller received a balanced defence of the performance, not from Dalberg but from Iffland (see NA 33 I, 58–59), the spirit of which is to insist that the playwright show respect for the actors as well as vice versa. He, Iffland, welcomes constructive criticism, referring back to Schiller's forewarning of reviews of performances in his *Ankündigung* to the *Rheinische Thalia*, and the fact that this detail from the *Ankündigung* is in his memory may suggest that Schiller's declared intention was taken as a threat by the Mannheim actors.[58] In the event Schiller must have thought better of giving untrammelled vent to his resentment in print, for his comments on the performances in the 'Repertorium der Mannheimer Schaubühne' are quite mild and circumspect. Nevertheless they unleashed new indignation against him, including, according to his letter to Dalberg of 19 March 1785, a tirade from Michael Böck (the original Karl Moor), whom Schiller both praised and criticized in moderate terms, which, given the fluctuating standard of performances, was quite reasonable: 'dieser Mann eröthet dennoch nicht, auf öffentlicher Bühne mit Gebrüll und Schimpfwörtern und Händen und Füßen gegen mich auszuschlagen, und auf die pöbelhafteste Art von mir zu reden' (NA 23, 182–83). On 27 March Dalberg wrote to Schiller:

---

58 See Kurscheidt's commentary on the letter, NA33/I, 131. On the controversy see also Herbert Stubenrauch, 'Schiller und die Schauspieler' in *Jahrbuch der Deutschen Schillergesellschaft*, 2 (1958), 43–59.

> Ich habe sage müssen, was ich ihres Repertorium wegen auf dem herzen hatte, weil ich, jemehr ich nachsinne, überzeugt bin, daß dergleichen Kritiken über schauspieler und Künstler nothwendig zerrüttungen und endlich gar den Zerfall eines theater Institutes bewürken müssen, welches ruhe und innere zufriedenheit voraussezt, wenn es von bestand seyn sol. (NA 33/I, 63)

Dalberg felt that his own method of raising standards by a kind of 'ästhetische Erziehung' helped maintain an *esprit de corps* but in practice he found this strategy hard to reconcile with the acknowledged need to gain greater publicity for the theatre.

These unhappy indicators of the tensions and rivalries at the theatre are supplemented by the evidence of a letter sent anonymously to Elector Carl Theodor and signed by an 'unterthänigstes pfälzisches Landeskind', in which Carl Theodor is apprised, perhaps by a member of the orchestra, of the fact that

> ein gewisser *Schiller*, der ein Deserteur aus der Ecole und militairischen chirurgischen Diensten des Dl. *Herzoges von Würtenberg* ist, die Gutherzigkeit unseres Theaterintendanten Baron von Dahlberg so zu hintergehen gewust habe, daß er von ihm als Theaterdichter bey dem hiesigen Nationaltheater mit 300fl. Gehalt, und noch 200 Zubuse, also 500fl., weilen die zweyte Aufführung seiner Stücke das Publikum nicht mehr sehen wollte, und also keine freye Einnahme zu hoffen war, für das verflossene Theateriahr engagiret worden. Seine drey dafür gelieferte Stücke die Räuber, Fiesko und Kabale und Liebe sind so voll Unsinn, und geben zu bösen Beyspielen sehr leicht Gelegenheit, daher die Aufführung des ersten in Straßburg verbothen worden. Bey dem Ueberfluse weit wohlfeilerer und besserer Stücke ward durch dieses am hiesigen Theater wahrhaftig überflüsigen Subjects der Kasse ein Abzug verursachet, auf den Landeskinder, und besonders die des Orchesters bey ihrer schmalen Besoldung durch die Genade *Euer Durchleucht* hätten Hofnung machen können. (NA 41/IIA, 230)[59]

Moral, aesthetic and financial objections all find expression here, and the letter-writer's envy is based on incorrect information about Schiller's salary, which was only 300 Gulden, 200 of which were paid

---

59 'Schiller als Mannheimer Theaterdichter. Zwei bisher ungedruckte Schriftstücke', *Mannheimer Geschichtsblätter,* 22 (1921), pp. 42–43. I am most grateful to Dr Martin Schalhorn for giving me a copy of this letter before it was printed in NA 41/IIA.

to him immediately to help him clear his debts.[60] In the light of this accumulated acrimony it is no wonder that Schiller turned his back so decisively on the theatre when he finally left Mannheim in April 1785 to accept the hospitality of four admirers from Leipzig.[61]

---

60 See Schiller's letter to Henriette von Wolzogen of 9 September 1783, NA 23, 110.
61 These were Christian Gottfried Körner and his fiancée Minna Stock, and Minna's sister Dora Stock and her fiancé Ludwig Ferdinand Huber.

Chapter Three
Iffland and Mannheim (1785–96)

Iffland, Dalberg and the Mannheim repertoire

As noted earlier, *Die Räuber*, though for ever associated with Mannheim, was anything but typical of the Mannheim style. Is it, however, correct to claim, as Martersteig does, that the theatre's style in its heyday (1785–92), and before it was hit by French Revolutionary upheavals, was Iffland's?[1] By the mid-1780s, as Iffland's career as a dramatist began to take off, Dalberg had clearly identified him as a highly talented and poachable asset; the widespread success of *Verbrechen aus Ehrsucht* on other German stages confirmed that fact. Iffland had also established himself as one of the most professionally-minded and artistically engaged actors in the company, being a member of the *Ausschuss* throughout its duration. But while Dalberg had a strong leaning towards sentimental, moralizing drama, he also had ambitions for the expansion of the repertoire that took him beyond the confines of the family drama. For example, the *Ritterstück* maintained its popularity into the 1790s (Joseph Marius Babo's *Die Strelitzen* (1790) being a particular success) and Shakespeare was tried in various adaptations. At the same time, Iffland's output and success as a playwright increased, and the family drama was further boosted by the arrival of August von Kotzebue (1761–1819) on the theatrical scene.

Meyer, the first *Regisseur* after Seyler, suggested apportioning the repertoire in a manner common to a number of theatres open three evening a week, namely opera or *Singspiel* on one day (in this

---

1   'Die Mannheimer Schule ist der Stil Ifflands […] der Triumph der Nuance – nicht der der Begeisterung', Max Martersteig, *Das deutsche Theater im 19. Jahrhundert. Eine kulturgeschichtliche Darstellung* (Leipzig: Breitkopf & Härtel, 1904), p. 104.

case Sundays), tragedy or serious drama on another (Tuesdays) and comedy on another (Thursdays).[2] Given that many Tuesday performances were of *Dramen* or *Schauspiele*, that is of non-tragic plays, it is clear that tragedy was being squeezed out and *Musiktheater* growing in its share of the available performance time. But Dalberg had a particular attachment to Shakespeare. Schröder had played the title role in his own adaptation of *King Lear* during his *Gastspiel* in 1780 and the following year Dalberg set Meyer, Iffland and Beil the challenge of each playing the part in Mannheim in consecutive months.[3] In 1783 *The Merchant of Venice* was premièred in Dalberg's own adaptation. Although he commended the performance, and Iffland's playing of Shylock in particular, the play was repeated only three times.[4] His version of *Julius Caesar*, premièred in 1785, in which Iffland played Cassius, proved very popular. Koffka records the attention paid to historical detail and the fact that the Elector Carl Theodor, who read Shakespeare in the original, particularly enjoyed the play and attended three performances.[5] Later Shakespeare adaptations staged by Dalberg were not successful. *Macbeth* (1788) was given in Heinrich Leopold Wagner's, by now fairly established, version. Pichler records that the Mannheim version had Macbeth die on stage with the words 'Verfluchter Ehrgeiz – ich sterbe – Dein Opfer!', another indication, if one were needed, of the penchant at the theatre for unambiguous morals.[6] *Timon of Athens* was premièred in 1789 and repeated only once.[7] The protocols record Dalberg's

---

2   Martersteig, *Protokolle*, p. 67.

3   Martersteig, *Protokolle*, p. 29. The actors, seeing the plan was over-ambitious, suggested it be deferred, and in the end only Iffland played the part in 1784 (see Walter, vol. 2, p. 290).

4   Martersteig, *Protokolle*, p. 66. Walter, vol. 2, pp. 379–418 gives an alphabetical listing of all performances at the Mannheim theatre from its beginning to 1803.

5   Koffka, p. 150.

6   Anton Pichler, *Chronik des Großherzoglichen Hof- und Nationaltheaters in Mannheim* (Mannheim: Bensheimer, 1879) p. 103. This volume contains a large amount of unpublished material, some of which was later also published in Walter, vol. 1. Dalberg used the witches' scenes from Gottfried August Bürger's translation.

7   This was a project under discussion during Schiller's days as *Theaterdichter*. See, for example, his letter to Dalberg of 24 August 1784 (NA 23, 154).

comment, 'Timon wurde durch Herrn Boecks Spiel [...] verdorben.'[8] The charge was one of sloppiness and inaudibility on the part of that actor, who played the title role, and of others in the cast. Dalberg's complaints preface general comments on the occasion of the last meeting of the *Ausschuss*. He is particularly concerned about the lack of professionalism that leads to egoism, a lack of concern for the performance as a whole and a manner of playing that conveys contempt for the play to the audience.[9] *Coriolanus* was premièred in 1791 and was Dalberg's last attempt to enlarge the Shakespearian repertoire. It survived only one performance.

Dalberg was keen to stage contemporary works he knew to be of literary importance. He had tried to put on Lessing's *Nathan der Weise* in 1779, the year it was published, but was prevented by Church opposition.[10] Also in 1779 he had tried to get a copy from Goethe of the latter's prose *Iphigenie auf Tauris* but Goethe would not send it.[11] When Schiller's *Don Karlos* was finally completed in 1787 he offered it to Mannheim and Dalberg put it on. An eagerly awaited play, which Schiller had begun to publish in 1785 while still in Mannheim, it was not very favourably received, in part because of its length. Trierweiler in the *Tagebuch der Mannheimer Schaubühne* wrote: 'dieses Stück, als literarisches Product betrachtet, wird immer in der gelehrten Welt Epoche machen, allein auf der Bühne kann es nie ein außerordentliches Glück erringen.'[12] Iffland took the role of Philipp. After three performances in 1788 it was not repeated until 1802.

---

8   Martersteig, *Protokolle*, p. 388.

9   Martersteig, *Protokolle*, p. 393. Already in 1786 Dalberg had told the *Ausschuss*: 'Es sei künftig Grundsatz unserer Bühne, mehr Anstrengung und Leben in solche Schauspiele zu bringen, wo der Schauspieler mehr thun kann, als der Dichter gethan hat' (*Protokolle*, p. 299).

10   Herbert Stubenrauch, *Wolfgang Heribert von Dalberg. Lebensskizze und Lebenszeugnisse*, Nationaltheater Mannheim: Bühnenblätter für die Spielzeit 1956/57 (Mannheim: Südwest-Werbung, 1957), p. 10.

11   Stubenrauch, *Wolfgang Heribert von Dalberg*, p. 10.

12   Trierweiler, *Tagebuch der Mannheimer Schaubühne*, 2 vols, (Mannheim: Schwan, 1786, 1787), vol. 2, p. 284. For a fuller account of the first performances of *Don Carlos* see Chapter 4.

Though Mannheim was in general not well disposed to works of the *Sturm und Drang*, Dalberg did stage three other plays in that style apart from Schiller's: Lenz's *Der Hofmeister*, Leisewitz's *Julius von Tarent* and Goethe's *Götz von Berlichingen*. The impetus for the experiment with *Der Hofmeister* came once more from Schröder's visit in 1780. Schröder had staged it successfully in Hamburg and in Mannheim it was performed eleven times during the eleven years to 1791. *Götz von Berlichingen* was not premièred until 1786, though Dalberg had clearly considered staging it earlier, for in 1782, after the première of *Die Räuber*, he encouraged Schiller to adapt it.[13] Famous and influential though it was, both as a literary work breathing the spirit of the *Sturm und Drang* and as the inspiration for many a subsequent *Ritterstück*, Goethe's chronicle play was difficult to realize successfully on stage. In Mannheim it was performed only three times in quick succession and then dropped. Koffka attributes its failure to the fact that by 1786 audiences were too accustomed to the *Ritterstück* and could not detect what distinguished *Götz von Berlichingen* from the many inferior products it had inspired, such as Törring's *Agnes Bernauerin*, which was performed eleven times in 1781 alone.[14] *Julius von Tarent*, as noted earlier, was not enthusiastically received at first but finally established itself in the repertoire. Though it has certain characteristic themes of the *Sturm und Drang*, the play is formally compact, observing the traditional unities, and generally fared better on stage than most *Sturm und Drang* dramas. Iffland commented in the *Ausschuss* on the play's première:

> That es dennoch die Wirkung nicht, die man erwartete, so liegt es daran, daß Bruder und Kindermord, wenn auch unvermeidlich gemacht durch die Situationen – diese Unvermeidlichkeit aber wieder von uns entfernt, gekältet durch blumigte Sprache – in der Kleidung unserer Zeiten – daß diese Gegenstände sind, die empören, und daß ein deutsches Publikum, wenn es das Schauspielhaus mit Schauder verläßt – es auch zugleich fast immer mit Mißvergnügen verläßt.[15]

---

13 Schiller was reluctant to adapt the play without the author's permission; see his letter to Dalberg of 1 April 1782 (NA 23, 32).
14 Koffka, p. 163.
15 Martersteig, *Protokolle*, p. 259.

This quotation should perhaps be read in conjunction with the actor's letter to Dalberg of 19 September 1784, discussed at some length in the previous chapter (see pp. 91–93), in which Iffland commented on the development of the repertoire (and on *Der schwarze Mann*). In the letter Iffland stresses the need to work on the 'Darstellung guter alter Stücke', plays of established reputation and popularity, and strongly urges Dalberg to limit the number of tragic dramas he attempts to introduce and sustain in performance. The disappointing audience response to *Julius von Tarent* dates from the spring of the same year as Iffland's September letter.

Iffland's instincts were arguably led more reliably than Dalberg's by the tastes of the Mannheim audience. The implication of his comment on Leisewitz's play is that material of a less extreme kind, which can be brought to a more reassuring conclusion, will be more acceptable to audiences. It may be going too far to suggest he was boosting by contrast the standing in the repertoire of the kind of play he wrote, for arguably he felt he was qualified professionally to comment on these matters. A certain wariness on his part, more fully expressed in the September letter, can perhaps be inferred regarding Dalberg's ambitions for the repertoire – a wariness perhaps characteristic of the professional towards the amateur, which Dalberg was. It also suggests a pragmatism about the repertoire that prioritizes the needs of the company over artistic ambitions.

The Mannheim style

Though a varied repertoire at Mannheim met with varied reactions from the audience, the 1780s saw the emergence of a distinctive Mannheim style. That such a style could emerge at all, and so comparatively rapidly, was due in large measure to Dalberg, who created the conditions in which a predominantly young company could mature and who saw the possibilities of welding it together. He had the confidence bestowed by amateur experience of the theatre, and the status of a performed playwright. He sensed he could create an institution unusual in the theatrical world, one not ruled by the whim of the *Prinzipal* but rather one based on what Martersteig calls 'eine Art josephinische Organisation.'[16] The analogy suggests that the actors were called to rational co-operation under Dalberg's benevolent authority. The co-operation was intended to cover not only the practicalities of theatre life (setting the repertoire, reviewing performances, dealing with infringements of the rules) but also the theatre's artistic progress. In October 1782 Rennschüb, later to become *erster Ausschuss*, suggested that the actors should read and report on plays to be considered for performance and Iffland supported this idea with a call for written reports.[17] Clearly, not all new potential productions were treated in this way but rather above all any that would represent a significant investment, and risk, on the part of the theatre. Iffland's report on Schiller's *Fiesko* is a case in point (see p. 75). This practice of reasoned appraisal of the suitability of new plays was complemented by Dalberg's attempt at a broader kind of aesthetic education. He introduced discussion questions on central matters regarding the aesthetics of the stage and invited written responses from members of the *Ausschuss*. An early example is the question that goes to the heart of the Mannheim project: 'Was ist Natur, und welches sind die wahren Grenzen derselben bei theatralischen Vorstellungen?'[18] The various and in part conflicting trends in the repertoire made this a vital topic. Other topics similarly embrace both the practical and the theoretical, for example: the boundaries of propriety on the stage; the use of pauses in acting; whether French classical plays can be successful in the repertoire; the definition of the term *Nationaltheater*.

Dalberg's own answer to the first question is summed up in a short disquisition presented to the last meeting of the *Ausschuss* in 1789, in which he restates his principle of balance between realism and idealization. For him nature is

> anschaulich lebendige Darstellung mancherlei Charaktere und menschlicher Begebenheiten, aus dem Kreise der Schöpfung genommen, und in dem engen

---

16   Martersteig, *Protokolle*, p. 413.
17   Martersteig, *Protokolle*, pp. 64–65.
18   Martersteig, *Protokolle*, p. 74.

Raum der Bühne nach gewissen Konvenienzen und bestimmten Regeln ge-
bracht.[19]

He emphasizes the importance of bringing sufficient contrast, sufficient light and shade into productions. His thoughts were prompted by
the guest performances at Mannheim of Franz Zuccarini, an actor who
had been with the company in its early days but had been whisked
away to Hamburg by Schröder in 1780. These performances gave
Dalberg occasion to compare the Hamburg and Mannheim styles,
demonstrating the continued benchmark represented by Hamburg for
Mannheim:[20]

> In den meisten Stücken wird hier der gewöhnliche Konversations-Ton zu viel
> beibehalten, es werden überhaupt zu wenig starke Schatten und Lichter ange-
> bracht, und indem die vorzüglichen Mitglieder unserer Bühne getreu bleiben
> wollen, vergessen sie, daß Natur im menschlichen Leben nicht Natur auf der
> Bühne ist, wohin etwas mehr Fresko, als Miniatur-Malerei gehört, Effekte her-
> vorzubringen.[21]

Konversations-Ton is precisely the term used by Goethe on several
occasions in the 1790s to criticize the overly natural style of
the Weimar actors; its use by both him and Dalberg suggests the
prevalence of this style on the stage of the time and corrects the
mistaken view that a director had to be aiming for a high degree of
stylization (as Goethe sometimes was and Dalberg generally was not)
in order to find fault with it.[22]

It is not known why Dalberg discontinued the meetings of the
Ausschuss in 1789. Iffland ascribes it to increased government responsibilities.[23] Perhaps he also tired of reiterating the same admonitions
and complaints and perhaps as a dilettante he had underestimated how
discouragingly slow the enterprise would be in delivering the improvements he sought. Through the years of the *Ausschuss* Dalberg's

---

19 Martersteig, *Protokolle*, p. 394.
20 At this point the Hamburg theatre, after several upheavals in the early 1780s,
    was again being led by Schröder.
21 Martersteig, *Protokolle*, p. 395.
22 See chapter 4, p. 146.
23 *Meine theatralische Laufbahn*, p. 58.

criticisms of the actors and performances remain fairly constant. He reproaches them for poor speaking, sloppy memorization, extemporization, lack of pace, lack of concern as individuals about the performance as a whole and for showing their opinion of the quality of the play through their manner of playing. In Chapter Two it was noted that Schiller complained to Dalberg in January 1785 about the, in his view, negligent performance of *Kabale und Liebe* (only its third on the Mannheim stage). Dalberg delegated to Iffland the task of replying to Schiller (and it is typical of Iffland that he defends the dignity of the actor), but addressing the actors themselves, in the private forum of the next meeting of the *Ausschuss*, Dalberg was very critical of their neglect of minor roles and of the lack of pace in the final acts of plays. He clearly felt, however, that such comments should be confined to discussions held within the theatre. The regularity with which this core set of criticisms was reiterated and the fact that they coincide markedly with Goethe's of the Weimar company suggests that at least some of the underlying causes lay in the circumstances of performance: constant change in the repertoire leading to a shortage of rehearsal time and a reliance on extemporization; virtuoso acting being favoured above ensemble playing because the actor had to gain prominence and favour with the audience.

Yet the members of the *Ausschuss*, and Iffland in particular, were assiduous supporters of Dalberg's efforts. In addition to their initiative to be involved in the evaluation of plays sent in for possible performance (and many reports are to be found in the minutes of the *Ausschuss*), in 1782 the decision was reached that for every play there should be a full reading rehearsal so that everyone in the cast should be aware how his or her part related to the whole.[24] Rennschüb, the *Regisseur* from 1783 to 1791, went on to be in charge of the Frankfurt National Theatre; Beck, a frequent member of the *Ausschuss*, later became *Regisseur* at Mannheim after Iffland's departure. So it is clear that Dalberg did foster professionalism in the company and received support in his aims from some of its members.

---

24   Martersteig, *Protokolle*, p. 87.

Iffland the actor

Martersteig sums up Iffland's basic preoccupations thus:

> Er war nicht der in seiner Kunst aufopferungsvoll den Großen sich anschlie-
> ßende Streiter für die ästhetisch–sittliche Wiedergeburt des Vaterlands, die er
> scheinen wollte; – er war ein gerade in den Instinkten der Masse fest-
> wurzelndes Talent; worauf es ihm ankam, das war nicht eine künstlerische
> Kultur des Theaters, sondern die Nobilitierung der Schauspielerei. Dieses Ziel
> hatte er im Auge als Schüler Dalbergs, als Meister der Mannheimer Jünger, als
> fruchtbarer Theaterdichter und endlich als Generaldirektor der Berliner
> Nationalbühne.[25]

Martersteig is certainly right in one important respect: for Iffland, acting was his primary calling, far more significant and fundamental to him than writing plays or being director of a theatre. Not a little condescension shows through Martersteig's judgment, the condescension of a viewpoint, typical of the later nineteenth century, informed by the near-deification of Goethe and Schiller and the consequent tendency to evaluate all other cultural phenomena in the light of their judgments and their aesthetic criteria. The implied 'ästhetisch–sittlich' purpose he presumes behind their work is set in contrast to the 'instincts of the masses', who, one infers, are concerned with entertainment and the confirmation of their prejudices. Martersteig implies a conflict typified by Iffland between the development of an artistically challenging theatre on the one hand and the striving of the virtuoso actor on the other to assert himself and his professional identity. This is arguably a false distinction. Iffland identified a greater professionalism on the part of actors as one key to an artistically more impressive theatre, a view that was later shared by Goethe, who particularly praised the example of professionalism Iffland gave to the Weimar company when he performed with them in 1796.[26] Martersteig's mention of the instincts of the masses is a pejorative way of referring to the reliable sense of the actor, playwright and later director for what

---

25   Martersteig, *Das deutsche Theater*, p. 104.
26   See chapter 4, p. 155.

would succeed in the theatre, often dramas such as his own with little depth or artistic significance but with fluent dialogue, lively character-ization and a happy ending. Iffland most certainly saw art as being at least in part in the acting itself, and many were the times that the Mannheim theatre put on plays that flopped because the acting was deemed afterwards not to have been up to scratch.

The words 'Nobilitierung der Schauspielerei' not only refer to the elevation of the actor's art and social position but are also meant as something of a sideswipe at Iffland's supposed social ambitions and his strong and indeed often controversial bond with the ruling aristoc-racies. Again this prejudice is misplaced. His ability to play the cour-tier when necessary was a useful asset all his life, for he understood the vital importance to a theatre of means and of the ruler's support. To Dalberg's credit, he also realized the advantages from an artistic point of view of making actors respected members of society and contributed to that process. In 1786, the year following the appearance of Iffland's first substantial publication on acting, his *Fragmente über Menschendarstellung auf den deutschen Bühnen*, he and Beck re-ceived an accolade that even a few years previously would have seemed impossible: they were made members of the *Kurpfälzische Deutsche Gesellschaft*.[27] Iffland had dedicated the work to the society, and the fact that he was received along with Beck indicates that the honour was going to him in his capacity as an actor. In Mannheim at least the actor was becoming a respectable citizen.

Fragmente über Menschendarstellung auf den deutschen Bühnen was published at Gotha, where Iffland began his career, by Ettinger, publisher of Germany's longest-standing theatre periodicals, the *Go-thaer Theaterjournal* and the *Gothaer Theaterkalender*.[28] Dalberg was keen to promote public awareness of the Mannheim theatre through

---

27   One of the vacancies (membership was restricted to 30) was caused by Schiller's departure from the Palatinate.

28   Iffland's first attempts at writing about acting, the 'Briefe über die Schauspiel-kunst', were published in the *Rheinische Beiträge zur Gelehrsamkeit* in 1781/82 (81/1, 65–69; 81/11, 364–73; 81/12, 451–56; 82/1, 50–59). A few pages each in length, they cover aspects of the young actor's development, such as the need to observe himself and others in order to achieve 'Wahrheit' and the superiority of nuanced playing over passion.

journalism, though the example of Schiller's plan for a *Mannheimer Dramaturgie* shows how uncertain he was about the benefits of criticism close to home of the performances. In November 1785 he called on members of the *Ausschuss* to write essays for publication[29] and in fact Iffland's *Fragmente über Menschendarstellung* derives in large measure from the responses he produced to Dalberg's series of questions to the *Ausschuss* from 1783 to 1785. These are prefaced by a review of the German stage and its recent history that reveals him as a clever publicist for the theatre because he attempts to bridge the gap between the literary world and the theatre world by taking his landmarks from literary developments.[30] He deprecates the dominance of French influence and the German theatre's lack of self-confidence. He decries the provincialism of outlook in Germany that resists embracing German theatre and he confidently claims that acting has made great strides in the previous fifteen years, paying tribute to Ekhof and to Sophie Hensel (later Seyler). He claims that Goethe, in particular with *Götz von Berlichingen*, gave German audiences the ability to respond to Shakespeare and that Shakespeare and Goethe gave playwrights courage to forsake the *Haupt- und Staatsaktion* and try out plays that display imagination and individuality. This section reads rather like a belated apologia for the *Sturm und Drang*. What Iffland says is the very opposite of what he says in the *Ausschuss* and in his revealing letter to Dalberg of September 1784, in which he reviews the repertoire, casting doubt on the value of *Die Räuber* to the Mannheim theatre and suggesting that audiences can stand only very measured amounts of Shakespearian or similar tragic drama. So the historical survey in the work reflects less Iffland's practical judgement as a man of the theatre and more his judicious sense of what line of literary approach will win the interest and approval of his readership. As we have seen, a lack of appreciation of the *Sturm und Drang* and an only moderate enthusiasm for Shakespeare were characteristic of

---

29   Martersteig, *Protokolle*, pp. 296–97.
30   'Ueber die Entstehung der deutschen Bühne und ihren Fortgang, nebst einer Berichtigung der Redensart "Die Nation hat und halt ihr Schauspiel", *Fragmente über Menschendarstellung auf den deutschen Bühnen. Erste Sammlung* (Gotha: Ettinger, 1785), pp. 10–30.

the theatre world at the time, but Iffland thinks it is more politic to let his readers believe that the theatre and literary spheres are communicating and sharing an agenda.

Iffland presents himself as an artist reflecting more on the practical conditions of his art than on its theoretical foundations.[31] His purpose is to raise the status of acting, by linking it not only to the important literary developments of the day but also to anthropological developments, thereby giving it something of a scientific turn. On the subject 'Was ist Natur? Und wie weit geht ihre Gränze auf der Bühne?' he writes: 'Der Augenblick nun, wo die Seele alle mächtigen Kräfte aufbietet um Menschen darzustellen, ist die Würkung des göttlichen Funkens, ist die hohe heilige Begeisterung.'[32] The use of the term *Begeisterung*, familiar from contemporary pre-Romantic poetics, turns acting by implication into a manifestation of the highest artistic creativity, a kind of poetry in motion. In fact, Iffland became renowned for acting based on a very different principle, that of detailed study and nuance, and he never excelled in tragic roles.[33] He was anything but an incarnation of inspiration. Again, one assumes that these words are chosen to elevate acting and align it with the newest trends in poetics.

At the same time, he gives definitions of his central term, *Menschendarstellung*, which he uses in preference to *Schauspielkunst* to mean acting. The underlying idea is that the actor portrays humanity in its complexity and multiplicity through close observation of detail and nuance. To do so, he must be aware of the 'Korrespondenz der Organisation des Körpers mit der Seele'.[34] Physical appearance, gesture, posture must all come together to boost the impression of a complete individual. Iffland was writing at a time when theories of the intimate connection between mind and body were making an impact on medicine (leading, amongst other things, to the early development of psychology), philosophy and aesthetics. 'Der ganze Mensch' must

---

31   As the reviewer in the *Allgemeine Literatur-Zeitung 1785. Supplemente*, pp. 186–87 comments, calling Iffland 'der Meister in der Schauspielkunst (p. 187).

32   *Fragmente über Menschendarstellung*, p. 35.

33   See Alafberg, p. 33.

34   *Fragmente über Menschendarstellung*, p. 47.

be the object of study and investigation.[35] Iffland's central ideas regarding acting and his practice are further illustrations of this anthropological turn.[36] His rejection of declamation and move towards greater realism are based on the notion that the body expresses the soul. Thus movement and gesture should emphasize the individual, the nuanced and the apparently spontaneous, rather than the stylized and stereotypical. With the neo-classical style in mind, Iffland contrasts the French stage with the German:

> Die Franzosen geben Vorstellungen
> Die Deutschen Darstellungen [37]

This anthropological turn dignifies the actor in two important ways. First, it strengthens the idea that in order to portray nobility of character on stage the actor must possess the associated virtues himself: 'Ohne selbst edles Gefühl zu haben, ist also die Vorstellung des Edlen nicht möglich.'[38] Iffland is aware that many actors' unsteady lives tend to confirm the public's prejudices against their profession but in mitigation turns attention to their uncertain working conditions, the power of the *Prinzipal* over them and the lack of pensions. By undermining the standard of acting, such conditions also undermine the aspiration to a national theatre. Secondly, the anthropological turn promotes the idea of the actor as educator, 'Volkslehrer', as Iffland

---

35   This anthropological turn has led since the 1980s to a new critical appreciation of the roots of the psychology of Schiller's early plays in the medical training he received at the Carlsschule, which emphasized the complex interaction of mental and physical processes. See, for example, Schiller's successful dissertation at the Carlsschule, *Über den Zusammenhang der thierischen Natur des Menschen mit seiner geistigen*. See Kenneth Dewhurst and Nigel Reeves, *Friedrich Schiller: Medicine, Psychology and Literature* (Oxford: Sandford, 1978) and Wolfgang Riedel, *Die Anthropologie des jungen Schiller* (Würzburg: Könighausen und Neumann, 1985).

36   For a full discussion of anthropology and acting, see Košenina. For a general characterization of Iffland's acting as a combination of realist and idealizing elements see Simon Williams, *German Actors of the Eighteenth and Nineteenth Centuries. Idealism, Romanticiam and Realism* (Westport, Conn. and London: Greenwood, 1985), pp. 29–39.

37   *Fragmente über Menschendarstellung*, p. 67.

38   *Fragmente über Menschendarstellung*, p. 55.

calls him, whose ability to present the psychology of a character to the audience in convincing ways supports the theatre's claim to be morally and socially useful.[39] Such arguments were commonplace in the second half of the eighteenth century, but, put by a practitioner whose plays also commanded moral, if not unequivocal critical, respect, they carried some weight with the reading public, if the review in the *Allgemeine Literatur-Zeitung* is indicative.[40]

Iffland devotes a chapter to the illnesses of actors and again the psychological turn is evident. 'Reizbarkeit' (the susceptibility to stimuli and impressions), a pre-requisite in a successful actor, makes his profession a danger to his health. The danger lies not only in physical over-exertion but in the stress on the mind and body caused by the effort of conveying the complexity of the human personality. Iffland therefore warns also against the prevalent *Rollensucht* among actors, the wish to appear only in leading roles, for this undermines the actor's constitution. He accuses *Prinzipale* of having insufficient regard for this aspect of their actors' wellbeing by rewarding only those who take prominent roles and so making it impossible for actors to gain recognition except at the cost of their health. A certain self-interest may be speaking here. Iffland was never the *jeune premier* and always specialized in character roles. Even while still in his teens at Gotha he was playing 'komische Alte'.[41] His concerns reflect a legitimate aspiration that talent and effort can be rewarded within what he hopes can become a more stable professional environment.

Though he was only in his mid-twenties when these essays were published, they contain the essence of Iffland's art: concern for psychological verity and nuance, attention to minute detail, and punctilious preparation. Iffland never wavered from these, seeing them as his strength, whether or not critics missed in his acting the mercurial and daemonic, qualities perhaps more readily associated with a suc-

---

39   *Fragmente über Menschendarstellung*, p. 62.

40   'Mit eben dem Vergnügen, welches man empfindet, wenn man einen Mengs über Mahlerey reden hört, lieset man hier die theoretischen Bemerkungen eines Mannes, der eben so großer Schauspieler als Schauspieldichter ist', *Allgemeine Literatur-Zeiting* (1785) *Supplemente*, Nr. 57, pp. 186–87.

41   See Chapter 1, p. 43.

cessful actor. His high professional standards were still untypical of actors in general. He continued to make a virtue of his specialization in character roles and was frequently commended by Dalberg in the meetings of the *Ausschuss*, for example for his Shylock in *The Merchant of Venice* and Cassius in *Julius Caesar*. As his writing career progressed he created prominent character parts for himself, such as Reinhold in *Die Hagestolzen* (1791), in which he was very popular. Later, at Berlin, he continued to act, often taking quite small roles as well as major ones, in order to maintain contact with the company and the public.

Apart from publishing essays on acting, Iffland's main method of raising his and the profile of acting in general was the *Gastspiel*. His first guest appearances were at Frankfurt on the occasion recorded in Chapter Two when Schiller's *Kabale und Liebe* was also given (see p. 84). The *Gastspiel* became a major part of Iffland's career up to his death. Quite a number of his plays were premièred in theatres, for example Hamburg, far from Mannheim or later Berlin because he was guesting there. The theatre in question therefore had the benefit not only of the actor but of a brand new play. The sheer energy involved in the travelling Iffland undertook is phenomenal and the renown he acquired by his travels made him, to Dalberg's disquiet, an increasingly sought-after commodity.

Iffland as a dramatist: 1784–89

Iffland's plays of the decade following his breakthrough drama *Verbrechen aus Ehrsucht* were his most successful. Those of his Berlin period, repeating many of the plots and motifs of his earlier phase, in general lacked the freshness of his early work and seemed increasingly routine.[42] After *Verbrechen aus Ehrsucht* he went on to capitalize

---

42   The most comprehensive studies of Iffland's dramatic works are: Karl Lampe, *Studien über Iffland als Dramatiker mit besonderer Berücksichtigung der ersten Dramen* (Celle: Ströher, 1899), Karl Heinz Klingenberg, *Iffland und*

on its success by remaining in the same milieu with his next play, *Die Mündel*, also premièred in 1784. It deals with the rivalry of two contrasting brothers, both wards of an upright merchant, Drawe, and with the plot by a corrupt minister to further the ambitions of the one brother, a friend of the minister's son, by destroying Drawe financially. The characters are clumsily drawn, the villainy insufficiently motivated and the intrigue rather far-fetched. The play was nevertheless a success when first performed, with its exposure of corruption in high places, a recurring motif in Iffland's work (though he always stopped short of criticism of the ruler). What is notable in the play is the use made of the contrasting rival brothers, the one, Ludwig, dissolute but redeemable, the other, Philipp, melancholy, forbidding and yet noble and self-sacrificing. Both are in love with their guardian's daughter and it is Ludwig who has won her affection. The popularity of *Die Räuber*, which uses the same theme of the contrasting brothers who are also rivals for the same woman's love, may have encouraged Iffland to rework the motifs, and the fact that *Julius von Tarent*, staged, as noted above (p. 102), earlier in the same year as *Die Mündel*, also uses them explains why they may have been in his thoughts. They are motifs typical of *Sturm und Drang* drama and Iffland may have reworked them to show that they can function in a non-tragic drama in a contemporary bourgeois setting without the addition of the shocking and extreme associated with Schiller's and Leisewitz's plays.[43]

The following year, 1785, saw the first performances of Iffland's most enduringly popular play, *Die Jäger*, which was still being staged almost a hundred years later,[44] the only work of his to remain so long

---

Kotzebue als Dramatiker (Weimar: Arion Verlag, 1962) and Sigrid Salehi, *August Wilhelm Ifflands dramatisches Werk* (Frankfurt am Main, Berne: Lang, 1990). See also Joseph Pinatel, *Le drame bourgeois en Allemagne au XVIIIme siècle* (Lyon: Riou, 1938), Horst Glaser, *Das bürgerliche Rührstück* (Stuttgart: Metzler, 1969) and Markus Krause, *Das Trivialdrama der Goethezeit 1780–1805. Produktion und Rezeption* (Bonn: Bouvier, 1982).

43 Klingenberg comments negatively: 'das Motiv der feindlichen Brüder erscheint ins Spießbürgerliche verwandelt' (p. 73).

44 It is recorded by Schäffer and Hartmann as being performed regularly at the Berlin theatre up to 1885, the last year covered by their survey. See C. Schäffer and C. Hartmann, *Die Königlichen Theater in Berlin. Statistischer Rückblick*

in the repertoire. It was the play with which Goethe opened the Weimar Court Theatre in 1791, and it exemplifies some of Iffland's central themes and illustrates his strengths as well as his weaknesses as a dramatist. Oberforstmeister Warberger (one of Iffland's favourite roles) and his family are set in contrast to that of the corrupt and ambitious family of the town's *Amtmann*, von Zeck, a member of the aristocracy. Von Zeck wishes to exploit his position to enrich himself at the expense of the community and attempts to draw Warberger into this corruption, aiming also to marry his daughter to Anton, Warberger's son. Anton, however, wishes to marry his parents' niece and ward but is told by them to wait for two years, whereupon von Zeck turns him against his father. Anton is unjustly accused of murder and the family seems to be at von Zeck's mercy, until the mystery is solved and harmony restored at the end. The play's main strength is in lively characterization, particularly that of Warberger with his sound fatherly values, and in natural dialogue. It makes good use of the contrast between town and country, the Warbergers being associated with uprightness and a modest and honest life lived out in natural surroundings. The plot illustrates Iffland's general lack of concern for precise cause and effect in the pursuit of striking contrasts; the charge against Anton, for example, is rather an unlikely development introduced to create tension.[45] Iffland concentrates instead on the creation of tableaux or illustrative scenes. Indeed the play's subtitle is *Ein ländliches Sittengemälde in fünf Aufzügen*.[46]

Die Jäger was first performed not at the Mannheim Theatre but at Dürckheim in the Palatinate by the amateur theatre group of the

---

auf die künstlerische Thätigkeit und die Personal-Verhältnisse während des Zeitraums vom 5. December 1786 bis 31. December 1885 (Berlin: Berliner Verlags-Comtoir AG, 1886), p. 44.

45 Klingenberg, for example, comments on Iffland's 'drastisch zugespitzte Scheinkonflikte' (p. 59).

46 A second version, in which some of the improbabilities are reduced, was published in 1789. On Iffland's changes to the play see Kurt Binneberg, 'Zwischen Schwärmerei und Realismus. Die beiden Textfassungen von A. W. Ifflands Drama *Die Jäger*', in *Textkritik und Interpretation. Festschrift für Karl Konrad Polheim zum 60. Geburtstag*, ed. by Heimo Reinitzer (Frankfurt am Main, Berne: Lang, 1987), pp. 161–75.

princely family of Leiningen, whose territories lay to the west of Mannheim. Iffland was frequently the guest of the family in the 1780s and early 1790s, forming a close friendship with Crown Prince Emich Karl.[47] His association with the family brings together features noted already in Iffland's career: a strong attachment, based on political conviction, to traditional ruling elites; a love of the aristocratic milieu; ambition for the standing of his profession, which he saw as honoured and made respectable through such aristocratic favour. It was a tendency that complemented a naturally conservative outlook, a belief, which emerges time after time in the dramas, that stability resides in a strong, patriarchal order. Iffland's father-figures are the key to many of his plays. If they are weak, such as old Ruhberg in *Verbrechen aus Ehrsucht*, they bring unrest and conflict into the family and destabilize its relations with the outside world. While individual members of the aristocracy may be portrayed as vain and corrupt, this criticism is never levelled at the ruler but only at those who act for him and abuse their authority.

Two further significant plays of the 1780s were *Bewußtseyn* (written 1786) and *Reue versöhnt* (1788), continuations of the story of Eduard Ruhberg. In his preface to *Bewußtseyn* Iffland explains how the play arose; he had received a report telling him that at a performance of *Verbrechen aus Ehrsucht* in Vienna the Emperor Joseph II had commented that he would not have been so lenient with young Ruhberg. Iffland defends the fact that, instead of ending the play with harsh punishment, he has tried to evoke pity and understanding, to which he attributes corrective powers. Nevertheless he feels it incumbent upon him to demonstrate, through a continuation of his hero's story, that Ruhberg must bear the consequences of his former lapses.[48] In *Bewußtseyn* he has risen to a position of respect in the service of a minister but is in constant fear that his past will be uncovered and worried about the now widowed mother he has left behind to be cared for by her son-in-law. A desire not to be a financial burden to his

---

47   See Wilhelm Herrmann, 'August Wilhelm Iffland und die Leininger Fürsten', *Mitteilungen des historischen Vereins der Pfalz*, 65 (1967), 208–29.

48   *Bewußtseyn. Ein Schauspiel in fünf Aufzügen* (Berlin: Decker, 1787), 'Vorrede', pp. v–viii.

family has prompted him to lead an independent life; circumstances, however, have forced him to accept employment in a sphere (an aristocratic one) in which he formerly came to grief. Indeed, Iffland's plot combines exploration of Ruhberg's unhappiness with criticism of the court milieu, through the creation of two unscrupulous courtiers who are alarmed by the favour shown to the young man and intrigue to bring about his downfall. Iffland delays the entrance of his central character until Act 2 so that he can give a clear portrayal of the perils of the court world that are about to engulf him, before we hear of his own unhappiness and fear, not only the result of past guilt but also of his hopeless love for the minister's ward.

Reue versöhnt was given its première in Mannheim in January 1788. Rather than concentrating on Ruhberg, the play shows the Walsing family, headed by a devoted but somewhat domineering *pater familias* who has taken Ruhberg in and treats him like a son. Mutual respect and tolerance are advocated, as Walsing, a widower, is made through Ruhberg's carefully judged counsel to see that to frustrate his daughter's hopes of marriage to an honourable officer is cruel and overbearing, while young Walsing is prevented by Ruhberg from absconding with some of his father's money and thus falling into the same folly that has made Ruhberg a semi-outcast. The officer, Major Randau, is cured of his irrational jealousy against Ruhberg, another example of repentance and reconciliation. Finally, Ruhberg is reunited with his mother and with Sophie, the woman he thought forever lost to him. As in the case of the other parts of the trilogy, Ruhberg is a colourless character, noble and lachrymose in equal measures, and the interest of the play is in the portraiture of Walsing and of lively secondary characters.[49]

In spite of Iffland's rapid rise to popularity as a stage writer, the reception of his plays in the literary world was always cool. A typical review in the *Allgemeine Literatur-Zeitung* of 1787 finds weaknesses in both plays discussed: lack of clarity of plot and characterization in *Die Mündel* and implausibility in *Die Jäger*. These are put down to careless writing. On the positive side:

---

49   On the trilogy's variations on the father–son conflict, see Niehaus, pp. 125–36.

Hr. Iffland hat zu keinem der Kunstgriffe Zuflucht genommen, denen manches mittelmäßige Schauspiel in unsern Tagen sein Glück zu danken gehabt hat [...]. Vom Studium Diderots geleitet, forscht er dem geheimen Gange der Natur nach; ohne die Regeln der Kunst aus den Augen zu verlieren, weiß er bald Menschen, wie es viel giebt, und die gewöhnlichsten Handlungen des Lebens mit täuschender Treue zu schildern.[50]

Some twenty years later Karl Heinrich Jördens's *Lexikon deutscher Dichter und Prosaisten* produces a very similar summary verdict on what was by then a much larger œuvre:

Schöne, rührende Familienverhältnisse und Szenen, interessante, edle Charaktere, tiefwirkende und doch so menschliche Situationen, wahre, reine Sprache der Natur, das sind die charakteristischen Merkmale, durch die er sich auszeichnet; eine gewisse originelle Herzlichkeit, welche man die *Ifflandische* nennen könnte, tiefe Menschenkenntniß, getreue Sittenschilderung, Leben und Wärme der Darstellung, und über das alles ein moralischer Zweck [...].[51]

The tone is that of wishing to do justice to a moderate talent with a clear gift for characterization and the creation of situations that speak to the experience of his audiences.

Iffland's later Mannheim years

Despite discontinuing the meetings of the *Ausschuss* in 1789, Dalberg remained a very important figure as intermediary between the Elector's court in Munich and the theatre, especially as the turbulence of the French Revolutionary wars brought the threat of closure. Only three more years of relative tranquillity still remained.

1789 saw two productions that heralded important developments that would become evident in the 1790s. The first was the première of Kotzebue's *Menschenhass und Reue*. August von Kotzebue became

---

50 *Allgemeine Literatur-Zeitung*, 10 November 1787, vol. 4, Nr. 270, p. 370.
51 Karl Heinrich Jördens, *Lexikon deutscher Dichter und Prosaisten*, vol. 2 (Leipzig: Weidmann, 1807), p. 532.

the most performed playwright of the next half century. His output, which included more than 230 plays and several novels, travelogues and historical and autobiographical writings, was even more prolific than Iffland's. Born in Weimar in 1761, Kotzebue studied law and took up a series of high-level legal and administrative posts in Estonia and Russia. He had some experience in the practical theatre world, first as short-lived *Theaterdichter* at the Burgtheater in Vienna in 1798 and later as director of the German theatre in St Petersburg. His anti-liberal polemics brought him notoriety in the post-Napoleonic period and he was assassinated in 1819 in Mannheim by a student, Karl Ludwig Sand, an event that provoked the promulgation of the Carls-bad Decrees, which imposed surveillance and censorship on the German universities as a move against demands for greater political liberty. Kotzebue's conquest of the German stage was rapid and Iffland quickly spotted the competition, writing to his sister in 1790 after seeing the former's play *Die Sonnenjungfrau*: 'Ich habe eben Cora gelesen – oder die Sonnenjungfer, Schauspiel von Herrn von Kotzebue. Dieser allein ist wohl ietzt mein Rival im würksamen Schreiben für die Bühne.'[52]

The second important première of 1789 was that of Mozart's opera *Don Giovanni*, which continued the success of *Die Entführung aus dem Serail* (premièred in Mannheim in 1785). The popularity of these works was surpassed in 1791 by that of *Die Zauberflöte*, the most popular opera ever performed on the German stage. *Don Giovanni* was given twenty-three times at Mannheim up to 1803, the year in which Dalberg stepped down as *Intendant*. *Die Zauberflöte* was performed sixty times from 1794 up to the same date. Although *The Marriage of Figaro*, *Così fan tutte* and *La clemenza di Tito* were comparatively less popular with audiences, the 1790s marked the start of the dominance of Mozart, music and libretto suitably adapted to the limitations of the company in question, on the German stage. Goethe and the Weimar court were Mozart enthusiasts and there the tendency is particularly marked.

In the years after the dissolution of the *Ausschuss* the artistic influence of Dalberg is harder to trace. The constant financial battle

---

52   Geiger 1, p. 27.

with rising costs made him ask repeatedly to relinquish his duties as *Intendant*.[53] He had put significant sums of his own into the enterprise and found it difficult to get them back. Late in 1790, in a memorandum to the Elector, he identifies the reasons for rising costs, which lie in the way the theatre has developed not only in Mannheim but in the German states generally in the previous decade.[54] At first, he says, the enterprise was buoyed up by its novelty for audiences. Operettas were a support and no-one minded the fact that they were out of date. But tastes began to change. Plays drawing on German history and requiring more elaborate sets and costumes came into fashion. Then with Mozart's *Entführung* the public demanded more and better operatic productions:

> Man forderte jetzt Compositionen von den berühmtesten Meistern, welche, theils aus dem Italienischen, theils aus dem Französischen übersetzt, mit einem kostspieligen Aufwande erscheinen mußten, wenn der Geschmack am Theater erhalten werden wollte.[55]

These musical works demanded a much higher standard of singing with attendant high production costs, which again rebounded on the costs and demands made of spoken theatre. Added to these costs, Dalberg writes, are those of acquiring good plays. Playwrights now had their plays printed only after they had sold manuscripts to interested theatres. Thus recent plays freely available in print were rarely the best. Dalberg also points to the rising cost of paying a company that has matured and developed over the years since its creation.

The *Intendant* was clearly concerned to reward members of the company who had shown it loyalty over a long period, and indeed the stability he was able to create in the company helped it ride out the turbulence of the French Revolutionary period. In his *Fragmente über Menschendarstellung* Iffland bemoans the damage to the actor's art brought about by his precarious circumstances and lack of pension

---

53   See Dalberg's letter to the Elector of 4 February 1791: 'Se. Ch. Drchl [...] haben mein wiederholtes Ansuchen, das ganze Theatergeschäft einem Andern in Mannheim übertragen zu dürfen, abgelehnt.' Quoted in Pichler, p. 119.
54   See Pichler, pp. 115–18.
55   Pichler, p. 117.

after a lifetime's labour. Dalberg was responsive to this complaint and in 1790 managed to secure better prospects for his long-serving actors in the form of life-long contracts and pensions of half their salaries.[56] Those included in addition to Iffland were Böck, the Becks, Mlle Withoeft, Gern, Beil, the Müllers and the Ritters. To control costs, however, the Elector decreed that salaries should be frozen and new contracts limited to one year.[57]

In October 1791 Rennschüb, who had been *Regisseur* for almost a decade, appeared on the Mannheim stage for the last time before taking up a new appointment as *Oberregisseur* at the newly built *Nationaltheater* in Frankfurt am Main. In 1792 the company elected Iffland unanimously as *Regisseur*.[58] His assurance to Dalberg of the need for impartiality and avowal of his subservience to Dalberg's wishes possibly gave the latter the confidence he needed that he had left the theatre, for which he now had little time or inclination, in competent and professional hands.[59] Fairness to and respect for his company as individuals was one of Iffland's ambitions at Mannheim and later at Berlin:

> Sind freilich nur wenige Schauspieler Künstler, so gewinnt dennoch eine Direktion, wenn sie alle als Künstler behandelt. Sie hat dann von den Schauspielern zu fordern, was sie ihnen vorher geleistet hat – Humanität [...] Ich habe gewünscht: Unterricht ohne Schulmeisterton, Ansehen durch Offenheit und Zutrauen, Festigkeit ohne Starrsinn zu bewirken.[60]

But from the early 1790s he became something of a controversial figure both in Mannheim and further afield. The city had experienced an influx of émigrés from France and from the left bank of the Rhine. Their presence sharpened the controversies already raging in the German states between royalists and sympathizers of the French Revolution.[61] Grétry's opera *Richard Cœur de Lion* was very popular with

---

56   Pichler, p. 115.
57   Pichler, pp. 118–19.
58   He had been acting *Regisseur* since the previous autumn.
59   *Meine theatralische Laufbahn*, pp. 95–96 and Pichler, pp. 120–21.
60   *Meine theatralische Laufbahn*, p. 96.
61   Perhaps surprisingly, one of Iffland's friends was the Mainz revolutionary Georg Forster. In 1790 he wrote to him: 'Es ist mir recht, wenn wir bleiben wie

émigré audiences in Mannheim. It was performed on 2 October 1791 and repeated on 4 October, shortly after the recapture of the fleeing French royal family at Varennes. At the end of the performance Iffland stepped forward and said in French (a language in which he was fluent): 'Möge der König einen Blondel finden, der sein Leben rettet!', thus clearly associating himself with the royalist sympathizers.[62] The strong attachment already noted to traditional authority and liking for aristocratic and courtly circles became controversial in the circumstances of the Revolution. Controversy was stoked when the Viennese court commissioned an anti-revolutionary drama, *Die Kokarden*, premièred in Leipzig in October 1791. The play was rarely performed and, significantly, never put on in Mannheim.

Though the influx of émigrés helped at first to boost theatre audiences in Mannheim, the next four years were to prove very turbulent, as the Palatinate became a theatre of war. On 30 January 1794 Iffland was instructed to dismiss the company. Bombardment of the city was feared and much of the population was preparing to flee. Iffland made ready to resist the long-term closure of the theatre, supported by the innkeepers of the city, who on Dalberg's suggestion petitioned the Elector to keep the theatre open. Dalberg himself supported their pleas to consider the economic viability of the city, a prominent reason why, on the removal of the Electoral court to Munich, the theatre had originally been created. He also reminded the Elector of the permanent contracts enjoyed by some members of the company.[63] The reply came that the Elector was sensible to the arguments but, in view of the 15,000 Gulden he had to pay as a subsidy, he wished Dalberg to suggest how that sum might be reduced.[64] The reopening of the theatre was approved from the beginning of March 1794 on

---

   wir sind. Es käme nichts beßers nach […] Fordern wir nicht zu viel von Fürsten? Es ist Mode, sie zu hassen und Mode sticht auch den Klügsten etwas an – ist es nicht Gerechtigkeitspflicht, sehr auf seiner Hut zu sein?' (*Georg Forsters Werke. Sämtliche Schriften, Tagebücher, Briefe*, ed. by the Akademie der Wissenschaften der DDR and the Berlin–Brandenburgische Akademie der Wissenschaften (Berlin: Akademie-Verlag, 1958–), vol. 18, pp. 414).

62   *Meine theatralische Laufbahn*, p. 92.
63   Pichler, p. 130.
64   Pichler, p. 131.

condition that Dalberg report after three months on possible savings. On 2 March it reopened with *Die Entführung*, but pressure remained on it to close. Dalberg even considered a scheme to retain the name 'Kurpfälzisches Nationaltheater' but to remove to another prominent city in the Elector's domains such as Cassel, Augsburg or Regensburg, away from the war-torn Rhineland.[65]

Further misfortune came in August 1794. On 14 August the actor David Beil died. On 17 August the Electress Elisabeth Auguste, who had remained in Mannheim on the removal of her husband to Munich so many years before and was a staunch supporter of the theatre, also died, whereupon the theatre closed for six weeks. When it reopened on 30 September 1794 the price of tickets had risen and Iffland was concerned that audiences would have to be kept especially satisfied. His advice to Dalberg was:

> um diese schwankende Stimmung zu schonen, um nirgends eine Explosion böser Laune zu machen die immer lange nachtönt – geben I. Ex. mit den ersten auszutheilenden zwei neuen Stücken, ja keine die zu fein, zu abstract sind, sondern solche, die *nicht* die *Reflexion*, sondern das *rohe Gefühl* beschäftigen, deren Erfolgs man also fast mathematisch gewiß sein kann.[66]

The season opened with the première of Iffland's own *Allzu scharf macht schartig*, which was repeated only three times up to 1803, and there were only four further premières that season, the emphasis being on tried and tested popular works. The most successful play premièred that year was Kotzebue's *Die Spanier in Peru*, a continuation of the popular *Die Sonnenjungfrau*. The greatest boost to the repertoire in 1794 was the introduction of Mozart's *Die Zauberflöte*. It was premièred on 29 March 1794 and performed eleven times by the end of that season and thirteen more in the next full season. With sixty performances up to 1803 it was the single most performed work at Mannheim during Dalberg's time as *Intendant*, a success repeated in many theatres in the German states.

The theatre was closed again on 24 December 1794 because of the French bombardment, which lasted eight days, and reopened on

---

65   Pichler, p. 135.
66   Pichler, pp. 137–38.

1 January 1795 with a performance of Spiess's *Klara von Hohen-eichen* (1790), a very successful *Ritterstück*, which was given as a benefit performance for those who had suffered damage as a result of the bombardment.[67] In summer 1795 the French were again bombarding the city and in September that year there was another two-week closure. The former opera house was destroyed and with it many of the theatre's sets, but the theatre building survived. From October it was occupied by Imperial forces. In December Dalberg was called to Munich leaving Iffland in charge. Though he reported from Munich that all was lost for the theatre, he won a reprieve in early 1796. Dalberg himself was then made President of the Palatinate, a high administrative office that naturally took him away from the theatre. On 12 July 1796 he told the company that the theatre was to be suspended for a year. They were given three months' salary and told to look for engagements elsewhere. What Dalberg probably did not anticipate was the protest of the garrison in Mannheim, which made him reverse his decision within two weeks.[68] The actors were, for the most part, able and willing to return. The notable exception to this was Iffland.

Dalberg, and Iffland himself, could well have considered that the actor had an unbreakable contract with Mannheim and unbreakable ties with the city. He owned a property on the banks of the Rhine. In 1785 he promised the Electress Elisabeth Auguste, who was particularly pleased with his short play *Liebe um Liebe*, written and performed to celebrate a royal wedding and the Electress's name day, that he would not leave Mannheim while she lived.[69] The Electress was now dead and Iffland's loyalty had been under strain for some years from attractive offers from leading theatres. In 1785 he had committed himself not to leave without Dalberg's consent as an acknowledgement of the latter's generosity in clearing his debts.[70] In

---

67   See Walter, vol. 1, p. 340. It was given 27 times between 1791 and 1803.

68   Pichler, p. 150.

69   *Meine theatralische Laufbahn*, p. 71.

70   Pichler quotes a letter from Schröder to Dalberg: 'Daß Iffland sich verbindlich gemacht hat in Mannheim zu bleiben, ist sehr klug von ihm, denn auf keinem anderen Theater in Deutschland würde er so gefallen' (Pichler, p. 92).

1790, when life-long contracts were being offered to the longest-serving members of the company, Iffland was considering an attractive offer from Vienna, through acceptance of which he would be able to clear the debts that had once more accrued. Dalberg again stepped in and produced enough money to offset the mounting costs of the interest on his debts.[71] By 1794 he was again contemplating a move, which he justified in part by suggesting that he was undervalued by Mannheim audiences, having arrived as a young man, who then worked his way up. In a letter to Dalberg of 2 February 1794 he tried to argue that his situation was of a particular and unusual kind. He claims his unprepossessing exterior had made his success harder to achieve: 'In einem Lande, wo das *Äußere* fast allein entscheidet wie hier, riß mein Äußeres nieder was mein Talent erbaut hatte.'[72] Later, he claims, what he wrote was regarded as cerebral and calculating. Even when his appearance was more solid and pleasing he was now seen as arrogant. These feelings of being unappreciated in Mannheim are compounded by opposition to the theatre on the part of several factions in the city:

> Diese Schauspielfreuden einzustellen gesellten sich zu den Franzosen die exjesuitischen Brüder mit ihren lojolistischen Zwecken, ferner die Parthey der alten Weintrinker, die die Künste hassen, obscurissimis! Aus Leuten, die die scheinbar starke Besoldung der Schauspieler anfeinden, die Privatursachen gegen uns einnehmen. Aus Democraten, die uns Aristokratenknechte nennen und hassen, die also in denen Stellen, wo Vermögen zu schaden war, entweder ergraute Dummheit oder gutmüthige Schwärmerei aufhetzten, um zum Zweck zu führen.[73]

Iffland turns what may have arisen from his own controversial position (as an acknowledged royalist sympathizer) into a prejudice against the actors in general. How far these protestations reflect his actual motivation is difficult to discern. In 1793 he made overtures to Berlin, building on the favour he had found with the Prussian King Friedrich Wilhelm II during the latter's stay in Mannheim in 1793. Again, as in the case of Vienna in 1790, when matters seemed to be coming to the point of decision, he made his debts, and this time his

---

71 See Walter, vol. 1, pp. 333–38.
72 Pichler, p. 139.
73 Pichler, p. 140.

war losses, an important factor in his thinking. Again, Dalberg showed himself willing to use his own money to ease Iffland's financial situation and keep him in Mannheim.[74]

In April 1796 Iffland arrived in Weimar for a three-week *Gastspiel*, a detailed account of which is to be found in the next chapter. Goethe had hopes of attracting him to Weimar to replace him as director of the court theatre and continued to hope, even after Iffland left Weimar again with the matter, though approved by Duke Carl August, still unresolved. His last performance at Mannheim was on 10 July. In September 1796, Dalberg having recalled the company after reversing his decision to suspend the theatre for a year, Iffland refused to return, claiming that no security for the future had been given.[75] In his autobiography he states that Dalberg had to withdraw the absolute guarantee of Iffland's pension that he had made earlier, admitting that losses to his own estates as a result of the French occupation might alter his ability to keep that commitment. Iffland suggests that this change of position depressed him, much as he understood Dalberg's concerns for his own family.[76] When he informed Dalberg in November that year of the handsome offer made to him by Berlin (a salary of 3000 Talers, a pension of 1200 Talers, one benefit performance a year and, crucially, settlement of his debts, which amounted to 14,000 Gulden or about 8000 Talers) the *Intendant* accused him of breach of contract and claimed he was as much under an obligation as other members of the company with life-long contracts not to enter into negotiations with another theatre.[77] Recriminations flew to and fro. Dalberg was deeply aggrieved, believing Iffland was using his debts and Prussia's willingness to pay them as an excuse to wriggle out of his commitments to Mannheim.[78] Later commentators have tended to take his part.[79] In his

---

74   Walter, vol. 1, p. 393 and Pichler, p. 142.
75   See Walter, vol. 1, p. 364.
76   *Meine theatralische Laufbahn*, p. 110.
77   Pichler, pp. 156–57.
78   Dalberg commented: 'So schrieb und handelte ein Iffland, Deutschlands dramatischer Sitten- und Tugendprediger!' (Walter, vol. 1, p. 408).
79   See, for example, Walter, vol. 1, p. 331: 'er verließ Dalberg und handelte ihm gegenüber in einer Art und Weise, die bei allem berechtigten Selbsterhaltungstrieb unschön und undankbar genannt werden muß.' See also Stubenrauch,

autobiography, Iffland, sensitive to criticisms, stresses Dalberg's cold-
ness and criticism of his financial handling of the theatre in the spring
of 1796.[80] Yet in the uncertain circumstances, where Dalberg's, and
more importantly the Elector's, support for the theatre was wavering
and the tribulations of war were likely to continue, an actor, playwright and director of Iffland's fame and talents was almost bound to
feel that he had given as much to Mannheim in the seventeen years he
had been there as Mannheim could expect, and that this was a theatre
that could offer him no scope or new challenge. In addition to the
popularity of his plays, his many *Gastspiele* had made him widely
appreciated as an actor. As a man, he was, as we have seen, deeply
bound to rulers and felt, rightly, that the Prussian king was personally
engaged in the project to bring him to Berlin, whereas his old patron-
ess the Electress of the Palatinate was now dead and Carl Theodor in
Munich was a distant and uncommitted figure. Dalberg's moral out-
rage may in part have been due, in spite of the respect he paid to the
actor, to his limited ability as a wealthy and independent aristocrat to
grasp the very modern professional ambition and self-confidence of
Iffland.[81]

The plays of Iffland's later Mannheim years (1790–96)

Iffland's fame as a dramatist rests on the success of his varied
depictions of the bourgeois family. The second phase of his work as a
playwright, however, demonstrates both the, arguably not always
very successful, broadening of his range and the creation of his
controversial reputation through plays, such as *Die Kokarden*, that
engage with contemporary political events. The two plays that made

---

    Wolfgang Heribert von Dalberg, p. 25 and Herrmann, *Thaliens liebster Sohn*,
    p. 47.

80   *Über meine theatralische Laufbahn*, pp. 122–23.

81   See Hugo Fetting, *Das Repertoire des Berliner Königlichen Nationaltheaters*,
    p. 31. Koffka, however, rejects this idea (p. 306).

his name in the 1780s were above all *Verbrechen aus Ehrsucht* and *Die Jäger*.[82] Between 1790 and 1796 Iffland penned twenty-two plays, a remarkable output given the turbulence of that period. His significant development was in the writing of comedy. In 1791 *Die Hagestolzen* was premièred in Mannheim and became one of his most enduringly popular plays. Inspired by Gotter's *Die Erbschleicher*, it demonstrates how comedy can combine the sentimental and the moralistic more palatably than can serious drama. In Hofrat Reinhold Iffland created one of his show-piece roles as an actor. The forty-year-old bachelor looks in vain for a wife among the town society, his attempts frustrated in part by his pious but grasping sister, who fears for her own prosperity and lends money at extortionate rates of interest. Reinhold flees the town to inspect a country smallholding leased to the poor but happy Linde, where he meets the latter's sister-in-law, Margarethe, and is captivated by her unspoilt charm and natural goodness. *Die Hagestolzen* was the play Goethe had in mind when he expressed his reservations in 1796 about Iffland's dramas:

> Er setzt überal Natur und Cultur in einen falschen Contrast. Cultur ist ihm immer die Quelle aller moralischer Verdorbenheit, wenn seine Menschen gut werden, so kehren sie in den Naturstand zurück, der Hagestolze geht auf seine Güther und heurathet ein Bauernmädchen [...] Die Idyllenszenen aus Arkadien, die in Ifflands Stücken so wohlgefallen, sind eine süsse, aber darum nur um so gefährlichere Schwärmerei.[83]

The change from the satire in the acts set in the town to the sentimental idyll of the country, though predictable and somewhat disappointing, is nevertheless handled with some charm, in spite of the fact that the difficulties of such a socially unacceptable marriage as

---

82 *Verbrechen aus Ehrsucht* gave rise to several imitations: for example, Röbiger's *Verbrechen aus Edelmuth*, Koller's *Verbrechen aus Liebe* and Palm's *Verbrechen aus Unschuld*.

83 Karl August Böttiger, *Literarische Zustände und Zeitgenossen. Begegnungen und Gespräche im klassischen Weimar*, ed. by Klaus Gerlach and Rene Sternke, 3rd edn (Berlin: Aufbau Verlag, 1998), pp. 89–90.

that between Reinhold and Margarethe are simply swept under the carpet.[84] Yet in a comedy such faults are more easily absorbed.

Another new departure was *Elise von Valberg*, also premièred in 1791, a play with a court setting in which a ruling prince and his consort play major roles. In a situation that has often been likened to that of *Emilia Galotti*, Elise is the object of the Prince's desire, mainly because the royal couple, married for the usual political and dynastic reasons, are estranged. Elise is blissfully unaware of the machinations at court to make her vulnerable to the prince's advances, but her much older brother (another Iffland role) is not and intervenes decisively to protect her. Elise herself, however, not only rescues her honour but brings about a reconciliation between the Prince and his wife by persuading her to put aside her resentment because of her superiority of birth (which has caused frostiness between them) and show him the affection that would stop him from straying. Iffland manages the difficult and highly improbable scene between Elise and the Princess with some skill.[85] Inevitably, the triumph of virtue is too easily achieved, and the absence of any probing of the values of the Prince makes the action in the end seem shallow.

Unquestionably the most controversial play Iffland ever wrote was *Die Kokarden*. It was commissioned by Emperor Leopold II, as Iffland is at pains to tell us in his autobiography:

Um diese Zeit wurde mir ohne Veranlassung, Einleitung, Zutun oder Verbindung, welche ich in Wien weder hatte noch jetzt habe, über Triest her auf Geheiß des Kaisers Leopold der Auftrag, gegen gewaltsame Staatsumwälzungen ein Schauspiel zu schreiben, und dazu das Thema gegeben, wie in der Mitte des vorigen Jahrhunderts die Könige von Dänemark die verlorene Souveränität wiedererlangt haben.[86]

---

84 On Goethe's continuation of the play see Friedrich Sengle, 'Goethes Nachspiel zu Ifflands Hagestolzen (1815)', in *Zwischen Aufklärung und Restauration. Sozialer Wandel in der deutschen Literatur (1700–1848)*, ed. by Wolfgang Frühwald and Alberto Martino (Tübingen: Niemeyer, 1989), pp. 307–16.

85 See Ernst Howald, '*Elise von Valberg*. Zur Ästhetik des Rührstücks', in *Philosophischer Eros im Wandel der Zeit* (Munich, Vienna: Oldenbourg, 1965), pp. 233–41.

86 *Meine theatralische Laufbahn*, pp. 93–94.

Instead of using the historical material suggested, Iffland chose to invent his own plot. A fictional uprising takes place in a small principality ruled over by a benevolent ruler. The peasants are led by two men of the bourgeoisie, who discredit themselves because of their complementary failings: Freund, the brewer, seeks personal gain and the chance to settle old scores, while for ideological reasons Magister Hahn, the rootless intellectual, stirs up the peasants to resentment against those above them in wealth and status, while being unable to offer any security against reprisals. Iffland's creation of Hahn as the demagogue and ideologue is remarkable evidence of his recognition of the power of ideas and journalism as a force in this new type of revolutionary change.[87] The characterization of the ruler as benevolent ('wie Fürsten sein sollen')[88] rather pre-empts the discussion and the invented plot thus exposes the difficulty of allegorizing contemporary events without bias or over-simplification. Family conflict is, as usual with Iffland, central to the play, as the minister Langenau finds his children on opposing sides in the uprising. Only three performances of the play are attested, significantly none in Mannheim, where the play would no doubt have fanned the flames in an already conflict-laden city. Besides that, it is not a very good play and arguably audiences looked for a respite from politics in the theatre. In his autobiography Iffland is concerned to correct the view that he was 'zu zahm, für die gute Sache der Menschheit Wahrheit zu sagen. Ich habe mich bemüht, diese nach meinen Kräften zu verbreiten [...] Aber eine Staatsverfassung zu untergraben, dahin habe ich nie arbeiten wollen'.[89] It was a commission that, in the volatile atmosphere, with hindsight he might have been better to avoid.

Die Kokarden was not the only play Iffland wrote at this time that was linked to contemporary politics, but on the other occasions, such as the coronation of the Emperor Leopold II (1790) and of

---

87 This aspect is explored by Wolfgang Martens in his article 'Der Literat als Demagoge. Zum Thema der poetischen Gefährlichkeit des Schriftstellers um 1790, entwickelt am Beispiel von Ifflands Antirevolutionsdrama *Die Kokarden*', in *Presse und Geschichte. Beiträge zur historischen Kommunikationsforschung I* (Munich: Verlag Dokumentation, 1977), pp. 100–36.

88 *Meine theatralische Laufbahn*, p. 94.

89 *Über meine theatralische Laufbahn*, p. 95.

Emperor Franz II (1792), the plays (*Friedrich von Österreich* and *Der Eichenkranz* respectively) he produced were uncontroversial celebrations of traditional monarchy and not written for adoption into the general repertoire. Several other plays were uncomplicated successes and widely performed, for example *Der Herbsttag, Die Reise nach der Stadt, Der Vormund* and *Die Aussteuer*. During the period 1786 to 1793 Iffland was the most performed dramatist at the Mannheim theatre. During the last Dalberg decade, up to 1803, he was overtaken at Mannheim, as he was everywhere, by Kotzebue. Although Kotzebue's dramatic output, by no means limited to the bourgeois family drama, was more varied than Iffland's (he was also a prolific translator and librettist), the preponderance of the family drama in the repertoire of spoken drama was firmly established by 1796. The Mannheim theatre in Iffland's last few years was inhibited by external turbulence and so it surrendered any claim it once had to be a leading stage. His move to Berlin, to a theatre actively supported by the monarch and with a budget far greater than Mannheim's, opened up possibilities undreamt of.

Chapter Four
Schiller, Goethe and the Weimar Court Theatre (1791–96)

Schiller left Mannheim for Leipzig on 9 April 1785 at the invitation of four admirers who had written to him the previous year: Christian Gottfried Körner and his fiancée Minna Stock and Ludwig Ferdinand Huber and his fiancée Dora Stock, Minna's sister. Körner, who became his lifelong friend, advanced money to free Schiller from financial obligations in Mannheim and also introduced him to the Leipzig publisher Georg Joachim Göschen, with whom the writer had many years of dealings, and who agreed to take over publication of the *Rheinische Thalia* (as the *Thalia*). Living close to the Körners in Leipzig and later in Dresden and relieved by his new friend's generosity of some financial pressures, Schiller immersed himself in historical study of the sixteenth century and in particular Philip II of Spain, in an attempt to make progress with the as yet unfinished *Don Karlos*. He had published the first act in the *Rheinische Thalia* before he left Mannheim; he then published two further instalments in the *Thalia* in 1785/86. Progress was slow because the complicated plot he had set in motion was difficult to bring to a conclusion within the confines of a five-act drama, while his historical reading produced new perspectives on the significance of the later sixteenth century as a period of progress and change. Having broken off publication in instalments, in 1787 he produced a book version of the completed work, which at 6282 lines was about 1000 lines longer than the last, now standard, version Schiller prepared for the 1805 edition of his works.

In October 1786, during his time in Dresden, he learned from his Mannheim friend, the actor Heinrich Beck, that Schröder wished to contact him. Schröder's earlier correspondence with Dalberg about the young playwright conveys both his admiration as well as disapproval of the evidence in the latter's work of the continued influence of the *Sturm und Drang* style, despite the fact that Schröder himself had brought several works of that literary movement to the stage in the 1770s. In 1785, clearly unaware of the expiry of Schiller's contract, he wrote to Dalberg: 'Sie haben das jetzt lebende größte dramatische Talent, Schillern bey sich und zwängen ihn nicht von dem Wege ab, auf dem er bis itzt wandelt' (FA 2, 1210). Schröder assumes here that Dalberg will have retained the services of such a talented writer. Beck subsequently let Schröder know that Schiller was at work on *Don Karlos* and thus that there was a possibility of staging it in Hamburg. Prompted by his friend, Schiller wrote to Schröder of his progress and promised future plays for the Hamburg theatre. Schröder invited him to come to Hamburg with a view to an appointment at the theatre but Schiller drew back. His few letters to Schröder suggest, alongside his strong admiration for the *Prinzipal* himself, a deep-rooted distaste for and disillusionment with the theatre. Trying to respond positively, he writes:

> Ich werde Sie sehen und mein beinahe erstorbenes Kunstgefühl für Theater wird neu in mir aufwachen. Von Ihnen hoffe ich diese Aussöhnung meiner Muse mit der Bühne, welche die meisten Theater die ich jetzo noch gesehen, mehr entfernt, als erleichtert haben. (NA 24, 101)

That hope was not sufficient to tempt him to commit himself to Hamburg. He agreed to visit the city where *Don Karlos* was to be premièred in the summer of 1787 but never completed the journey.

In spite of his reluctance to work in the theatre world, Schiller was eager to make what money he could from acting versions of his new play, and prepared manuscripts for sale to various interested theatres before he sent off the book version to Göschen.[1] First he supplied Schröder with an acting version in the original blank verse rather than in the prose required by most theatres, where verse speaking had become a rare accomplishment. Schröder was concerned about Catholic sensibilities in a city with many foreign embassies, and as a result the Cardinal Inquisitor, to Schiller's regret, was omitted. The two men also considered how to handle the role of Domingo, who in the Hamburg version is no longer explicitly the King's confessor.

---

1   For extensive treatments of the acting manuscripts and for details of performances, see BA 3, 860–80 and NA 7/II, 482–501.

Schröder himself played Philipp, the première (on 29 August 1787) seems to have been a success and the play was repeated the very next evening and performed a further four times that year.[2] Its length caused all theatres problems and led to cuts being made that further dislocated an already perilously complex action. Religious sensibilities also had to be taken into account elsewhere and the play was sometimes given in the 'Perez' version, in which Domingo is replaced by 'Staatssckretär' Antonio Perez. In Mannheim the play was given in a verse version adapted by Dalberg from Schiller's manuscript, in which Domingo was changed into a Jesuit, to allow Dalberg a means of indirectly criticizing Ignaz Frank, a Jesuit court preacher known for his anti-Enlightenment views.[3] To Schwan, who informed him about the Mannheim première, Schiller was philosophical about the muted audience reaction:

> Es ist nicht mehr als billig, daß sich die Theatralische Göttinn für die wenige Galanterie die mich, beim Schreiben, für sie beseelte, an mir gerächt hat. Indeßen, wenn mein Carlos auch ein noch so verfehltes *Theaterstück* ist, so halte ich doch dafür, daß unser Publikum ihn noch zehenmahl wird aufführen sehen können, ehe es das *Gute* begriffen und ausgeschöpft hat, was seine Fehler aufwägen soll. (NA 25, 53)[4]

Contemporary reviews are responsive to Schiller's great dramatic moments – Posa's farewell to Elisabeth, his death, Carlos's scenes with Lerma – as well as to the work's flaws.[5] Schiller was only too

---

2   See BA 3, 862. Further detail on the changes for the Hamburg première is given in Hans Knudsen's article 'Die Hamburger Uraufführung des *Don Karlos* und ihre Darsteller', *Die Scene*, 8, Hefte 10–12 (1918), 134–37.

3   See Schiller's letter to Körner, 25 April 1788: 'Ifland soll den König geheult, Böck den Marquis aber gut vorzüglich gut gespielt haben' (NA 25, 49); also BA 3, 865.

4   Schiller had heard in the meantime that the second performance had been better received; see NA 25, 483.

5   The *Tagebuch der Mannheimer Schaubühne* recorded, for example: 'Der Plan ist nicht gut, er ist zu gedehnt; das Interesse ist zu sehr getheilt [...]. Don Karlos ist nicht ganz richtig geschildert; gleich in der ersten Scene mit dem Beichtvater giebt er sich zu sehr blos [...]. Doch in dem Stücke sind Scenen, die theatralisch, erschütternd, rührend sind.' See *Tagebuch der Mannheimer Schaubühne*, 2 vols (Mannheim: Schwan, 1788), vol. 2, pp. 284–85.

aware of them himself, for they were the main reason why he abandoned the writing of plays for the next decade.

If Mannheim caused him a crisis in relation to the theatre, *Don Karlos* caused him one in relation to tragedy itself. The compositional difficulties of the play undermined his confidence, and though, after its publication, he entertained plans for new dramas such as *Der versöhnte Menschenfeind* and *Die Maltheser*, he did not have the assurance to carry them through.[6] *Don Karlos* marked the beginning of a transition to a new style – thereafter he wrote only verse plays[7] – but it also convinced him that he could not write another play until he had achieved greater mastery of dramatic form. He thus set out on a theoretical journey through aesthetics and philosophy that took almost a decade. He concerned himself with the practicalities of dramatic construction, with the moral and aesthetic problem of taking pleasure in the portrayal of suffering, with the nature of the sublime, with the calling of the artist and with the function of art itself as a humanizing and transforming force in the individual and in society. During this process, he never abandoned the conviction that his true vocation was to write high tragedy.

In 1787, however, Schiller's immediate future seemed to lie in the direction of historiography. He was completing his *Geschichte des Abfalls der vereinigten Niederlande von der spanischen Regierung*, published in 1788, the product of his background reading for *Don Karlos*. In the summer of that year he set out on what was to be a temporary absence from Dresden for Weimar (and possibly Hamburg) but in the end established himself in the small state of Sachsen–Weimar–Eisenach, where he remained for the rest of life. The most illustrious inhabitant of his new world was Goethe, who returned in 1788 from his Italian journey, but their first meeting did not establish mutual sympathy. Goethe recorded later that he saw in the younger

---

6   Whereas the plans for *Der versöhnte Menschenfeind* were abandoned in the late 1780s, those for *Die Maltheser*, a play that would feature a chorus, were periodically resurrected up to 1803.

7   One of his first stylistic exercises after *Don Karlos* was to make translations of Euripides's *Iphigenia in Aulis* and part of *The Phoenician Women*. These appeared in Schiller's journal, *Thalia*.

writer the author of *Die Räuber*, a work that reminded him unpleasantly of a style he had long rejected and which seemed particularly distasteful to him after his Italian experiences.[8] Schiller was disappointed by Goethe's indifference, yet even so Goethe was instrumental in securing for him a professorship in history at the University of Jena, which, although not salaried, gave him for the first time a respected position in the social hierarchy. Schiller lived for the next ten years in Jena, marrying Charlotte von Lengefeld in 1790. His life became more secluded after 1792 when he almost succumbed to a pulmonary infection that left him an invalid for the rest of his life. It was therefore a particular confluence of circumstances that brought him back to practical involvement with the theatre. The first vital link was the establishing in 1794, after several years of only distant contact, of his friendship and alliance with Goethe, who in 1791 had become *Intendant* of the Weimar Court Theatre.[9]

Goethe would not have had the commitment and energy to conduct the Weimar experiment in a non-naturalistic style of drama if he had not had Schiller, whom he trusted, whose aesthetic outlook he shared and who could write plays that audiences wanted to see, to work with him. Schiller would not have written new plays with the theatre so prominently in mind if he had not been reintroduced to the practical world of theatre by Goethe, primarily through the production of *Wallenstein*. In time, the Weimar Court Theatre provided Schiller with a stage that would perform his later plays as he wrote them, and indeed the company became adept at verse speaking. The fact that together Goethe and Schiller had such prestige in the cultural environment meant that Iffland's ambitious vision for the Berlin National Theatre, when he became Director there at the end of 1796, could be realized through cooperation with these two men.

---

8   See his famous account of his first meetings with Schiller, entitled 'Glückliches Ereignis', MA 12, 86–90.

9   For a fuller account of the establishment of the friendship between Goethe and Schiller, see Chapter 5.

Weimar: From amateur dramatics to the creation of the Court Theatre

When Goethe came to Weimar at the invitation of the young Duke Carl August in 1775 there was no standing theatre in the little dukedom[10] because, as noted in the Introduction, fire had destroyed the palace theatre in the Wilhelmsburg in May 1774.[11] For the previous three years the Seyler–Ekhof company had been playing in Weimar at the invitation of the regent, Duchess Anna Amalia. After the fire she mediated the company's move to Gotha. For most of the next decade theatrical performances in Weimar were provided by two amateur groups, one composed of the court and nobility and one of the *Bürger* (led by the entrepreneur, dramatist and translator Friedrich Justin Bertuch), which then came together under Goethe's leadership. He was already a successful dramatist and stage writer, not only with *Götz von Berlichingen* and *Clavigo*, but also with *Erwin und Elmire* (first performed in 1775), the libretto he based on an episode from Goldsmith's *Vicar of Wakefield* (1766). Amateur theatre was one of the passions of the age and the enthusiasm for it of the Weimar court and citizens was to sustain some eight years of sometimes quite ambitious productions, until around 1782, when Goethe was so burdened with administration that activities petered out. Thereafter and for the next twenty years there was only the very occasional production. In 1783 the Graz actor and *Prinzipal* Joseph Bellomo was granted permission to perform in Weimar and he and his company remained until the creation of the Court Theatre in 1791.

Performances of the amateur theatre took place in a building that was also used for balls and other entertainments and so the stage had to be suitable for erecting and dismantling as required.[12] They were

---

10   Bruford (*Germany in the Eighteenth Century*, p. 335) gives the size of Sachsen–Weimar–Eisenach around 1800 as c. 760 modern-day square miles with a total population of 106,400. Weimar had c. 7500 inhabitants.
11   See p. 19.
12   For the fullest account of the amateur theatre with details of the repertoire, see Gisela Sichardt, *Das Weimarer Liebhabertheater unter Goethes Leitung*

open to the public free of charge, as they had been when professional companies had played. This accessibility was not maintained when there were performances at the small royal palaces of Ettersburg and Tiefurt, both a short distance outside Weimar, where the audience was confined to the court and to a small number of guests. Ettersburg and Tiefurt provided the opportunity for open-air performances and so Goethe supplied some works specifically for outdoor performance, such as *Die Fischerin*, his Singspiel of 1781 or his 1780 translation of part of Aristophanes's *The Birds*.[13]

The problems of the impermanent stage in Weimar were finally relieved in 1780, when a new theatre and ballroom (the *Redoutensaal*) on the Esplanade (now the Schillerstrasse) was completed, more or less where the National Theatre stands today. This served for theatre performances until the extensive renovations of 1798. By 1780 the heyday of the amateur theatre was over but there was now a permanent *Kulissenbühne* that could then be used by Bellomo's company, which began playing in January 1784. The new theatre was a tall building with a gallery. Two high doors opened to the garden at the back. There were five or six pairs of *Kulissen* and a rising stage to enhance the perspective they created. From the time of Goethe's first involvement in early 1776 to 1783, by which time productions had more or less ceased, about one hundred performances are attested.

(Weimar: Arion Verlag, 1957). For other useful accounts Heinz Kindermann, *Theatergeschichte der Goethezeit* (Vienna: Bauer, 1948); W. H. Bruford, *Culture and Society in Classical Weimar* (Cambridge: CUP, 1962), pp. 120–36; Leonhard Schrickel, *Geschichte des Weimarer Theaters von seinen Anfängen bis heute* (Weimar: Pause, 1928), pp. 59–76; Marvin Carlson, *Goethe and the Weimar Theatre* (Ithaca and London: Cornell University Press, 1978); Peter Huber, 'Goethes praktische Theaterarbeit' in *Goethe Handbuch*, vol. 2, *Dramen*, ed. by Theo Buck (Stuttgart: Metzler, 1996), pp. 23–30 (for a bibliography on Goethe as a theatre director, see the same volume, pp. 41–42). An introduction for the general reader is provided in Dietrich Fischer-Dieskau, *Goethe als Intendant* (Munich: DTV, 2006), pp. 19–87.

13   On Goethe's *Singspiele*, see Markus Waldura, 'Die Singspiele', in Theo Buck (ed.), *Goethe Handbuch*, vol. 2, *Dramen*, pp. 173–94; Thomas Frantzke, *Goethes Schauspiele mit Gesang und Singspiele 1773–82* (Frankfurt am Main and Berne: Lang, 1998); Tina Hartmann, *Goethes Musiktheater. Singspiele, Opern, Festspiele, 'Faust'* (Tübingen: Niemeyer, 2004), esp. pp. 59–134.

Over thirty of these performances were of works by Goethe himself, the most frequently given being his *Erwin und Elmire*, for which the Dowager Duchess composed a new score. The only serious play of his to be performed and at the same time the most significant production by the amateur group, was the original prose version of *Iphigenie auf Tauris* (1779), in which the court singer Corona Schröter played the title role and Goethe played Orest.

The remainder of the repertoire was not unlike that of many professional companies of the time, that is a mixture of opera/ *Singspiel* and comedy, with very few serious plays. Apart from *Iphigenie*, only Voltaire's *Mahomet* (probably performed in French) and *Kalliste* (1782) by Karl Friedrich Siegmund von Seckendorff (1744–85) were serious dramas. French (Molière, Beaumarchais, Destouches), Italian (Gozzi, Goldoni) and English (Cumberland, Colman/Garrick) comedies were played, as well as a small number of German ones, for example *Minna von Barnhelm* and J. J. Engel's popular *Der Edelknabe* (1774).[14] Notably absent from the repertoire were sentimental dramas of the kind made popular by Diderot, Sedaine and Nivelle de la Chaussée. These were prominent in the repertoires of commercial companies and their absence suggests that court taste was hostile to the prevailing sentimentalism of that decade. Indeed it is satirized in Goethe's *Der Triumph der Empfindsamkeit*, a comedy dating from the early 1770s, which he revised in 1778 for its première by the amateur group. Some of the works performed were favourites taken from Seyler's repertoire: the operas *Der Faß-binder* (Faber/Audinot), *Das Milchmädchen und die beiden Jäger* (Schwan/Anseaume) and the comedies *Der Postzug* (Ayrenhoff), *Der Poetische Dorfjunker* (Destouches), *Der Spieler* (Regnard) and *Der Westindier* (Cumberland). Although relations between the Weimar and Gotha courts were close, the Weimar repertoire does not seem to have been influenced by that of the newly-created Gotha Court Theatre under the leadership of Ekhof and Reichard. Only three plays were common to their repertoires: Beaumarchais's *Le Barbier de*

---

14   Sichardt gives a full list of all attested performances on pp. 130–72.

Seville, Engel's *Der Edelknabe* and Lessing's *Minna von Barnhelm*.[15] This absence of sentimental moralizing from the Weimar productions no doubt coincided with Goethe's personal tastes. His comment of 1773 to his Strasbourg friend Johann Daniel Salzmann, 'Wir haben Sittlichkeit und lange Weile' (WA IV, 2, 66), was made about post-Gottsched theatre, from which the traditional comic person of Hanswurst had been banished but where wit had not taken his place. It suggests that to be able to work and perform away from the constraints of the commercial theatre and with the liberty bestowed by the court environment to disregard the bourgeois tendency to preach was welcome to him. In his *Iphigenie auf Tauris*, which is crucially concerned with moral action, he shows goodness and a tentative hope finally winning through, but only after great suffering and a desperate gamble on the part of the heroine.

Bellomo's company was not formally engaged in Weimar as a court theatre group but nevertheless came under the jurisdiction of the royal household in certain matters and an *Intendant* was appointed by the court to oversee it. From 1788 this task was performed by Franz Kirms, who would become Goethe's right-hand man, when the latter assumed responsibility for the theatre, and took care of much of the correspondence and financial matters. Bellomo was obliged to issue firm contracts to his company, not to engage new actors without permission from the court and to present his proposed repertoire for court approval. In return he received the right to use the *Redoutensaal* free of charge, with free heating and lighting, ticketing, wardrobe and props (these remained the property of the court). He also had free use of the court musicians. In addition, the court added a subvention of 320 Reichstaler a year.[16]

Bellomo's repertoire was composed of the typical mixture of the time. About half consisted of comedies and about a quarter of *Sing-*

---

15   See Schlösser, *Vom Hamburger Nationaltheater zur Gothaer Hofbühne*, pp. 75–78.
16   For a concise account of Bellomo's time in Weimar see Ernst Pasqué's *Goethes Theaterleitung in Weimar. In Episoden und Urkunden*, 2 vols. (Leipzig: Weber, 1863), vol. 1, pp. 30–40 and Bruno Satori-Neumann's *Die Frühzeit des Weimarischen Hoftheaters unter Goethes Leitung (1791 bis 1798)*, Schriften der Gesellschaft für Theatergeschichte, 31 (Berlin: Elsner, 1922), pp. 9–11.

spiele and comic opera (*opera buffa*). The remainder of the repertoire was made up of serious plays and tragedies (the latter much in the minority). In addition to the popular contemporary dramatists such as Iffland, Gotter and (from the late 1780s) Kotzebue, Bellomo played Shakespeare (*Hamlet, Macbeth, King Lear, Othello, Julius Caesar*), Lessing and the early Schiller, as well as Goethe's *Götz von Berlichingen* and *Clavigo*. The standard seems to have been very mixed. In 1788 an article appeared in Bertram's journal *Annalen des Theaters* with the title 'Ueber die Bellomoische Schauspielergesellschaft'. The anonymous author reviews over forty performances between November 1787 and March 1788. The result is not flattering to the hardworking company, which was obliged by contract to put on a new play each week and a new opera every second week. Individual performers were sometimes impressive but the performances that were judged satisfactory as a whole were few. The comments are confined to acting rather than being directed at other aspects of the performance. Andreas Einer (also known as Krako), an actor who reappeared for a time in the Weimar company in the court theatre's early years, is thus described in a performance of Iffland's *Die Jäger*: 'Herr Einer als Anton, tobte wie ein angeschossenes Thier herum und polterte die schönsten Szenen so schlecht, als wüste er gar nicht was er sprach, und das war auch der Fall.'[17]

As a result of the general dissatisfaction with the standard of the company, by the end of the 1780s Duke Carl August was planning for a new, post-Bellomo era, namely the creation of a court theatre partially commercial and partially supported by court subsidy. Goethe was circumspect in his response, hinting in a letter of 6 February 1790 at the strife such an enterprise can bring with it:

> Daß Sie sich, unter den gegenwärtigen Umständen, noch mit der mechanischsten aller Wissenschaften, dem deutschen Theater abgeben mögen, läßt uns andere Verehrer der Irene hoffen, daß diese stille Schöne noch eine Zeitlang regieren wird (WA IV, 9, 172–73).

---

17 'Ueber die Bellomoische Schauspielergesellschaft. Weimar den 24. Mai 1788', *Annalen des Theaters*, Heft 2 (1789), 43–51 (p. 49).

To Johann Friedrich Reichardt (1752–1814), composer and royal *Kapellmeister* in Berlin, he justifies his pessimism, alluding to his ruler's consultations with Schröder, and touches on aesthetic problems that will be at the heart of his own involvement with the theatre:

> Von Kunst hat unser Publikum keinen Begriff und so lange solche Stücke allgemeinen Beyfall finden, welche von mittelmäßigen Menschen ganz artig und leidlich gegeben werden können, warum soll ein Direktor nicht auch eine sittliche Truppe wünschen, da er bey seinen Leuten nicht auf vorzügliches Talent zu sehen braucht, welches sonst allein den Mangel aller übrigen Eigenschaften entschuldigt.
>
> Die Deutschen sind im Durchschnitt rechtliche, biedere Menschen aber von Originalität, Erfindung, Charakter, Einheit, und Ausführung eines Kunstwercks haben sie nicht den mindesten Begriff. Das heißt mit Einem Worte sie haben keinen Geschmack. (28 Feb. 1790, WA IV, 9, 180–81)

The inference is that Schröder has made some connection between the repertoire and the need for morally upstanding actors. This was a familiar theme in theatrical circles: the assumption was that if only the status of actors could be raised, if only they could be regarded as respectable members of society, there was some hope of making theatre-going respectable for (middle-class) audiences and the acting profession attractive to people of real talent. Goethe exposes the unresolved conflict that had dogged theatrical debate in the eighteenth century between the moral and aesthetic aims of theatre and shows he thinks that no artistic progress can be made by striving to make theatre a place where respectable plays are put on to respectable audiences by respectable actors.

By the end of 1790 it was clear that Bellomo's contract would not be renewed for a further year and he announced that he would be leaving for Graz.[18] His last performance was on 5 April 1791, when Kotzebue's *Das Kind der Liebe* (1790) was played. A small scandal was created by the recitation of a farewell address, which in its published form contains words of gratitude to the court:

---

18 'Als Hr. Bellomo endlich den für uns so vortheilhaften Entschluß faßte, Weimar zu verlassen, und nach Graz zu gehen, wurde ihm dazu aller möglicher Vorschub geleistet, und die Sache gelang', 'Chronologie des Theaters zu Weimar', *Annalen des Theaters*, Heft 20 (1797), 63–64.

In dieser Stadt, wo Carl August, der Vater seines Landes
Wo der geliebte Fürst, den Musen Tempel weiht
[…]
hier, wo Luisens Hand mit jedem Tage sich verjüngt,
hier, wo Amalia für Wissenschaft thronet,
hier wurde unsre Kunst geliebt, beschützt, belohnet.[19]

The section of the poem from which these lines were taken was omitted from the recitation.

Carl August cast around for a director for the new court theatre, but it was not very likely that anyone of renown from the theatre world would be attracted to such a precarious enterprise in a small provincial capital. Gradually, everything seemed to point to the desirability of Goethe's taking the post, at least in the short term. Since his return from Italy his administrative responsibilities had lain in the cultural field, so it was difficult for him to resist this new addition. A *Fürstliche Theater-Commission* under the aegis of the *Hofmarschallamt* was formed, with Goethe in overall charge. Additional actors were sought to supplement a group retained from Bellomo's company. These new members included Anton Genast, a tenor specializing in character roles, whose recollections of his theatrical career at Weimar were recorded by his son Eduard and, though very respectful, are an important source of information about the day-to-day experience of the company.[20] Goethe tended to draw the actors from far afield, looking – no doubt for reasons of economy – for emerging talent rather than for actors of renown. Everyone had to be able to sing and some members of the company, for example Christian Benda, son of the Gotha *Kapellmeister* Georg, were chiefly engaged for their singing abilities. One of the most questionable appointments was that of the *Regisseur* Franz Fischer, who had had a relatively undistinguished career up to that point. He failed to maintain order in the company and was not retained after Easter 1793.[21]

---

19   *Annalen des Theaters*, Heft 8 (1791), p. 14.
20   Eduard Genast, *Aus dem Tagebuch eines alten Schauspielers*, 4 vols (Leipzig: Voigt & Günther, 1862–66).
21   Looking back from the safe distance of 1822 at that period in his memoir *Campagne in Frankreich 1792* Goethe claims that Fischer 'wußte die einheimischen [Schauspieler] gut zu behandeln, wodurch ein innerer Friede sich über das

Goethe's first task as director was not, however, to engage the actors but to secure the rights of the new troupe to play the summer season, as Bellomo had done, at Lauchstädt, a small but quite fashionable spa close to Merseburg in Saxony, frequented in the summer months by the Saxon nobility and by Leipzig merchants and their families. Already on 10 January Goethe was writing to the Dresden court on behalf of Carl August:

> Bellomo verläßt den hiesigen Ort und es wird sich eine neue Truppe hier etablieren. Nun wünschen Durchl. der Herzog, daß das Bellomoische Privilegium auf die neue Weimarische Schauspieler übertragen werden möge. Man wird sich mit Bellomo wegen seines Lauchstädter Hauses abfinden und hofft überhaupt daß die künftige Gesellschaft besser als die bißherige exhibiren soll. (WA IV, 9, 39)

With a population of around 600 the town was very small and the spa visitors were naturally keen for entertainment during their stay. The theatre was also popular with the students of Halle. Bellomo was given permission in 1785 to build a theatre, a very plain oblong building with twenty rows of seating, partially raised, and a stage with five pairs of *Kulissen*. The accumulated income from the Lauchstädt season was considerable, as costs were low. Doebber estimates that forty Lauchstädt evenings brought in as much as a hundred in Weimar, though in time the building became badly run down and in need of repair.[22] The Weimar company also supplemented their income with occasional summer seasons in Erfurt and Rudolstadt. Bellomo was pressurized by time and by Kirms's canniness into a, for him, not very advantageous sale of the theatre and its contents.[23] The concession was granted and that summer the Weimar company moved as usual to Lauchstädt.

The new court theatre opened on 7 May with a performance of Iffland's *Die Jäger*, not only a popular play but one that existed in

---

ganze verbreitete' (MA 14, 504). He may simply wish to be kind to a man who was not kept on and later fell on hard times.

22   Adolph Doebber, *Lauchstädt und Weimar. Eine theatergeschichtliche Studie* (Berlin: Mittler, 1908), p. 43.

23   Doebber, pp. 36–38.

Bellomo's repertoire and could therefore be put on without delay.[24] The prologue Goethe wrote for the opening night announces the aesthetic for which he would strive in the coming years and which at that point he still regarded as a somewhat distant prospect:

> Nun dächten *wir*, die wir versammelt sind
> Euch manches Werk der Schauspielkunst zu zeigen,
> Nur an uns selbst; so träten wir vielleicht
> Getrost hervor, und jeder könnte hoffen,
> Sein weniges Talent Euch zu empfehlen.
> Allein bedenken wir daß Harmonie
> Des ganzen Spiels allein verdienen kann
> Von Euch gelobt zu werden; daß ein jeder
> Mit jedem stimmen, all mit einander
> Ein schönes Ganze vor Euch stellen sollen;
> So reget sich die Furcht in unsrer Brust. (MA 4.1, 192)

Goethe announces the principle of harmonious playing rather than the pursuit of individual virtuosity. This would remain his central aim during his time at the theatre, though in 1791 he must have known he was far from achieving it. Many years later, in his memoir *Campagne in Frankreich 1792* (1822) he wrote:

> Was mir bei diesem Unternehmen aber besonders zu Statten kam, war der damals überhand nehmende Natur- und Konversationston, der zwar höchst lobenswert und erfreulich ist, wenn er als vollendete Kunst, als eine zweite Natur hervortritt, nicht aber wenn ein jeder glaubt nur sein eigenes nacktes Wesen bringen zu dürfen, um etwas Beifallswürdiges darzubieten. Ich aber benutzte diesen Trieb zu meinen Zwecken, indem ich gar wohl zufrieden sein konnte, wenn das angeborne Naturell sich mit Freiheit hervortat, um sich nach und nach durch gewisse Regeln und Anordnungen einer höheren Bildung entgegen führen zu lassen. (MA 14, 503)

Goethe's retrospective comments present a rosy and streamlined picture of events; in fact his attempt at influencing the company towards

---

24 The most detailed history of the early years of the theatre is Bruno Satori-Neumann's *Die Frühzeit des Weimarischen Hoftheaters*. The following account is indebted to it. See also Julius Wahle, *Das Weimarer Hoftheater unter Goethes Leitung. Aus neuen Quellen bearbeitet* (Weimar: Verlag der Goethe-Gesellschaft, 1892).

a more stylized and uniform manner of playing was a great deal more difficult than these words suggest. But the emphasis on ensemble playing, on a move away from a naturalistic to a more stylized acting technique and on the acquisition by the actors of a shared dramatic idiom is repeated in Goethe's letters and in other contemporary documents such as the Prologue quoted above. In the *Campagne in Frankreich 1792* he refers significantly to the kind of groundwork he wanted to do:

> Da ich Teil an der Direktion genommen, so war es mir eine unterhaltende Beschäftigung gelind zu versuchen, auf welchem Wege das Unternehmen weiter geführt werden könnte. Ich sah gar bald, daß eine gewisse Technik aus Nachahmung, Gleichstellung mit andern und Routine hervorgehen konnte, allein es fehlte durchaus an dem was ich Grammatik nennen dürfte, die doch erst zum Grunde liegen muß, ehe man zu Rhetorik und Poesie gelangen kann (MA 14, 503)

By 'Grammatik' he means a set of acknowledged parameters within which a harmonious style of acting could develop. This 'Grammatik' would be based on a common idea of performance and its aesthetic aims. That aesthetic depended on the actor's willingness to cultivate a style in tune with the ensemble as a whole. More practically, it also suggested a flexible attitude towards playing major and minor roles and an attempt to suppress strong regional accents and variations in speech. A letter to Reichardt of 30 May 1791, from the early days of the first season, illuminates the meaning of 'Grammatik' further:

> Im Ganzen, macht mir unser Theater Vergnügen, es ist schon um Vieles besser, als das vorige, und es kommt nur darauf an, daß sie sich zusammen spielen [...] und aus dem abscheulichen Schlendrian in dem die mehrsten deutschen Schauspieler bequem hinleiern, nach und nach herausgebracht werden. Ich werde selbst einige Stücke schreiben, [...] und sehen, ob man sie nach und nach an ein gebundenes, kunstreicheres Spiel gewöhnen kann. (WA IV, 9, 263–64)

By 'kunstreicher' Goethe does not mean that individuals should develop stage mannerisms but that their acting style should be determined by a general aesthetic concept and discipline of performance.

These would be the aims guiding Goethe throughout his work at the theatre but arguably it was not until Schiller's active participation that they would come anywhere near to being realized. In the early years to 1796 Goethe's involvement in the practicalities of staging was limited; he relied on the *Regisseur*. For the first years of the theatre his artistic ambitions were at least partly submerged under the practicalities of keeping the repertoire and the performances going and the audiences coming. At an early stage he took advice from Schröder on ticketing and on secure financial arrangements, measures that had not been necessary when attendance was free. He also introduced the *Abonnement* or season ticket in order to build up a regular and committed audience.

On 24 December 1792 the following announcement in Goethe's own hand went out to the members of the theatre company:

> Die Oberdirektion des hiesigen Theaters sieht sich, durch mehrere eintretende Umstände, bewogen – sämtlichen Schauspielern und Schauspielerinnen, die biß zu Ostern bestehende Contrakte hiermit aufzukündigen, und selbige zu veranlaßen, sich in Zeiten nach anderweitigem Engagement umzusehen.[25]

Fischer had proved unable to weld the actors into a cohesive ensemble.[26] A small incident during the company's summer season in Erfurt in 1791 illustrates his difficulty. On 25 September a performance of Schiller's *Don Karlos* was planned. Earlier, on 14 September, a letter from Carl Krüger, one of the actors not subsequently re-engaged at Weimar, tells of his meeting with Schiller, who was staying at Erfurt at the time. Before Krüger went in to see Schiller, Fischer told him that he, Fischer, would play the role of Philipp. Krüger expresses his contempt for Fischer through his exclamation, '*Fischer. Der König*?' Clearly Krüger had hoped to play the coveted role himself. Schiller, deploying all his diplomatic skill and charm, seems to have suggested Krüger take the role of Domingo,

---

25   Thüringisches Hauptstaatsarchiv Weimar, Generalintendanz des DNT Weimar, Nr. 1/1, Blatt 5.

26   There may also have been a financial motive: Kirms wrote to Fischer that the management was compelled 'das Theater in einer kleineren Form zu continuieren' (Thüringisches Hauptstaatsarchiv Weimar, Generalintendanz des DNT Weimar, Nr. 1/1, Blatt 7), but that may have been an excuse to mask the real reasons.

worauf ich antwortete daß es mir hertzlich leid thäte, ihm seine erste Bitte abschlagen zu müßen – indem ich mit Bewilligung der Oberdirektion keine Spitzbüben mehr spielte, zumalen eine so kleine unbedeutende Rolle wie diese wäre – ohnerachtet ich Anspruch mit Recht auf den König machen könnte.[27]

This anecdote indicates the vanity and touchiness of the actors, the sense of rivalry and lack of respect for Fischer. It also illustrates the tendency for some actors to confuse the proper place of moral judgment and to conclude that they were too good to play villains. The dismissal of the whole troupe with effect from Easter 1793 was followed by the re-engagement of several actors, minus the disruptive elements. The directorial duties were assumed after Fischer's departure by Heinrich Vohs, a talented young actor who had made his debut with the company in May 1792 and would later be the first Max Piccolomini. The new era that Vohs hoped to inaugurate in the company is announced in a memorandum that was circulated along with a proposed set of theatre rules (*Theatergesetze*), modelled on those of the Mainz National Theatre and common in the theatre world. Vohs bemoans the pervasive effects of 'Unordnung':

> Traurig wärs wenn schon aller Künstler-Stolz bey uns so sehr erloschen wäre, daß es uns große Aufopferung kosten solle, einem Schlendrian zu entsagen, der doch nur der einzige Grund dieser Unordnungen war. – doch nein! Mit Recht darf ich stolz darauf sein, Mitglied einer Gesellschaft zu sein, wo ich so oft den Wunsch äußern hörte, daß jeder, die Kunst erschwerende Unfug gänzlich möge abgeschaft werden.[28]

The appeal to see themselves as artists is typical of a generation emerging in the final two decades of the eighteenth century and yet it was often precisely the pretensions fostered by the concept of art that exacerbated rivalries within the company. The rules governed matters such as punctuality at rehearsals and performances, and the props and

---

27 Letter from Krüger to Kirms, 14 September 1792: Thüringisches Hauptstaats-archiv Weimar, Sammlung Pasqué, Sammlung Convolut A, XI, Blatt 204.

28 Promemoria of 7 March 1793: Thüringisches Hauptstaatsarchiv Weimar, Gene-ralintendanz des DNT Weimar, Nr. 1/1, Blatt 9.

clothing for which the actors were responsible.[29] They also forbade the exchanging of roles without permission and the introduction of outsiders into the rehearsals. They did not bear on aesthetic matters at all and were thus very different from the *Regeln für Schauspieler*, which encapsulate Goethe's artistic principles for young actors.[30] The rules were signed by all members on 7 March 1793. As one might have predicted, they did not prevent squabbles and rivalries, one of which made Vohs stand down as *Regisseur* in 1796. From then on three of the actors, referred to as *Wöchner*, took it in turns on a weekly basis to put the company through its paces.

There is no doubt that even at an early stage Goethe had an eye to the formation of a repertoire with some durability. He was very conscious of the strain that constant change placed on the company, commenting later:

> Ich habe in meiner Praxis [...] als Hauptsache gefunden, daß man nie ein Stück oder gar eine Oper einstudieren lassen solle, wovon man nicht guten Sukzeß auf Jahre hin mit einiger Bestimmtheit voraussieht [...] Die Sucht, immer etwas Neues haben und ein mit unsäglicher Mühe einstudiertes gutes Stück oder Oper nur einmal höchstens zweimal sehen zu wollen [...] ist ein wahrer Verderb des Theaters und ein Mißbrauch der Kräfte des ausübenden Personals, der gar nicht zu verzeihen ist. (MA 19, 511–12)

At the same time, Weimar was a small town with only about 7,500 inhabitants. Although the theatre's audience was often boosted at the week-end by students from Jena, there was a very limited pool of potential theatre-goers and they naturally wanted variety and a chance to see new and talked-about plays and operas. The court also made its demands from time to time, when there was a birthday, festivity or a visiting prince or dignitary. Out of the 600 productions during Goethe's time 104 were of works that were given only once (the

---

29 The *Theatergesetze* are printed in Jutta Linder, *Ästhetische Erziehung. Goethe und das Weimarer Hoftheater* (Bonn: Bouvier, 1990), pp. 136–41.

30 First published in 1824, these principles, summing up the Weimar style, originated in instruction in fluent and harmonious acting that Goethe gave around 1803/04 to two new Weimar actors, Pius Alexander Wolff and Karl Franz Grüner. They were drawn up from the actors' notes by Johann Peter Eckermann.

majority short comedies).[31] At the Berlin National Theatre during Iffland's time 751 separate works were given (drama, opera and ballet), of which 63 were played only once.[32] The city environment, even at a theatre that was open every night of the week, made it easier to find an audience for works that were not destined to survive in the repertoire.

The first full Weimar season, which began in October 1791, saw some extension of the repertoire in the direction of more aesthetically challenging works. Among the new productions was Shakespeare's *King John*, in Eschenburg's translation, which Goethe directed himself. It featured the stage debut of the talented actress Christiane Neumann, then only twelve years old. *Der Groß-Cophta*, one of the few plays Goethe wrote during his early years in charge of the theatre, was also staged at the end of 1791 and his *Clavigo* and *Die Geschwister* were performed after Christmas, though in general Goethe did not take his position as *Intendant* as an opportunity to have his own plays performed. *Hamlet* was played, again in Eschenburg's translation, though with the final scene omitted to give a non-tragic ending (in Schröder's often-played version Hamlet lives on to rule Denmark). Mozart's *Don Giovanni* was performed and became, like all of Mozart's operas, a firm favourite at Weimar. Schiller's *Don Karlos* was given in February 1792 and *Die Räuber* in a new production later that season. Shakespeare's *Henry IV, Part 2* was also new to the repertoire.

The remainder of the repertoire in that first season showed a heavy reliance on the popular playwrights of the day: Brandes, Babo, Schröder, Christoph Friedrich Bretzner, Johann Friedrich Jünger, as well as Iffland and Kotzebue. Between a quarter and a third of the works given were *Singspiele* and operas by, for example, Dittersdorf, Anfossi, Cimarosa and Mozart. There was also a need for translations and adaptations of foreign works, which in the early years were often carried out by Christian Vulpius (1762–1827), brother of Goethe's

---

31   For the most complete repertoire see Carl August Hugo Burkhardt, *Das Repertoire des Weimarischen Hoftheaters unter Goethes Leitung, 1791–1817*, Theatergeschichtliche Forschungen, 1 (Leipzig: Voss, 1891).

32   A breakdown of the Berlin repertoire by number of performances by play is given by Hugo Fetting, *Das Repertoire des Berliner Königlichen Nationaltheaters,* Appendix, pp. 70–87.

Christiane and a successful writer of popular fiction, who was engaged first by Bellomo and then by Goethe for the extensive work of adaptation. The company set about building up a library of texts, for even German works had to be prepared for performance. The work of adaptation was often most extensive in the case of operas and *Singspiele*. In the absence of copyright laws, indeed in the absence often of published versions of these works, theatres were very free with the scores and librettos circulating in manuscript form. They had to be tailored to the available talent. Arias that went beyond the singers' capacities were simplified or cut. The *durchkomponiert* opera still existed almost exclusively in the Italian tradition and was performed in that form virtually only at the great court opera houses such as Dresden or Berlin. Operas performed at smaller theatres such as Weimar's almost always replaced recitative with spoken dialogue, and this practice could be extended according to the company's musical capacities. As far as translations of foreign plays were concerned, the popularity and abundance of Iffland's and Kotzebue's plays meant that by comparison with the 1770s and even the 1780s there was less reliance on a constant stream of French comedies in translation. Foreign plays (mainly comedies) apart from Shakespeare's performed that year in Weimar were by Gozzi, Holberg, Cumberland, Beaumarchais, Voltaire and Sheridan.

Iffland's first visit to Weimar and Schiller's adaptation of *Egmont*

As far as repertoire, style and artistic standard were concerned, the Weimar theatre in the first five years of its existence did not distinguish itself, despite Goethe's good intentions, from other similar theatres. Carl August's subsidy covered about one third of the costs and so the enterprise had to make money to survive.[33] It could not

---

33   Burkhardt, p. xxxiv.

afford high salaries and hence had no actors of renown. The account above has revealed something of the turbulence, quarrels and rivalries that regularly disrupted the smooth running of the operation. The man who would give Goethe a new lease of life as *Intendant* and help him try to realize some of his vision of a harmonious and distinctive style was Schiller. But Schiller was physically and mentally removed from the theatre in the early 1790s. It was the visit of Iffland to Weimar for a series of guest performances that began the process of his return to active engagement with it.

In view of this, as yet unsuspected, future of theatre collaboration with Schiller and the national significance the Weimar theatre would acquire as a result, it is ironic that Iffland's visit was in part designed to ease Goethe's exit from that theatre. On several occasions during this early period he made comparisons between the theatre and his other interests and commitments, such as building projects and his work in the natural sciences, thus highlighting his sense of the former's impermanence. To the former royal tutor Carl Ludwig von Knebel he wrote on 5 October 1791:

> Eine doppelte Beschäftigung hält mich hier zurück die Ausgabe des optischen Versuchs und die Einrichtung des Schauspiels, jenes macht mir mehr Freude als dieses, denn ich kann hoffen dort etwas reelles und bleibendes zu leisten, wenn die vorübergehende Theater Erscheinung nicht einmal ihre Wirckung in dem Augenblick äußert für den sie bestimmt ist. (WA IV 9, 285–86)

This feeling intensified to the point where late in 1795 he asked Carl August to release him from his theatre duties.[34] Carl August did not, however, want to lose Goethe's unique combination of talents for the post. Nevertheless, Goethe cast around for a suitable replacement. Schiller's name entered the discussion but the Duke was not inclined to follow that suggestion.[35] For some time Goethe had been trying to attract Iffland to Weimar for a *Gastspiel*. Now that he had agreed and

---

34   See Carl August's reply of 20. 12. 1795 in: *Briefwechsel des Herzogs–Groß-herzogs Carl August mit Goethe*, ed. by Hans Wahl, 3 vols (Berlin: Mittler, 1915), vol. 1, pp. 204–05.

35   Wahle quotes Carl August as commenting that Schiller's appointment would be 'wohl schwer ausführbar' (p. 59). There is no indication that Schiller himself knew of this suggestion or would have wanted the job.

the future of the Mannheim Theatre was in doubt amid the upheavals caused by the French Revolutionary wars, the actor might, Goethe hoped, be open to offers. He arrived in Weimar on 28 March 1796 and left on 25 April, during which time the question of a permanent appointment was broached, Carl August having given his approval. Pasqué claims that Iffland, perhaps understandably, was not entirely candid about his commitments or his plans during these negotiations.[36] While the issue was still considered live in Weimar, he was offered the directorship of the Berlin National Theatre, clearly a much more lucrative, prestigious and secure proposition than an offer from the provincial and underfunded Weimar theatre, if Iffland was going to take the serious step of breaking his obligations to Mannheim. Sensitive to the impression of deviousness he could have given, Iffland later, in December 1796, assured Kirms that he had not expected any offer from Berlin while he was at Weimar and that the King of Prussia's willingness to pay his debts was crucial.[37] The difficulty was got over and Iffland returned to Weimar to play again in 1798, 1810 and 1812.

In Weimar, as elsewhere, Iffland's plays were a mainstay of the repertoire in the 1790s. From about 1804 their popularity seems to have begun to fall off in Weimar and even in Berlin.[38] Perhaps the moralizing streak began to lose favour with audiences, for whom Kotzebue's less judgmental tone was more congenial. Goethe was not an admirer of Iffland's plays. Not only did he criticize the frequent improbabilities of the action and the false contrast of nature and culture, he felt Iffland had failed in the writer's task, 'da vielmehr das Geschäfft eines Schauspieldichters in unserem Zeitalter seyn sollte, zu zeigen, wie die Kultur von Auswüchsen gereinigt, veredelt und liebenswürdig gemacht werden könne.'[39] He was nevertheless an admirer of Iffland's acting ability, which undoubtedly outshone that of the Weimar company, and of his professionalism. Writing to Schiller

---

36   For the full correspondence relating to Iffland's visit see Pasqué, vol. 1, pp. 253–75.
37   See Pasqué, vol. 1, p. 267: 'Freund, die Schulden haben entschieden.'
38   See Chapter 7 for further details.
39   Böttiger, *Literarische Zustände und Zeitgenossen*, pp. 89–90.

on 2 May during the 1798 *Gastspiel*, which Schiller was unable to attend, he comments:

> an ihm zu rühmen ist die lebhafte Einbildungskrafft, wodurch er alles was zu seiner Rolle gehört zu entdecken weiß, dann die Nachahmungsgabe wodurch er das gefundne und gleichsam erschaffne darzustellen weiß, und zuletzt der Humor, womit er das Ganze von Anfang bis zu Ende lebhaft durchführt. [...]
>
> Indem er als ein wirkliches Natur und Kunstgebilde vor den Augen des Zuschauers lebt, so zeigen sich die übrigen, wenn sie auch ihre Sache nicht ungeschickt machen, doch nur gleichsam als *Referenten*, welche eine fremde Sache aus den Acten vortragen. (NA 37/I, 284)

Iffland's combination of 'Genie, Kunst und Handwerk' that Goethe mentions in the same letter seems to him exemplary. He later looked back on Iffland's first visit as marking a new era in the history of the theatre, for Iffland not only shone in his own right but gave the actors a sense of what could be done on stage. He knew how to divest himself of his individuality, rather than always playing himself, an ability Goethe knew his actors needed in order to cultivate a more idealized style: 'Von dieser Zeit an haben mehrere unserer Schauspieler, denen eine allzuentschiedene Individualität nicht entgegen stand, glückliche Versuche gemacht, sich eine Vielseitigkeit zu geben, welche einem dramatischen Künstler immer zur Ehre gereicht.'[40]

For the four weeks of Iffland's first visit to Weimar thirteen plays were agreed on for performance, six of which were by Iffland himself: *Scheinverdienst*, *Dienstpflicht*, *Der Spieler*, *Die Hagestolzen*, *Die Aussteuer* and *Der Herbsttag*. The other plays were Gemmingen's *Der teutsche Hausvater*, Babo's *Die Strelitzen*, Dalberg's *Die eheliche Probe*, Kotzebue's *Die Sonnenjungfrau*, Schröder's *Stille Wasser sind tief*, Schiller's *Die Räuber* (Franz Moor was still one of Iffland's *Paraderollen*) and, most importantly as far as future impact on the theatre was concerned, Goethe's own *Egmont*.[41] The play had been

---

40 'Weimarisches Hoftheater', MA 6.2, 693.
41 The performances attracted the extravagant praise of Karl August Böttiger, headmaster of the grammar school in Weimar, who attempted to capture them in detail in his series of essays entitled *Entwickelung des Ifflandischen Spiels in vierzehn Darstellungen auf dem Weimarischen Hoftheater im Aprillmonath 1796* (Leipzig: Göschen, 1796). This account atomized Iffland's performances

premièred in Mainz in 1789 and had been performed in Weimar by Bellomo's troupe in 1791 before their departure, but it had not enjoyed much success. The review in Bertram's *Annalen des Theaters* was uncomplimentary: 'Es war schrecklich, die Ausbrüche der dramatischen Kunst in diesem Schauspiele ansehen zu müssen. Wehe dem Autor, dessen Meisterstück in die Hände solcher dramatischer Tagelöhner fällt! Und wehe dem, der den Jammer mit ansehen muß.'[42] The journal had a tradition of being rude about Bellomo's company and the reviewer distinguishes between the play and the playing, but such a reception may have been the reason why *Egmont* was not one of the plays in Bellomo's repertoire that Goethe immediately took over when he became the *Intendant*. It may have left him on the other hand with a lingering wish to give the work a better chance on the boards.

In 1794, as Goethe and Schiller finally overcame the barriers and prejudices between them and moved towards friendship, Schiller, making his first extended visit to Goethe, tells his wife, Charlotte: 'Er hat mich gebeten, seinen Egmont für das Weim*arische* Theater zu corrigieren, weil er es selbst nicht wagt, und ich werde es auch thun.'[43] This plan was then shelved and resurrected at short notice in 1796 for Iffland's visit. It is not clear what prompted Goethe to make the original suggestion in 1794, but it is possible that he attached a special significance to it as a gesture of friendship, bearing in mind that Schiller had published a review of *Egmont* on its publication in 1788 that levelled some severe criticisms at the play. Schiller wrote the review shortly after completing *Don Karlos* and while he was working on his *Geschichte des Abfalls der vereinigten Niederlande von der spanischen Regierung*, so his mind was full of the compositional problems of the former and the historical details of the latter. He was critical of Goethe's failure, as he saw it, to motivate his hero's behaviour adequately. Unlike the historical Egmont, who had a wife and numerous children whom he did not want to subject to hardship by fleeing, Goethe's character is unmarried with a doting mistress. Thus his

---

in a way that brought ridicule on Böttiger (see Chapter 7 for Ludwig Tieck's response in *Der gestiefelte Kater*). Iffland was not involved in writing it.

42   *Annalen des Theaters*, 8. Heft, 1791, 80–81.
43   Letter of 20 Sept 1794 (NA 27, 49).

failure to react to the warnings he receives about the danger from Alba in favour of dallying with Klärchen seems irresponsible, and in Schiller's view he forfeits our sympathy.[44] He also objected to the play's operatic ending with its vision of the goddess of freedom with Klärchen's features crowning Egmont with a laurel wreath. *Egmont* arguably reminded Schiller too much of the kind of character drama he wanted to move away from and of the difficulties he had had in finishing *Don Karlos*, in which creating a coherent and well-motivated plot had been almost impossible. By contrast, he praised *Iphigenie auf Tauris* when Goethe published the blank verse version in 1788, seeing its economy of means, its compact plot and its clarity as exemplifying all he had failed to achieve himself in *Don Karlos*.[45] The fact that in spite of the *Egmont* review Goethe entrusted him with the adaptation of his play suggests a touching gesture of confidence, as well as perhaps a hope that Schiller's earlier criticisms would ensure that he would make the work more effective on stage and thus extend the theatre's repertoire. Goethe wrote to Iffland during the latter's stay in Weimar:

> Mit dem größten Vergnügen sehe ich dann der Bearbeitung und Aufführung Egmonts entgegen. Es ist das Eigenste was mir hätte begegnen können, daß ein Stück, auf das ich in mehr als einer Hinsicht längst Verzicht gethan habe, mir durch Schillern und Sie so unerwartet wiedergeschenkt wird. (WA IV, 30, 59)

In fact, though it was a useful reintroduction for Schiller to stage writing, the *Egmont* adaptation was never repeated at the Weimar theatre during Schiller's lifetime and reveals the very different approaches of Goethe and Schiller not only to drama but also to the aesthetics of performance.

Schiller began work on *Egmont* just at the point where he was returning to dramatic writing. He decided finally against pursuing the

---

44   'Nein, guter Graf Egmont […] Wenn es Euch zu beschwerlich ist, Euch Eurer eignen Rettung anzunehmen, so mögt Ihrs haben, wenn sich die Schlinge über Euch zusammenzieht. Wir sind nicht gewohnt, unser Mitleid zu verschenken': 'Über Egmont, Trauerspiel von Goethe' (NA 22, 203).

45   See my articles 'Schiller and Goethe's *Egmont*', *Modern Language Review*, 77 (1982), 629–45 and 'Schiller and Goethe's *Iphigenie*', *Publications of the English Goethe Society*, 54 (1984), 101–22.

plan for *Die Maltheser* and in favour of the Wallenstein project.[46] The *Egmont* adaptation reveals his deepest concerns as a dramatist – a wish to create a coherent and swiftly moving linear action and to embed the hero in an inescapable chain of events. Both Egmont and Wallenstein are charismatic heroes, who believe they can carry the day by sheer force of personality and who perish because in their separate ways they both suffer from a fatal blindness with regard to their true position. The question of how to create a tragic sequence of events had preoccupied Schiller since *Don Karlos*,[47] and his changes to *Egmont* reflect that concern as well as a practical need to make Goethe's play easier to stage. He modifies Egmont's 'Sorglosigkeit' into something more morally charged, into a sense of duty to his people and a resistance to coercion. The action is compressed and streamlined: Goethe's play involves twelve scene changes, Schiller's version only seven. The role of the Regent, Margarethe von Parma, is cut altogether. The vision of the goddess of freedom in the final scene, which in his review Schiller had complained was a 'Salto mortale in eine Operwelt' (NA 22, 208), is turned into a dream that Egmont recounts but the audience does not see.

Goethe was later to recall in conversation with Eckermann that Schiller had always, 'auch in seiner schönsten Zeit', been characterized by 'ein gewisser Sinn für das Grausame'. He continues:

> So erinnere ich mich noch recht wohl, daß er im *Egmont* in der Gefängnisszene, wo diesem das Urteil vorgelesen wird, den Alba in einer Maske und in einen Mantel gehüllt im Hintergrund erscheinen ließ, um sich an dem Effekt zu weiden, den das Todes-Urteil auf Egmont haben würde. Hiedurch sollte sich der Alba das unersättlich in Rache und Schadenfreude darstellen. Ich protestierte jedoch und die Figur blieb weg. (MA 19, 130–31)

In fact, the evidence points to Goethe's memory being faulty, for other recollections suggest that the figure of 'der Vermummte' introduced by Schiller did appear in the 1796 production. Genast writes: 'Schiller

---

46   See his letter to Körner of 21 March 1796 (NA 28, 209).
47   The *Egmont* review and the essay 'Über die tragische Kunst' (1792) are important evidence of this. The preoccupation with inevitability carries through into the planning of *Wallenstein*, during which Schiller studied Aristotle's *Poetics*.

rezitierte und spielte zuweilen in den Proben vor [...] Daß Alba im *Egmont* im fünften Akt als Henker mit großem roten Mantel und tief ins Gesicht gedrücktem Hut erscheinen mußte, geschah auf seine Anordnung.'[48] When the play was repeated in Weimar in 1806, however, the *Regiebuch*, which still exists, retains only the presence of 'Ein Vermummter im Hintergrund', who is not unmasked as Alba, but remains anonymous, though clearly suggesting a figure of doom.[49]

What Goethe's recollection shows is his disapproval of this *coup de théâtre* and the 1806 *Regiebuch* suggests an attempt to tone it down. While Siedhoff proposes (though there is no actual evidence for this) that the introduction of the figure could have been a concession to Iffland, who enjoyed such theatrical effects, Goethe clearly recalls it as typifying a difference between himself and Schiller with regard to stage practice.[50] This difference cannot be defined as merely a matter of taste. Rather it indicates a more fundamental difference between these two men with regard to how the play and audience interact. Both saw art as elevating and refining the individual, but Goethe's temperament, instincts and *Weltanschauung* led him to conceive of the aesthetics of performance in terms of harmony, whereas Schiller's aesthetic was based on conflict; while ultimately the play restores serenity through transcendence, the process is one in which the spectator's senses must be powerfully affected by the action of the play. This fundamental matter will be discussed in detail in the next chapter. In 1829 Goethe explained to Eckermann why he tolerated Schiller's radical interventions in his play: 'Man ist oft gleichgültiger als billig [...] Und dann war ich in jener Zeit mit anderen Dingen tief beschäftigt. Ich hatte sowenig ein Interesse für Egmont wie für das Theater' (MA 19, 290). The fact that between Iffland's visit and the première of *Wallenstein* the *Egmont* adaptation was not repeated and

---

48 Genast, vol. 1, pp. 112–13. Eduard Genast further recalls his father's fellow actor Graff, who played Alba in 1796, protesting on future occasions against any suggestion of omitting 'der Vermummte', with the words, 'Schiller hat es so gewollt!' (p. 113).

49 The fullest discussion of this matter is in Sigrid Siedhoff's study: *Der Dramaturg Schiller. 'Egmont'. Goethes Text – Schillers Bearbeitung* (Bonn: Bouvier, 1983), pp. 151–55.

50 Siedhoff, p. 155.

that Goethe did not ask Schiller to take on any other stage adaptation during that time (though he later produced several with considerable success) might suggest that Goethe had not taken that first experience of collaboration as a promising beginning.

Although the original plan for the casting of the play put Iffland in the role of Alba, he in fact appeared as Egmont.[51] Possibly Weimar could not find anyone suitable for the role. Certainly it was not an ideal one for Iffland, who was already growing somewhat corpulent and had never specialized in playing young romantic leads.[52] Later, in the 1801 Berlin production of Schiller's adaptation, he took the part of Oranien. His visit to Weimar brought him into contact again with Schiller, whose comment to Goethe on hearing of the projected *Gastspiel* late in 1795 was: 'Es würde mich freuen, einen alten Bekannten wieder zu sehen' (NA 28, 127) The visit does not seem to have led to a new friendship between the two men. Only a few months later – for 1796 was the year of the *Xenien*, the satirical distichs Goethe and Schiller wrote to take their revenge on everyone and everything they disapproved of in the literary world – he was writing 'Shakespears Schatten', in which he specifically pillories the dominance in the theatre of sentimental drama, which has marginalized heroic tragedy almost completely. The poem features a dialogue in the underworld between Shakespeare and a contemporary writer:

"Also sieht man bei euch den leichten Tanz der Thalia
　　　Neben dem ernsten Gang, welchen Melpomene geht?" –
Keines von beiden! Uns kann nur das christlich-moralische rühren,
　　　Und was recht populär, häuslich und bürgerlich ist.
"Was? Es dürfte kein Cäsar auf euren Bühnen sich zeigen,
　　　Kein Achill, kein Orest, kein Andromacha mehr?"
Nichts! Man siehet bei uns nur Pfarrer, Kommerzienräthe,
　　　Fähndriche, Sekretairs oder Husarenmajors (NA 2/I, 306)

---

51   On the original plan for casting see Günter Schulz, 'Zwei Schiller-Autographen', in *Jahrbuch der Deutschen Schillergesellschaft*, 3 (1959), 19–33.

52   As even the extravagantly laudatory Böttiger has to admit: see *Die Entwicklung des Ifflandischen Spiels,* p. 353.

Schiller writes to Goethe that he wishes to spare Iffland's feelings and asks if Goethe's secretary will send him a few occupations of characters from Schröder's and Kotzebue's plays, but in fact Iffland's plays are full of characters of similar occupations and Schiller surely knew that and that his readers would not make the distinction.[53] These distichs spring from a new engagement with drama and the theatre and from a consequent awareness of how his own *Wallenstein*, though only embryonic, ran decidedly counter to popular taste.

When Iffland returned for a second *Gastspiel* to Weimar in the spring of 1798 Schiller did not attend at all. This was, admittedly, because he had been ill and was under pressure with other commitments. But the comments he makes in response to Goethe's reports of Iffland's visit suggest some ongoing low-level hostility towards, or at the least reservations about, Iffland.[54] Schiller seems unable or unwilling to separate the actor and the playwright, as Goethe did, admiring the one, and criticising the other. He was at that point simply less interested in acting than Goethe and, understandably, less interested also in the small improvements that might be achieved at the practical level of performance at the Weimar theatre. But by the autumn of 1798 Schiller was completing *Wallenstein* and Iffland, now established at the Berlin National Theatre, had heard of it and was eager to secure it as soon as he could for Berlin. It was to be the start of a curious symbiosis that gave decisive direction to the shaping of the German repertoire.

---

53   Letter to Goethe of 31 July 1796 (NA 28, 275).
54   For example, he criticizes Iffland's choice of Gotter's and Benda's *Pygmalion* for one of his Weimar performances and states that he does not admire the actor in tragic roles; see NA 29, 228 and 232.

Chapter Five
Aesthetic Education I: Schiller's *Wallenstein*

Looking back in 1802 at the eleven years' history of the Weimar Court Theatre, Goethe wrote of Iffland:

> Die Weisheit, womit dieser vortreffliche Künstler seine Rollen von einander sondert, aus einer jeden ein Ganzes zu machen weiß und sich, sowohl ins Edle als ins Gemeine, und immer kunstmäßig und schön, zu maskieren versteht, war zu eminent, als daß sie nicht hätte fruchtbar werden sollen.[1]

Thus Iffland's *Gastspiel*, according to Goethe, helped bring about a transition from the first period of the theatre's development to its second because at least some of the company were able to profit by his example and overcome the 'falsch verstandener Konversationston' and their 'unrichtiger Begriff von Natürlichkeit' (MA 6.2, 693) and move towards greater artistry. The second transitional point was marked by the reintroduction of verse drama with the première of *Wallenstein*. The third phase saw the consolidation of this achievement and extension of the repertoire, culminating in the experiment with the use of masks for the production of Terence's *Adelphoe* (*Die Brüder*). The theatre is now, from Goethe's 1802 perspective, in its fourth phase.

Goethe's periodization seems artificially neat today and probably did so in 1802, for it implies that the Weimar theatre's progression towards its distinctive style was the product of planning and foresight rather than being, as it was, mainly the unforeseen result of particular

---

1   'Weimarisches Hoftheater', MA 6.2, 694. This essay was written in response to controversy surrrounding the staging of A.W. Schlegel's *Ion* and Goethe's objection to and attempt to suppress publication of the critical review written by Böttiger for the *Journal des Luxus und der Mode* (on this controversy see MA 6.2, 1186–90). The essay's programmatic character and somewhat dictatorial tone aroused adverse comment but it nevertheless contains certain key statements regarding the aesthetic conception underlying the Weimar theatre experiment.

circumstances. The link Goethe makes from *Wallenstein* back to Iffland's first *Gastspiel* is probably the most tenuous, for Goethe's comment to Schiller in 1798 during the second *Gastspiel* about the Weimar company being like *Referenten* by comparison with the great actor (see p. 155) does not bespeak great progress since Iffland's first *Gastspiel* of 1796. It would also be wrong to infer from Goethe's periodization that the repertoire changed in any significant way between April 1796 and September 1798. The breakthrough to a new vision of what the theatre could achieve came with the staging of *Wallenstein* and with Goethe's resolve in encouraging the ailing and sometimes hesitant Schiller to let the Weimar theatre introduce the world to the new work.

A brief analysis of the repertoire for the period between Iffland's *Gastspiel* and the end of the 1798 season confirms that it is hard to detect any change to the patterns established in the theatre's first five years. Burkhardt lists forty-four premières for the period May 1796 to September 1798. Nine were of operas or *Singspiele*, of which the most enduringly popular was Mozart's *Così fan tutte*, adapted by Vulpius and entitled *So sind sie alle*. Paisiello's *Die Müllerin* and Wranitzky's *Oberon. König der Elfen* were two further successes of that period. The thirty-five plays were all comedies, with four exceptions: Hagemeister's *Die Jesuiten* (1787), Klingemann's *Die Maske* (1797), Leisewitz's *Julius von Tarent* and Rambach's *Otto mit dem Pfeile* (1796). The most successful playwright was Kotzebue, seven of whose plays were given their Weimar première during this period, the three most popular, judging by the number of performances up to 1817, being *Der Wildfang* (1798), *Die Corsen* (1798) and *Die silberne Hochzeit* (1799). Five Iffland plays were performed in Weimar for the first time, of which the most successful by some way was the comedy *Der Hausfriede* (1797).[2] Also beginning a successful run were two plays by Heinrich Beck, the Mannheim actor and now *Regisseur* there, which had already established themselves elsewhere in the popular repertoire. These were *Die Schachmaschine* (1795) and

---

2   Burkhardt records twenty-one performances up to 1817. The others were *Das Gewissen*, *Leichter Sinn*, *Die Erinnerung* and *Der Komet*, the latter a one-act comedy.

Die Quälgeister (1792), an adaptation of Shakespeare's *Much Ado About Nothing*.

Schiller's *Wallenstein* was therefore a distinct departure from the general trend of the repertoire and it was a decision with lasting, though at that time probably unforeseen, consequences when Goethe seized the opportunity to make the work the focus of the theatre's 1798/99 season. The three parts were first performed in October, January and April and so spanned much of the theatre year. The two men had discussed the work's progress at every stage and so Goethe was in no doubt that, even in its original conception as a five-act play with a prologue, it would make heavy demands on the company's resources. On the other hand, it was clearly a work of suitable importance to inaugurate the remodelled neo-classical interior of the theatre, to which Schiller subsequently alludes in his 'Prolog' (NA 8, 3–4). The fact that *Wallenstein* also inaugurated Goethe's and Schiller's theatrical partnership, which lasted until the latter's death in 1805, makes this a suitable point at which to examine the aesthetic premises that underpinned that partnership.

Aesthetic education: Reconciling differences

When their first encounters in 1788 failed to establish a mutual sympathy, the two men remained at an apparently fixed and polite distance. In 1794, however, Schiller invited Goethe to be a contributor to and member of the editorial panel of his new journal project, *Die Horen*, and Goethe accepted. Shortly after, on 20 July, came the famous discussion after the meeting of the *Naturforschende Gesellschaft* in Jena, when the two men found that, in spite of their differences of temperament and outlook, intellectual exchange was possible. Goethe's much later account of the meeting is his short memoir 'Glückliches Ereignis' (1817).[3] The issue was how nature could be

---

3   It was first published in the context of Goethe's writings on plant and animal morphology; see MA 12, 86–90.

presented as a unified whole rather than as a collection of fragments. Goethe expounded to Schiller his notion of the *Urpflanze*, the primal plant that for him was visible in the structure of all individual plants. Schiller famously denied that such a concept could be based on experience but must be an idea in the Kantian sense (not wholly divorced from experience but not entirely derived from experience), while Goethe persisted, as he self-deprecatingly says, in his 'hartnäckige[r] Realismus'.[4] The battle ended in a truce; neither was the victor but both had gained a sense that communication had taken place and, more importantly, that further communication would be possible and desirable.

Schiller's account of the meeting is brief; in a letter to his friend Körner he reports that he and Goethe had had a long conversation 'über Kunst und Kunsttheorie':

> Wir hatten [...] uns die Hauptideen mitgetheilt, zu denen wir auf ganz verschiedenen Wegen gekommen waren. Zwischen diesen Ideen fand sich eine unerwartete Uebereinstimmung, die um so interessanter war, weil sie wirklich aus der größten Verschiedenheit der Gesichtspunkte hervorging. Ein jeder konnte dem andern etwas geben, was ihm fehlte, und etwas dafür empfangen. (NA 27, 34)

The possibility of reciprocity had thus been glimpsed. Shortly after that breakthrough Schiller wrote his so-called birthday letter to Goethe on 23 August, in which he expounded the idea that, if Goethe had been born in the south, in Greece or Italy, he would have been surrounded by an environment that gave rise to an idealizing art. Being born in the north he had instead had to work his way by rational thought to the ideals of the art of antiquity, which are at odds with the 'wilde und nordische Natur' around him (NA 27, 26). He then had to turn these reflections into intuitions that could be productive for the creative imagination. Thus Goethe's philosophical instincts are in harmony with the purest results of speculative reason and he reaches similar conclusions to the man of speculative mind (Schiller), though by a contrasting route.

---

4   'Glückliches Ereignis', MA 12, 89.

Schiller went on to theorize the difference between himself and Goethe as writers in his last great treatise, *Über naive und sentimentalische Dichtung* (1795/96). The naïve poet, who is more typical of the ancient world, has an immediate perception of external reality and can present it without interposing his personality between it and the reader. The sentimental (in this idiosyncratic Schillerian sense) writer lacks this singleness of perception and inevitably presents external reality along with his own response to it. He is more typical of the modern world, in which thought and feeling are divorced and there is an almost universal sense of a gulf between reality and the ideal. For Schiller, Goethe was a naïve poet (in this specialized sense) and thus untypical of his age, while Schiller, painfully aware of his speculative and reflective consciousness, saw himself as a sentimental poet. The otherness of Goethe challenged him and forced him to justify what kind of poet he could be.

The treatise is a fascinating late contribution to the *Querelle des anciens et des modernes* and a vindication of the modern that indicates a recovery of confidence on Schiller's part.[5] For although contact with Goethe's very different type of poetic consciousness made him question his vocation as a poet, it also gave him renewed impetus to excel in that branch of poetry – tragedy – for which he believed he had a particular talent. While contemplating and writing the treatise in 1795 he began to write poems again.[6] In March 1796, just before Iffland's first Weimar *Gastspiel*, he decided to embark on the *Wallenstein* project. The new possibilities opened up by the play and by collaboration with Schiller gave Goethe renewed energy as *Intendant* and was part of the general rebirth of creativity that Goethe attributed later to Schiller's friendship:

---

5 The *Querelle des anciens et des modernes* was a controversy that raged at the end of the seventeenth and was periodically reanimated in the eighteenth century about whether the writers of antiquity must be regarded as unassailable models for modern writers or whether they could be rivalled or surpassed by writers employing new forms and styles. Hence it concerned the criteria on which literary judgments should be based.

6 Among them 'Die Macht des Gesanges', 'Das Ideal und das Leben', Das verschleierte Bild zu Sais' and 'Der Tanz'.

> von der ersten Annäherung an war es ein unaufhaltsames Fortschreiten philo-
> sophischer Ausbildung und ästhetischer Tätigkeit [...] für mich war es ein
> neuer Frühling, in welchem alles froh nebeneinander keimte und aus aufge-
> schlossenen Samen und Zweigen hervorging.[7]

If Schiller saw in Goethe a type of poet he could never be and
could only admire and love, and if he reached his conclusions by a
speculative rather than an intuitive route, he concurred with Goethe on
the principles of art. Both men held to the belief that art must express
external reality, not as a copy but rather by searching out its essence.
In so doing it imposes a form upon that reality that would seem the
opposite of the natural. Only through the imposition of that form do
the accidents of the material fall away to allow the work of art to
become a symbol, an expression of the true through the beautiful. For
both men the ancients had instinctively grasped this principle and thus
their works remain timeless monuments of perfection. For both men
art itself was the central human activity and had a vital civilizing function in society. Schiller set down his thoughts on the subject in his
treatise *Über die ästhetische Erziehung des Menschen in einer Reihe
von Briefen* (1794). There he expounds the idea that the response
to art activates in us a condition in which, if only momentarily, the
warring sides of our being, the drive to experience (*Stofftrieb*) and
the drive to order and give meaning (*Formtrieb*), are brought into
harmony in what he calls the *Spieltrieb* (play drive). This aesthetic
response can be produced only if art is free from any utilitarian or
moral purpose and is recognized as obeying its own laws. In a
revolutionary age both men believed that change for the better could
begin only with the individual and so work its way through to society
and state. The artist therefore has a very specific task; in striving
always for the best, for what he judges to be of highest artistic merit,
he provides a perpetual challenge to those around him.[8] In the ninth

---

7   Goethe, *Tag- und Jahreshefte* (MA 14, 34).
8   I use the masculine pronoun deliberately. Although their practice was more
     progressive than their theory, Goethe and Schiller saw genuine artistic talent as
     exclusively granted to men. This did not prevent their actual relations with
     female artists and writers from being cordial and in some cases supportive and

letter of *Über die ästhetische Erziehung des Menschen* Schiller paints an idealized portrait of the artist, in part inspired by Goethe, who, prophet-like, gives his age not what it wants but what it needs:

> Der Künstler ist zwar der Sohn seiner Zeit, aber schlimm für ihn, wenn er zugleich ihr Zögling oder gar noch ihr Günstling ist. Eine wohlthätige Gottheit reisse den Säugling bey Zeiten von seiner Mutter Brust, nähre ihn mit der Milch eines bessern Alters, und lasse ihn unter fernem griechischem Himmel zur Mündigkeit reifen. Wenn er dann Mann geworden ist, so kehre er, eine fremde Gestalt, in sein Jahrhundert zurück; aber nicht, um es mit seiner Erscheinung zu erfreuen, sondern furchtbar wie Agamemnons Sohn, um es zu reinigen. (NA 20, 333)

These are stirring words, which perhaps dispose the reader to overlook the fact that Schiller himself was at this time a person of only very limited independent means, who needed his prince and his public. The letter form should not obscure the fact that Schiller uses a rhetor in the work, rather than speaking as himself, as he might in a private communication.[9] They also highlight the fact that aesthetic education must not be confused with didacticism; Goethe's and Schiller's works are marked by complexity and ambivalence and confound those who seek straightforward moral teaching.

Yet the theatre presents particular problems for the artist who wishes to keep moral and commercial pressures at bay. Goethe was entrusted with oversight over an enterprise that received only a modest subvention from the ruler. He could certainly not afford to turn it into a place where only plays that he and Schiller considered to be high art were performed. The early policy of the theatre, as outlined in the previous chapter, was to maintain a balance of the usual elements, namely comedy, serious drama and opera/*Singspiel*, with tragedy included only rarely. The Duke, himself an adherent of the French classical style, had wisely held back from trying to impose this on other theatre-goers. In the years of Schiller's involvement with the theatre, plays by Iffland and Kotzebue continued to take up a large share of

---

their creative writing from projecting a more complex and liberal view of women's potential than their letters and criticism.

9 A point emphasized by Victoria Rippere in *Schiller and 'Alienation'* (Berne, Frankfurt am Main, Las Vegas: Lang, 1981).

the spoken repertoire. The success of *Wallenstein*, however, paved the way for an experiment in introducing a number of more demanding works, usually in verse and performed in a stylized manner.[10] This stylization depended crucially on declamation, on the ability to speak verse comprehensibly and with conviction. A wish to improve the standard of speaking on stage had been among Goethe's early ambitions for the theatre (and *Don Karlos* had been performed in verse in Weimar in 1792), but it was not until the company was faced with the challenge of the world première of a new, three-part verse drama in *Wallenstein* that he was prompted to work seriously to raise the standard of speaking. Other elements, such as the creation of ensemble playing and attention to harmonious visual effects, also assumed importance for prestige productions and led to the emergence of a distinctive style, unique in German theatre at the time, though neither universally admired nor welcomed by many in the theatre world.[11]

---

10   In her essay 'Drama and Theatrical Practice in Weimar Classicism' Jane K. Brown provides some statistical analysis of numbers of performances and average runs of individual authors and of the balance of the different components of the repertoire that provides an overview during Goethe's directorship: see *The Literature of Weimar Classicism*, ed. by Simon Richter, The Camden House History of German Literature, 7 (Rochester, NY: Camden House, 2005), pp. 133–64 (pp. 137–43). For a comparison of the repertoire in Weimar, Berlin and Mannheim in 1803, see Chapter 7, pp. 244-45.

11   One of the best known and most extensive attacks on the Weimar aesthetic in performance was *Saat von Göthe gesäet dem Tage der Garben zu reifen. Ein Handbuch für Aesthetiker und junge Schauspieler* (Weimar and Leipzig: n.p., 1808), published anonymously but written by a former Weimar actor, Carl Reinhold, after he watched the company's *Gastspiel* in Leipzig in 1807. He accuses Goethe, through the pursuit of 'Idealism', of setting back the German theatre and of producing monotony through stylization: 'Jeder Charakter auf der Bühne muß nicht bloß etwas *veredelt*, welches ja schon die dummen *Realisten* lehren, sondern *vergöttert*, oder wenigstens *verheldet* werden' (p. 15). Later historians of the theatre also express respectful doubts, for example Heinrich Laube: 'Ja, die hohle Declamation, die steifen, gezierten Manieren, der kalte Formalismus sind durch die Weimar'sche Schule geradezu geweiht worden und haben auf dem deutschen Theater [...] Leben und Wahrheit des Dramas niedergehalten': *Heinrich Laubes Gesammelte Werke*, ed. by H. H. Houben, 50 vols (Leipzig: Hesse, 1909), vol. 31, pp. 71–72.

Although Goethe and Schiller were united in their belief that the theatre could be a place where the beautiful, conceived according to classical principles, could have its unique effect on the human mind, they nevertheless found themselves at times at variance over matters of staging and over the means theatre should use to achieve its impact. As discussed in the previous chapter, Schiller's *coup de théâtre* in *Egmont*, his introduction of the disguised figure of Alba in Egmont's prison whom Egmont then unmasks, provided an instance. In two men whose temperament and cast of mind were so different, such disagreements signalled more than a clash of preferences or taste, for they were indicative of a fundamental difference in outlook deriving from their contrasting attitudes to the material world. One can explore this difference by looking at a number of instances of how both men use the words *Natur* and *Kunst* in their writings for the theatre in this period.

Goethe's concept of the *Urpflanze*, which was engaging his mind at the time of the Jena scientific meeting, encapsulates his vision of nature, his wish to see the material world in its fullness and variety and also to grasp simultaneously its underlying unity and unchanging structures. That wish finds its parallel in his view of art. In art external reality has to be transformed in such a way that its ideal content is revealed. The sonnet 'Natur und Kunst', first delivered in public as part of the little play *Was wir bringen* (written and performed for the re-opening of the renovated Lauchstädt theatre in 1802), but dating from some years earlier, encapsulates the paradoxical idea that only by the pursuit of an art that shapes and limits can nature be revealed:

> Natur und Kunst sie scheinen sich zu fliehen,
> Und haben sich, eh man es denkt, gefunden;
> [...]
> Wer Großes will muss sich zusammenraffen.
> In der Beschränkung zeigt sich erst der Meister,
> Und das Gesetz nur kann uns Freiheit geben. (MA 6.1, 780)

Schiller's attitude to the material world was more ambivalent. He was always torn between wanting to assert the value of the earthly and temporal and wanting to transcend them. This ambivalence expressed itself in his aesthetics. The treatise *Über naive und sentimentalische*

171

Dichtung is centrally concerned with art and nature and provides an example of how his attitude to nature can change within a single work, giving rise to notorious shifts of meaning in the text. In describing the ancient Greeks as naïve in the early part of the treatise, he talks of their being in unreflective harmony with nature, in other words the external world, rather than experiencing, as moderns do, a sense of loss or longing when confronted with certain natural scenes or objects. For moderns, Schiller suggests, nature exists as an ideal that is at such times projected onto the external world. As the treatise develops he has to find a term to denote the actual external world ('wirkliche Natur') people experience, in order to distinguish it from ideal nature ('wahre Natur'), which exists only as a concept. The connotations of 'wirkliche Natur' are thus negative, nature devoid of ideal content and in need of the ennobling properties of art.

The mistrust of the material world is clear also in Schiller's writings on the sublime, most of which are concerned with the sublime as a response to tragedy and with the possibility of reformulating the traditional Aristotelian theory of the evocation of pity, fear and the resulting catharsis, using categories drawn from Kantian philosophy. In *Über das Pathetische* and *Über das Erhabene* he employs the Kantian distinction between the phenomenal world, the world of our experience, and the noumenal world, which enables us to frame laws (including moral laws) that bestow order on our experience. In tragedy the spectator experiences pity and fear when watching the sufferings of the tragic figure. The playwright's task, however, is not only to evoke these responses but to create in the spectator an imaginative experience of the suffering subject's continued potential, even if not realized in the play, to act as a free moral being and thus transcend the purely physical. The exhilaration this creates in the spectator, though balanced by pity and fear, is what Schiller means by the sublime in tragedy. The treatise *Über das Erhabene*, published in 1801 but probably written around 1794/95, demonstrates that his notion of the sublime rests on a negative appraisal of the material world:

> Das Erhabene verschafft uns also einen Ausgang aus der sinnlichen Welt, worinn uns das Schöne gern immer gefangen halten möchte. Nicht allmählig […], sondern plötzlich und durch eine Erschütterung, reißt es den selbständigen

Geist aus dem Netze los, womit die verfeinerte Sinnlichkeit ihn umstrickte. (NA 21, 45)

In this passage the beautiful is associated with the material and sensuous and the sublime with an impulse to free oneself from the shackles of the earthly.[12]

Two years later, in 1803, Schiller published the essay 'Über den Gebrauch des Chors in der Tragödie' as a preface to *Die Braut von Messina*, his experiment in neo-classical tragedy with a chorus. It contains some programmatic statements of the artistic intention of the Weimar Court Theatre at that time, most famously the aim 'dem Naturalism in der Kunst offen und ehrlich den Krieg zu erklären' (NA 10, 11), the chorus itself being a strikingly anti-naturalistic device. Schiller restates Goethe's principle of the paradoxical relationship between art and nature:

> Wie aber nun die Kunst zugleich ganz ideell und doch im tiefsten Sinne reell seyn – wie sie das Wirkliche ganz verlassen und doch aufs genaueste mit der Natur übereinstimmen soll und kann, das ists, was wenige fassen, was die Ansicht poetischer und plastischer Werke so schielend macht, weil beide Forderungen einander im gemeinen Urteil geradezu aufzuheben scheinen. (NA 10, 9)

He makes a distinction between 'das Wirkliche' and 'die Natur' that is analogous to that between 'wirkliche Natur' and 'wahre Natur' in *Über naive und sentimentalische Dichtung*. The essay also restates some of Schiller's fundamental ideas about the sublime that again suggest an ambivalence towards the material world:

> Die wahre Kunst aber hat es nicht bloß auf ein vorübergehendes Spiel abgesehen, es ist ihr ernst damit, den Menschen nicht bloß in einen augenblicklichen Traum von Freiheit zu versetzen, sondern ihn wirklich und in der That frei zu *machen*, und dieses dadurch, daß sie eine Kraft in ihm erweckt, übt und ausbildet, die sinnliche Welt, die sonst nur als ein roher Stoff auf uns lastet, als eine blinde Macht auf uns drückt, in eine objektive Ferne zu rücken, in ein

---

12   David Pugh discusses this ambivalence towards the material world as an aspect of Schiller's appropriation of the Platonic tradition in *Dialectic of Love: Platonism in Schiller's Aesthetics* (Montreal and Kingston, Ont.: McGill-Queen's University Press, 1996). My discussion here is indebted to his approach.

freies Werk unsers Geistes zu verwandeln und das Materielle durch Ideen zu beherrschen. (NA 10, 8–9)

Even allowing for Schiller's habitual polarization of arguments and the strongly rhetorical character of this essay in particular, we have here a clear statement of his conviction that freedom, and that includes aesthetic freedom, is predicated on a tension between the material and the ideal, in which the ideal realm subdues the material realm.

A practical result of these contrasting views of the material world on the part of Goethe and Schiller is their differing estimations of what should be shown on stage. Schiller was much more open to powerful stage effects because he believed that only when we are strongly engaged, firmly held in the chains of the material world by our sympathic responses to suffering, can we then experience the liberation brought by the sublime. Goethe's aesthetic of performance was more contemplative. His concern for visual harmony posits an audience that admires and responds to the beauty of the work and its realization. His *Regeln für Schauspieler*, which originated in instruction in acting given to two new Weimar actors, Pius Alexander Wolff and Karl Franz Grüner, arose in the same period as 'Über den Gebrauch des Chors in der Tragödie', and lay stress on clear speaking, graceful and harmonious movement and decorum on stage.[13] They imagine the audience as contemplative, even detached, observers. This approach led him to resist some of Schiller's ideas for making the visual impact of the play more immediate and theatrically effective. Paradoxically, it was Schiller, in whose thinking the plastic arts were never very influential, who on occasions called for greater visual impact on stage and Goethe, the lover of the plastic arts, who tended to resist.

A small but significant negotiation that springs from this difference arose in preparation for the staging of *Wallenstein*. For the première of *Wallensteins Lager*, which opened the newly remodelled theatre, Schiller wrote a prologue in iambic pentameter, which was delivered by Heinrich Vohs, the actor who played Max Piccolomini in the first performance of the subsequent two parts of the work (NA 8,

---

13   MA 6.2, 703–48. See Chapter 4, note 30 (p. 150).

3–6). Schiller begins by alluding to the new interior ('Und sieh, sie hat sich neu verjüngt!': NA 8, 3) and deftly links the images of the masks of tragedy and comedy depicted on the main curtain to the central themes of the play ('Der scherzenden, der ernsten Maske Spiel': NA 8, 3); the words *Ernst, Scherz* and *Spiel* are key terms in the two main parts of the drama, in which we see Wallenstein toying with the idea of rebellion and then being faced with the all too serious consequences of things he has said and appearances he has given in jest. The prologue had already been sent to the printer for inclusion in Schiller's annual poetry anthology, the *Musenalmanach* for 1799, when Goethe suggested some amendments for the *Lager* première. A copy of Goethe's amended version was discovered in the 1980s in the Goethe and Schiller Archive in Weimar. The section beginning 'Doch euren Augen soll ihn jetzt die Kunst/Auch eurem Herzen menschlich näher bringen' (NA 8, 5) is removed, most probably because Wallenstein himself was not going to appear that evening, indeed not for some months. The biggest change is to the closing few lines, which in the original version contain an apology for the use of rhyme:

> Ja danket ihr's [der Muse], daß sie das düstre Bild
> Der Wahrheit in das heitre Reich der Kunst
> Hinüberspielt, die Täuschung, die sie schafft
> Aufrichtig selbst zerstört und ihren Schein
> Der Wahrheit nicht betrüglich unterschiebt,
> Ernst ist das Leben, heiter ist die Kunst. (lines 131–36, NA 8, 6)

Goethe's version reads:

> Ja, danket ihr daß sie das düstre Bild
> der Wirklichkeit mit bunten Farben schmückt.
> Ernst ist das Leben, heiter sei die Kunst! (FA 4, 298)

Schiller's version identifies the use of rhyme as a means of stylization that reminds the audience that the play is not life but an artificial world. The use of the words *Täuschung* and *Schein* is familiar from his aesthetic writings, particular *Über die ästhetische Erziehung des Menschen*. There, *Schein* is a key term in his argument about how works of art affect the imagination. Our awareness of art objects as art, as a sort of honest deception, allows us to contemplate them under

175

different criteria from those we apply to the rest of our lives, namely the moral and the utilitarian, and this allows them to become symbols of our inner experience.[14] This set of abstract concepts is not readily accessible in the form of live delivery and more suitable to readers of the published prologue. Goethe tries to preserve something of Schiller's contrast by picking up the image of 'das düstre Bild' and setting it in opposition to 'bunten Farben', an apt allusion to the colourful appearance of the camp scenes about to follow on stage. Most significant is the change to the final line from 'heiter ist die Kunst' to 'heiter sei die Kunst'. Schiller's original formulation contains in it a stark contrast, between life as potentially, perhaps inherently, tragic and art as a realm that allows us escape by transporting us to serenity. His strict antinomies, underpinned by a Kantian rigorism, as well as his tendency to devalue the material world, were unpalatable to Goethe, who, in the course of simplifying the material for the benefit of a live audience, managed to neutralize any conflict with his own, arguably more pragmatic, artistic viewpoint.[15] He presents art as reality adorned with many colours, an image he uses elsewhere to suggest the heightening and intensification that art brings to life. It is also appropriate that he extends the picture image because of his habit of talking of theatre in terms of a picture.[16] Schiller clearly accepted the small changes, grateful no doubt for the commitment

---

14   This idea is elaborated in Suzanne Langer's influential study *Feeling and Form. A Theory of Art developed from 'Philosophy in a New Key'* (London: Routledge and Kegan Paul, 1953). See also E. M. Wilkinson's article 'Schiller's Concept of *Schein* in the Light of Recent Aesthetics', *German Quarterly*, 4 (1955), 219–27.

15   See Anita and Jochen Golz, '"Ernst ist das Leben, heiter sey die Kunst": Goethe als Redakteur des "Wallenstein"-Prologs', in *Im Vorfeld der Literatur. Vom Wert archivalischer Überlieferung für das Verständnis von Literatur und ihrer Geschichte*, ed. by Karl-Heinz Hahn (Weimar: Böhlau, 1991), pp. 17–29 and Norbert Oellers, 'Die Heiterkeit der Kunst. Goethe variiert Schiller', in *Edition als Wissenschaft. Festschrift für Hans Zeller* (Beihefte zu *Editio*, 2), ed. by Gunter Martens and Winfried Woesler (Tübingen: Niemeyer, 1991), pp. 92–103.

16   See, for example, the *Regeln für Schauspieler*: 'Das Theater ist als ein figurenloses Tableau anzusehen, worin der Schauspieler die Staffage macht' (MA 6.2, 705).

Goethe was showing to the successful staging of his new work and aware that his more complex ideas would appear later in print.

The premières of *Wallenstein*

Wallensteins Lager opened the new season on 12 October 1798 and was followed by the two longer parts of the drama, *Die Piccolomini* and *Wallensteins Tod*, on 30 January and 20 April 1799 respectively. It shared the evening with Kotzebue's popular drama *Die Corsen*. Thereafter the three parts of the play were usually performed in rapid succession, often on consecutive theatre evenings, though very occasionally *Wallensteins Lager* was performed without the other two parts because it was a convenient length to fill out an evening's programme with another short play and was well known to the Weimar audiences. Schiller had not even finished the second and third parts of *Wallenstein* when the first was premièred. He joined Goethe in Weimar on 10 September and in the days following the two men considered the structure of the work, Schiller deciding finally on a division of the action into two full-length plays. To balance these and to provide a piece that could be played separately from them, he had to expand the camp scenes to about twice their existing length. He returned to Jena with the task of completing the new version in a little over two weeks.

The opening of the 1798 theatre season was also the inauguration of the remodelled interior of the theatre building. On his visit to Switzerland in 1797 Goethe met the Swabian artist and architect Nicolaus Thouret in Stuttgart and brought about his engagement on the Weimar palace reconstruction, where he contributed in particular to the interior design, and on the theatre renovation.[17] Work began in mid-July 1798 and finished in September. Goethe reported to Schiller

---

17   For details of the renovation see Alexander Weichberger, *Goethe und das Komödienhaus in Weimar 1779–1825*, Theatergeschichtliche Forschungen, 39 (Leipzig: Voss, 1928), pp. 35–55.

on 14 July 1798 that the new auditorium would hold about two hundred more than the old one and yet not seem empty at performances that were less well attended.[18] A new extension was built for stage sets. The old auditorium was wider than the stage on either side and was brought in to be the same width, while the stage was shortened. An elegant loop of arches on the ground floor supported a tier of boxes composing the upper level and above that was a gallery supported by graceful neo-classical columns. The slightly shortened stage had six pairs of *Kulissen*. The sharp-tongued Caroline Schlegel wrote to her brother-in-law Friedrich:

> [Goethe] hat das weimarische Comödienhaus inwendig durchaus umgeschaffen, und in ein freundliches glänzendes Feenschlößchen verwandelt. Es hat mir erstaunlich wohl gefallen. Ein Architekt und Dekorateur aus Studtgart ist dazu her berufen und innerhalb von 13 Wochen sind Säulen, Galerien, Balcone, Vorhang verfertigt und was nicht alles geschmückt, gemahlt, verguldet, aber in der That mit Geschmack. Die Beleuchtung ist äußerst hübsch, vermittelst eines weiten Kranzes von englischen Lampen, der in einer kleinen Kuppel schwebt, durch welche zugleich der Dunst des Hauses hinaus zieht. Göthe ist wie ein Kind so eifrig dabei gewesen, den Tag vor der Eröfnung des Theaters war von früh bis spät Abends da, hat da gegessen und getrunken und eigenhändig mitgearbeitet. (FA 4, 800–01)

Much was at stake for Schiller in putting a new play out into the world. After his almost twelve-year dramatic silence the expectations riding on any new play would be high. While he felt he had gained the theoretical clarity he needed to return to his true vocation, that of tragedian, in choosing to dramatize the Wallenstein material he had set himself a Herculean task. During his period of theoretical reflection he had focused on the need for simplicity and clarity of plot. *Don Karlos* still haunted him as an example of how a play ought not to be written. Immediately after finishing it he turned to classical Greek drama in search of the key to the construction of a lucid linear plot. Yet when he set himself the task of a new drama, he chose to treat a subject that required panoramic breadth as well as lucidity. Also, by his very ambiguity the figure of Wallenstein created the possibility of exploring an immense richness of themes, which Schiller did not wish

---

18   NA 37/I, 326.

to sacrifice to the demands of theatrical viability. By placing alongside his central figure two contrasting ones, Octavio and Max Piccolomini, he created scope for parallel and contrasting encounters in which the central themes – loyalty, tradition and change, self-determination – are argued out.

The expansiveness of the play was encouraged by Schiller's decision late in 1797 to write it in blank verse, in spite of his original intention to use prose. With a sense of relief he wrote to Körner on 20 November 1797: 'es ist unmöglich, ein Gedicht in Prosa zu schreiben' (NA 29, 158). It was the obvious choice for a high tragedy combining elements of the classical and Shakespearian traditions but further underscored how far he was bucking the trend of drama and theatre. In fact, performance was not foremost in his mind as the work progressed. Early in 1798 there was a suggestion that Schröder might come to Weimar in the autumn to play the title role. Schiller's response was:

> Wenn ich überhaupt nur mit einigem Interesse daran denken soll, für das Theater zu schreiben, so kann es nur dadurch seyn, dass ich für Schrödern zu arbeiten denke. Denn mit ihm, fürchte ich, stirbt alle Schauspielkunst in Deutschland und noch weiter aus.[19]

When the plan looks as though it will not come off Schiller writes in May 1798 to Goethe: 'Ich weiss kaum wie ich es mit Schrödern halten soll, und bin beinahe entschlossen, die ganze Idee von der Repræsentation des Wallensteins fallen zu lassen.' Then mentioning various practical difficulties he says:

> Ich denke daher, meinen Gang frey und ohne bestimmte Theaterrücksichten fortzusetzen und mir wo möglich die Stimmung zu bewahren. Ist der Wallenstein einmal fertig und gedruckt, so interessiert er mich nicht mehr, und alsdann kann ich auf so etwas noch eher denken. (NA 29, 232)

Writing to Körner in September 1798 about his decision to divide the main action of the play into two parts he says: 'Ohne diese Operation wäre der Wallenstein ein Monstrum geworden an Breite und Ausdehnung, und hätte, um für das Theater zu taugen, gar zuviel Bedeutendes verlieren müssen' (NA 29, 280). He concedes that the three-part play

---

19   To Bottiger, 25 January 1798 (NA 29, 193–94).

will make fewer demands on the theatre by requiring fewer actors at any given moment, but this is clearly a secondary consideration and poetic quality takes precedence over theatrical viability.

It takes precedence also over contemporary fashion, but Schiller nevertheless took comfort in the evidence of the limitations of the appeal of his erstwhile rival and the family drama, writing to Goethe in August 1798:

> Ich freue mich den Theaterbau mitanzusehen, und glaube Ihnen, daß der Anblick der Bretter allerlei erwecken wird. Es ist mir neulich aufgefallen was ich in einer Zeitschrift oder Zeitung las, daß das Hamburger Publicum sich über die Wiederhohlung der Iflandschen Stücke beklage und sie satt sey. Wenn dieß einen analogischen Schluß auf andere Städte erlaubt, so würde mein Wallenstein einen günstigen Moment treffen. Unwahrscheinlich ist es nicht, daß das Publikum sich selbst nicht mehr sehen mag, es fühlt sich in gar zu schlechter Gesellschaft. Die Begierde nach jenen Stücken scheint mir auch mehr durch einen Ueberdruss an den Ritterschauspielen erzeugt oder wenigstens verstärkt worden zu seyn, man wollte sich von Verzerrungen erhohlen. Aber das lange Angaffen eines Alltagsgesichts muß endlich freilich auch ermüden. (NA 29, 271–72)

Knowing he was challenging contemporary taste, he takes up that very theme in the 'Prolog' to *Wallenstein*, linking the Weimar theatre's material renewal with the playwright's response to the renewed challenge created by contemporary events to leave behind the familiar domestic world:

> Die neue Ära, die der Kunst Thaliens
> Auf dieser Bühne heut beginnt, macht auch
> Den Dichter kühn, die alte Bahn verlassend,
> Euch aus des Bürgerlebens engem Kreis,
> Auf einen höhern Schauplatz zu versetzen,
> Nicht unwert des erhabenen Moments
> Der Zeit, in dem wir strebend uns bewegen.
> Denn nur der grosse Gegenstand vermag
> Den tiefen Grund der Menschheit aufzuregen.
> Im engen Kreis verengert sich der Sinn
> Es wächst der Mensch mit seinen grössern Zwecken (lines 50–60, NA 8,4)

In an age of upheaval it is the duty of the dramatist, he says, to transport the audience out of its narrow bourgeois sphere and onto a higher plane, otherwise the theatre is put to shame by 'des Lebens Bühne' (line 69) and the opportunity of imaginative expansion of the mind and heart is missed. Yet he also pays homage to Iffland the actor, using the occasion to remind the audience of the distinguished acting that has taken place in the theatre[20] and thus he draws audience, writer and actors into an elevated vision of their common artistic enterprise.

Goethe anticipates the sentiments of the 'Prolog' in his own announcement of the performance in the *Allgemeine Zeitung* of 12 October 1798.[21] The author of *Wallenstein*, he reports, wonders how the 'Wagestück' of putting on a verse play will succeed:

> Da man in Weimar vor einer gebildeten und gleichsam geschlossenen Gesellschaft spielt, die nicht bloß von der Mode des Augenblicks bestimmt wird, die nicht allzu fest am Gewohnten hängt, sondern sich schon öfters an mannigfaltigen originalen Darstellungen ergötzt hat, und, durch die Bemühungen der eignen Schauspieler sowohl als durch die zweimalige Erscheinung Ifflands, vorbereitet ist, auf das Künstliche und Absichtliche dramatischer Arbeiten zu achten, so wird ein solcher Versuch desto möglicher und für den Verfasser desto belehrender sein. (MA 6.2, 642)

The audience is thus primed for the performance and flattered as being more discerning and exclusive than most audiences. In fact, this was probably not just flattery but to some extent true.[22]

Goethe took immense pains with the production of *Wallensteins Lager*. His friend, the artist Heinrich Meyer, was instructed to gather as many woodcuts depicting camp life in the Thirty Years' War as he could to serve as a guide for the stage grouping of characters. Rehearsals were already advanced when Schiller decided to add the Capuchin friar's comic sermon, borrowing for inspiration from Goethe

---

20 See lines 15 to 25.

21 'Weimarischer, neudekorierter TheaterSaal. Dramatische Bearbeitung der Wallensteinischen Geschichte durch Schiller (Auszug eines Briefes aus Weimar)': MA 6.2, 639–42.

22 See Iffland's letter of 10 February 1799 to Schiller regarding *Wallensteins Lager*. Contrasting Weimar with Berlin he writes: 'Ganz ein anders ist das in Weimar, wo kein Militairstaat ist, der Zirkel der Zuschauer fast eine verstandne Gesellschafft ist' (NA 38/I, 35).

a copy of the works of Abraham a Santa Clara, the seventeenth-century Augustinian preacher known for his wordplays. Genast played the role of the Capuchin, for which he became famous in the company. Contemporary engravings based on the well-known painting of the production by Georg Melchior Kraus depict various characters and moments from the action in a single panoramic scene (see illustration). If the costumes are accurately depicted, then it is clear that much attention was given to their authenticity. Unlike the printed version of the text, the stage version began with a song as the curtain went up, to which both Goethe and Schiller contributed stanzas and which was sung to a well-known tune by Reichardt from *Claudine von Villa Bella* (1776), Goethe's *Singspiel*. As the first stanza indicates, the song gives a rough and in part humorous picture of the ruthlessness and impermanence of the soldier's existence:

Es leben die Soldaten
Der Bauer gibt den Braten,
Der Gärtner gibt den Most,
Das ist Soldatenkost. (FA 4, 301)

The song thus contrasts with the greater sophistication of the closing chorus, in which various characters we have met in the *Lager* scenes – a *Kürassier*, a *Jäger*, a recruit – take the individual stanzas and are differentiated. In particular the *Kürassier* (from Max Piccolomini's regiment) stands out by his nobler interpretation of the nature of a soldier's freedom.[23]

Schiller came to Weimar for the dress rehearsal. He was particularly concerned about the verse-speaking. The verse form used in *Wallensteins Lager*, the rhyming doggerel known as *Knittelvers*, was used in the sixteenth century by the poet Hans Sachs and revived by Goethe for parts of his *Faust*, though when *Wallensteins Lager* was premièred only the unfinished *Faust. Ein Fragment* (1790) had been published. By its jerkiness and rhyme it reinforces the colloquial, direct and at times jesting tone of the dialogue of *Wallensteins Lager*.

---

23 In the version of *Wallensteins Lager* performed at the première a *Scharfschütz* and a *Rekrut* are assigned stanzas given in the printed version to a *Dragoner* and the *Wachtmeister*; see FA 4, 335–56.

Contemporary accounts suggest that the actors acquitted themselves quite well as verse speakers, and the evening was judged to be a success.[24] Caroline Schlegel, no admirer of Schiller, records: 'Göthens Mühe war auch nicht verloren; die Gesellschaft hat exzellent gespielt, es war das vollkommenste Ensemble und keine Unordnung in dem Getümmel' (FA 4, 801). Schiller's report to Körner is more guarded but none the less satisfied:

> Das Vorspiel ist nun in Weimar gegeben. Die Schauspieler sind freilich mittelmässig genug; aber sie thaten was sie konnten, und man mußte zufrieden seyn. Die Neuerung mit den gereimten Versen fiel nicht auf, die Schauspieler sprachen die Verse mit vieler Freiheit, und das Publikum ergötzte sich. (NA 29, 295)

Goethe's review praises Heinrich Vohs's delivery of the 'Prolog', saying his skill in handling the lines of blank verse gave grounds for hope for the reception of the following parts of the play and for the possibility that the theatre might be cured of its 'Rhythmophobie, von dieser Reim- und Taktscheue, an der so viele deutsche Schauspieler krank liegen' (MA 6.2, 643).

No sooner was the première over than Schiller was under great pressure to finish the two main parts. On 31 December he sent Goethe the version of *Die Piccolomini* that was performed, cut by four hundred lines from its original length to reduce the playing time. The division between the two final parts of the work came at what is now the end of *Wallensteins Tod* Act 2 because Schiller wanted *Die Piccolomini* to end with the final parting of Max and Octavio. This unbalanced division was adjusted for the printed version of the work, for, though it made for a swift and concentrated third part, Schiller had to concede in time that the second part had proved too long for the

---

24 An anecdote is recorded by the actor Friedrich Ludwig Schmidt concerning an extra – numerous extras had to be taken on for the performance – who had a very small speaking part and was urged by Schiller, 'Lassen Sie mir keinen Fuß aus'. The man looked down in puzzlement and reassured the poet that he would omit anything rather than his feet. Quoted in *Dichter über ihre Dichtungen. Friedrich Schiller*, ed. by Bodo Lecke, 2 vols (Munich: Heimeran, 1970), vol. 2, pp. 308–09.

stage, an instance of performance having an impact on the final printed shape of the work.

Conscious of the task involved in rehearsing such a long verse play, Schiller came to Weimar on 4 January and remained there for some five weeks. He and Goethe took immense pains to practise the verse-speaking with the cast. Amalie von Voigt records:

> Den jüngern Schauspielern wurde der Unterschied zwischen skandiren, rhythmisch sprechen, oder die Verse wie Prosa herabrollen, verständlich gemacht, auch die ältern fügten sich, nur einige, die unbelehrbar waren, wurden bey Seite geschoben. (FA 4, 837)

The Weimar public awaited the performance with great expectancy. The German–Danish naturalist and philosopher Henrich Steffens recalled the mounting excitement:

> Die Spannung, mit welcher man dieser Aufführung entgegensah, war merkwürdig. [...] Man hörte in der ganzen Stadt von nichts Anderem sprechen. Frauen und Töchter intriguirten gegen einander, um sich wechselseitig zu verdrängen; wer einen Platz erhalten hatte, pries sich glücklich. (FA 4, 840)

The performance seems to have been moderately successful, given its length and the fact that the audience is offered no ending. Johann Jakob Graff, who played Wallenstein, was felt not to be altogether equal to the great role, though Schiller appreciated the trouble he had taken to memorize the lines and speak them clearly. After the second performance, which seems to have been more favourably received, the playwright thanked him in a gracious letter for his 'treffliche Recitation' (NA 30, 27). Two other successes of the evening were Vohs as Max Piccolomini and Caroline Jagemann as Thekla. Jagemann seems to have been particularly striking for the way in which she responded to the character Schiller had created, who is strong and composed, her father's 'starkes Mädchen', resisting the stereotype of the sentimental heroine portrayed by subsequent Theklas, 'die vor Rührung zerflossen, und die des Feldherrn ächte Tochter zu einem liebessiechen Mägdlein im bürgerlichen Schauspiel herabzogen.'[25] Her fine singing

---

25   Amalie von Voigt's memoirs quoted in FA 4, 838.

naturally made Thekla's song a highlight of the performance.[26] The other main roles were taken by Schall as Octavio (one of the weaknesses of the production), Leissring as Terzky, Cordemann as Illo, Genast as Isolani, Malcolmi as Buttler, Mad. Wolff-Malcolmi as the Duchess and Mad. Teller, a new arrival in the company, as Countess Terzky.

Schiller himself was gratified not only by the production and its reception but also with his own ability to enjoy something like a normal life in Weimar. Proximity to the court and his close relationship with Goethe laid many social obligations on him of a kind he had been used to avoid in Jena, in order to preserve his strength for his work. Surprisingly, he had been able to spend the five weeks in Weimar society without falling victim to his habitual 'Krämpfe'. With clear surprise and satisfaction he tells Körner: 'so hab ich in diesen 5 Wochen wieder als ein ordentlicher Mensch gelebt und mehr mit- gemacht, als in den letzten 5 Jahren zusammen genommen' (NA 30, 29). As he congratulated the poet on the success of *Die Piccolomini*, Duke Carl August expressed the wish that he might spend more time in Weimar, which raised in Schiller the hope that the Duke was willing to help provide the means to realize that wish. His head al- ready full again with dramatic plans, he recognized that proximity to the theatre was a necessary stimulus.[27] Carl August responded with an increase in Schiller's income of 200 Talers. The move to Weimar, at first envisaged as being for the winter months, became permanent and was of course an implicit undertaking on the playwright's part to involve himself with the Weimar theatre more generally. It took place in the final weeks of 1799 and was delayed by the life-threatening ill- ness of his wife Charlotte after the birth in October 1799 of their third child, Caroline. She succumbed to a fever, lost consciousness and the

---

26 See Goethe's report for the *Allgemeine Zeitung* (FA 4, 835).
27 To Carl August, 1 September 1799: 'Da zugleich meine dramatische Beschäfti- gungen mir die Anschauung des Theaters zum nächsten Bedürfniß machen und ich von dem glücklichen Einfluß desselben auf meine Arbeiten vollkommen überzeugt bin, so hat alles dieß ein lebhaftes Verlangen in mir erweckt, künftig- hin die Wintermonate in Weimar zuzubringen' (NA 30, 93).

distraught writer spent many nights at her bedside. She then made a slow but complete recovery.

After the première of *Die Piccolomini* Schiller and Goethe returned to Jena on 7 February and Schiller was again hard at work, completing *Wallensteins Tod* and sending it to Goethe on 17 March. On 26 and 27 March the play was sent to the Weimar theatre so that rehearsals could begin. Schiller himself left Jena with Goethe on 10 April in order to assist. The première took place on 20 April, after *Wallensteins Lager* and *Die Piccolomini* had been repeated on 15 and 17 April respectively. A second performance was given on 22 April. The demand for tickets was so great that the prices were put up by a third or even a half. The cast was the same as for *Die Piccolomini*. This time Schiller was less guarded in his report to Körner:

> Der Wallenstein hat auf dem Theater in Weimar eine außerordentliche Wirkung gemacht, und auch die unempfindlichsten mit sich fortgerissen. Es war darüber nur Eine Stimme, und in den nächsten acht Tagen ward von nichts anderem gesprochen. (NA 30, 47)

Goethe, who recognized that *Die Piccolomini* was a difficult play to make work on its own, wrote to Wilhelm von Humboldt on 24 May 1799 that the third part of the play 'aus den vorbereitenden Kelchblättern, wie eine Wunderblume unversehens hervorstieg und alle Erwartungen übertraf' (WA IV, 14, 97).

The *Wallenstein* season was thus a momentous one for Schiller. He had re-established, indeed enhanced, his reputation as Germany's foremost dramatist, surprising the world with a work entirely lacking the extravagances and wildness of his early style. He could fill a theatre with a performance of a demanding verse play that ran counter to the trend of contemporary theatre in content and style. He had experienced the thrill of seeing his own play performed under his own guiding hand. He had engaged in practical theatre work in partnership with Goethe and come out of his seclusion without being physically destroyed by the demands made on him.

What of Goethe? His reflections on the importance of the *Wallenstein* project are summed up in the letter quoted above to Wilhelm von Humboldt. The effort has brought everyone 'Mühe' and 'Genuss':

> Doch hat das eigentliche Unangenehme und Unbequeme der Vorbereitung
> Schiller selbst mir abgenommen. Er hat sich in Absicht auf Gesundheit und
> Stimmung bey dieser Thätigkeit sehr wacker gehalten und durch diesen neuen
> und von allen Seiten schweren Versuch gar viel gewonnen. (WA IV, 14, 96)

The fact that Schiller had found the strength to be active in the theatre
opened up for Goethe too the possibility of future collaboration and of
making his theatre duties an aesthetic project, even in a small provincial theatre like Weimar's. If one had the courage, the audience could
respond:

> Man hat auch bey diesem Unternehmen gesehen, dass man eigentlich alles
> wagen kann, sobald man mit Genie, Geist und Überlegung wirkt. Das erste
> Stück, *Wallensteins Lager*, hat die Menschen nicht allein sogleich mit dem
> Reim ausgesöhnt, sondern sogar dessen Bedürfniß erweckt und durch seine
> Lebhaftigkeit eine gute Sensation gemacht. Das zweyte, *die Piccolomini*, hat
> den Beyfall aller erhalten, welche es ganz hören konnten oder mochten [...]
> *Wallenstein* zuletzt hat alle Stimmen vereinigt. (WA IV, 14, 96–97)

The production had opened up the theatre as a new branch of the
Weimar experiment.

Chapter Six
Aesthetic Education II: Weimar and Berlin

As soon as Iffland got wind of the fact that Schiller had a new play nearing completion, he tried to secure an acting manuscript, declaring himself willing to pay any sum the playwright required.[1] With his customary optimism Schiller had allowed his publisher Cotta to announce the publication of the play for Easter 1799, and Iffland was anxious to put it on while it was still a rarity. Schiller's reply was dated 15 October, just after the première of *Wallensteins Lager*, and is striking for the amount of work that was clearly still to do and the writer's underestimate of the time he would need to do it. He asked Iffland for a large sum, namely 60 Friedrichsd'or (about 300 Talers) and promised to send details of sets and costumes from the Weimar production. Iffland paid it without demur but pressed Schiller hard for the manuscript, fearing the play would be printed before he could get his production on stage. He wrote on 17 November, 'gern gebe ich – Wallenst*ein* – 60 Pistolen dafür [...] Aber um *Beschleünigung* bittet Ihr Iffland' (NA 38/I, 7), and on 4 December, 'Darf ich die Absendung der Schauspiele dringend erbitten? Ausschreiben. Decorationen. Garderobe pp nehmen Zeit und mehr als Alles ist es mir Pflicht die Ungeduld des Publikums zu befriedigen!' (NA 38/I, 12). The theatre director explained his importunity not just as the result of his eagerness to see Schiller's new work on stage and to give it suitable preparation and rehearsal time but also of financial circumstances relating particularly to Berlin:

Indem ich darauf rechnen durfte, habe ich keine Anstalt zu einer Oper von Gluck und Sachini gemacht. Etwas der Art, ist das Publikum im Jenner und Februar zu sehen gewohnt. Dies Beiden Monathe, sind die ErtragsMonathe, und

---

1   See his letter of 5 October 1798: 'Das Publicum verlangt mit Sehnsucht danach. Von mir rede ich nicht [...]. Ich werde mit Freuden die Bedingungen erfüllen, welche Sie so gütig sein wollen, dafür vestzusetzen' (NA 37/I, 362).

irgend ein Werck, was um diese Zeit Geist und Sinn beschäfftigt, macht ein plus und – wenn es zur rechten Zeit nicht da ist – ein minus von 4000 Thaler. In diesen Monathen, muß eine große Vorstellung des National Theaters, den königl*ichen* großen Opern, welche *frei* gegeben werden, das Gegengewicht halten. Piccolomini und Wallenstein, sollen mit Anstand und Aufwand gegeben werden. Beides erfordert Zeit. (NA 38/I, 18)

Schiller sent the bulk of *Die Piccolomini* on 24 December 1798 and Iffland was extravagant in his praise for it. On 10 February 1799, however, only eight days before the première, he informed Schiller that for political reasons *Wallensteins Lager* would not be put on:

Es scheint mir und schien mehreren bedeütenden Männern ebenfalls bedenck-lich, in einem militairischen Staate, ein Stück zu geben, wo über die Art und Folgen eines großen stehenden Heeres, so treffende Dinge, in so hinreißender Sprache gesagt werden. Es kann gefährlich sein, oder doch leicht gemißdeütet werden, wenn die Möglichkeit, daß eine Armee in Maße deliberirt, ob sie sich da oder dorthin schicken laßen soll und will, anschaulich dargestellt wird. Was der wackere Wachtmeister, so characteristisch über des Königs Szepter sagt, ist, wie die ganze militäirische Debatte, bedencklich, wenn ein militäirischer König, der erste Zuschauer ist. Ganz ein anders ist das in Weimar, wo kein Militairstaat ist, der Zirkel der Zuschauer fast eine verstandne Gesellschafft ist, die keinen Mißverstand gegeben finden kann, weil sie keinen nehmen will. Der Anfrage bin ich ausgewichen. Das Theater hat keine Censur, ich hüte mich lieber, etwas zu thun, wodurch wir eine bekommen könnten. Bei den Anfragen ob das Vorspiel gegeben würde, habe ich geantwortet, die Kosten wären zu groß. Ich will mich lieber über diesen platten Grund tadeln laßen, als den eigentlichen Grund nennen. (NA 38/I, 34–35)

The privilege of being without external censorship (and the fear of losing that privilege) caused Iffland to exercise strict self-censorship on behalf of the theatre. Throughout his time in Berlin he showed himself extremely careful not to make his theatre politically contro-versial, a policy reinforced by his sense of personal loyalty towards the monarch. He was particularly concerned that Schiller should be discreet and not reveal the true reason why the play would not be performed, for he feared a negative backlash in the popular press. Schiller's reply[2] suggests serene acceptance; he was, after all, used to varieties of censorship exercised in the German states and Iffland was

---

2   See his letter to Iffland of 18 February 1799 (NA 30, 30).

still paying him the agreed sum despite the decision not to perform the *Lager*.[3]

The first Berlin performance of *Die Piccolomini* was on 18 February 1799. The *Regiebuch*[4] suggests the careful planning Iffland himself put into the production; his sketch of the banquet scene, for example, shows his attention to Schiller's stage directions. He even called in the director of the Berlin observatory, Professor Bode, to give advice on the astrological tower.[5] The rehearsals were mainly in the hands of the *Regisseur*, Ferdinand Fleck (1757–1801), who was doubtful about the play's impact: 'Ein weites schönes Meer, fast jede Stelle ein erhabener Gedanke. Schön und ruhig wird der denkende Zuschauer sich hinüber wogen lassen, aber der nur zahlende? Wird er nicht Sturm und Gewitter wünschen?'[6] The première was not a great success, in part because Iffland played the longer version sent to him before Schiller, in his haste to send the play off, had checked the playing time. The result was that the performance lasted some five and a half hours and was thereafter cut. Iffland's own report to Schiller is subdued:

> Es gehört zu vicles dazu, dies große Ganze auf ein mahl und in allen seinen Theilen zu umfassen, als daß die Wirkung auf die Menge, so lebhaft sein könnte, wie die Berührung gewöhnlicher, allen Menschen bekannter Gegenstände, sie wohl veranlaßt. (NA 38/I, 46)[7]

---

3   When *Wallensteins Lager* was played during the summer season at Lauchstädt, which belonged to the Protestant territory of Merseburg, it was the Capuchin who caused concern and had to be replaced from 1800 onwards by a 'Feldschulmeister'. See NA 38/II, 493.

4   See Julius Petersen (ed.), *Schillers 'Piccolomini' auf dem Kgl. National-Theater zu Berlin. Ifflands Regiebuch der Erstaufführung am 18. 2. 1799* (Berlin: Gesellschaft für Theatergeschichte, 1941).

5   Petersen, p. 9.

6   Letter to Iffland, quoted by Ruth Freydank in '"Es ist Ihr Triumph, nicht meiner …" Ifflands Berliner Schiller-Inszenierungen', *Theater der Zeit*, 5 (1987), 22–25 (p. 23).

7   Karl Ludwig Woltmann wrote in the *Jahrbücher der preußischen Monarchie*: 'Die Hauptursache aber, daß dieses Schauspiel nicht so aufgenommen wurde, wie man es seinem Gehalte nach erwarten sollte, liegt in dem Grundfehler der modernen Kultur, über welchen sich nur wenige erheben, daß wir weit mehr das

Iffland's own performance was crucial to the play's effect.[8] He shrewdly chose the role of Octavio and seems to have brought his famous attention to nuance and detail to the part. In the banquet scene, for example: 'Er war emsig bemüht zu sprechen, als merke er auf nichts und sah doch alles.'[9] Wallenstein was played by the renowned Fleck, whose interpretation of the role in performances up to his death in December 1801 has gone down in theatre history as definitive. His saturnine quality combined with an ability to convince the audience both of the character's mystical side and of his charismatic leadership. Both his and Iffland's declamation were commended by Woltmann.[10] After his death Iffland took over the part, though tragic heroes were neither his preference nor his forte.

The first Berlin performance of *Wallensteins Tod*, preceded the evening before by a performance of *Die Piccolomini*, was on 17 May and was well received. Iffland made sure considerable rehearsal time was invested. Johann Friedrich Unger, the Berlin publisher, reported to Schiller:

> Die Vorstellungen selbst machten große Wirkung auf das Publikum, welches nicht aus den gewöhnlichen alltäglichen Komödiengehern bestand. Es war der feiner Theil Berlins, und es waren gewiß ein paar sehr schöne Tage, sowohl für die Schauspieler als Zuhörer. So allgemeine Stille, solche grosse Aufmerksamkeit erblikt man gewiß selten. (NA 38/I, 110)

August Wilhelm Schlegel's disingenuously expressed fears in a letter to Goethe, that the Berlin audience was 'von Natur prosaisch, und durch Gewöhnung im höchsten Grade Kotzebuisirt', and therefore unlikely to respond to the work, proved unfounded.[11] Friedrich Eberhard Rambach, writing in the *Jahrbücher der preußischen Monarchie*,

---

Interesse der Neugierde, als des Kunstsinnes zu allem mitbringen. Ueber ihn ein mehreres zu sagen, würde ganz unnütz sein' (FA 4, 867).

8   Schiller wrote of the première of *Die Piccolomini* in Weimar, 'Octavio fürcht ich geht hier ganz verloren' (NA 30, 25).

9   Woltmann, FA 4, 868.

10   See FA 4, 868–69, 871.

11   Letter of 4 Februar 1799. See Karl-Heinz Hahn and others (eds), *Briefe an Goethe. Gesamtausgabe in Regestform,* 7 vols (Weimar: Böhlau, 1980–2004), vol. 3, p. 34.

summed up his review thus: 'Wir zweifeln, ob irgend eine deutsche Bühne eine Vorstellung dieser Dramen geben könne; die dem Dichter so genügen würde, wie die unsrige' (FA 4, 880).

It was not only in Berlin and Lauchstädt that censorship or fears of censorship affected performances. Kotzebue, at the time resident playwright at the Burgtheater in Vienna, entered into negotiations with Schiller to put on *Wallenstein*. He had already created rivalries at the theatre by bringing in new actors and seeming to neglect established ones and was finally in effect driven from his post in conservative Vienna by the mere rumour that he had Jacobin sympathies. Explaining the censor's reasons for opposing the production, he writes: 'Erst fand er das Sujet wegen des Hofes bedenklich, dann wegen der Familie Wallenstein, und endlich wegen des ganzen Publikums' (NA 36/I, 26–27). The work was not performed in Vienna until 1814.

Schiller's later dramas on the Weimar and Berlin stages

Maria Stuart

Even before *Wallensteins Tod* was premièred Schiller's mind was working on his next project, and from the start this next play was to be more suitable for the stage than *Wallenstein*. His study of the Greeks and his concern to create a lucid, linear action had certainly left their mark on the plot of *Wallenstein*, but, though originally intending to write a five-act play with a prologue, he had in the end combined those elements with epic breadth. The huge burden of work on that play once lifted, he still felt the challenge of classical simplicity and economy of means. In early April 1799 he was discussing Euripides with Goethe and others and ordering a translation of his plays from his publisher Cotta. On 26 April he wrote to Goethe of the Mary Stuart material: 'Besonders scheint er sich zu der Euripidischen Methode [...] zu qualifizieren, denn ich sehe eine

Möglichkeit, den ganzen Gerichtsgang zugleich mit allem politischen auf die Seite zu bringen, und die Tragödie mit der Verurtheilung anzufangen' (NA 30, 45). His luxuriant imagination still produced a play charged with action, one in which there are two centres of interest and two main characters – arguably a double tragedy. But from the start this was going to be a compact work suited to the needs of performance.

Schiller hoped also that he would be able to write quickly. The protracted and burdensome work on *Wallenstein* left him with a determination to find projects that could be finished, staged and earn him some money. After completing the preliminary work, he began writing *Maria Stuart* on 4 June 1799 and completed it in early June 1800, shortly before the première on 14 June. Other projects interrupted him, notably the translation and rehearsal of Shakespeare's *Macbeth*, first given on 14 May 1800, and before it his involvement in staging Goethe's translation of Voltaire's *Mahomet* on 30 January. Personal circumstances – his wife's serious illness following the birth of the couple's third child and the move to Weimar at the end of 1799 – intervened. While still at quite an early stage of work, in the autumn of 1799, he was already casting around for the next project, considering once again the *Maltheser* plan, for example, which he had toyed with in the 1780s and rejected in favour of *Wallenstein* in 1796. This restlessness was not only characteristic of his temperament but indicative of the immense release of creative energy following the completion of *Wallenstein*. He was pleased with his relative speed and wrote to Körner that 'bei zunehmender Uebung und größerer Sicherheit in der Ausführung'[12] he would be able to speed up to the point of being able to finish a play in six months.

Schiller took the main responsibility for rehearsing the company and began in May 1800, before the play was even finished. He then withdrew to the ducal palace at Ettersburg, accompanied only by his servant, to write the final act of the play in the second half of May. The première on 14 June was held to be a great success. The play was given thirty-six performances in Weimar up to the end of Goethe's directorship. There were two controversial moments, however, which

---

12   Letter of 28 July 1800 (NA 30, 181).

led to modifications in subsequent performances. The Weimar public was shocked by the physical ardour shown by Mortimer (played by Vohs) for Maria (played by Mad. Vohs) in Act 3. More importantly, it was shocked by the communion scene in Act 5, which was the subject of discussion even before the première. Carl August was informed that a communion scene was to be put on stage and on 10 June he wrote to Goethe asking him to ensure that nothing offensive should take place:

> Ich erinnere dich daran, weil ich der prudentia mimica externa Schilleri nicht recht traue. So ein braver Mann er sonsten ist, so ist doch leider die göttliche Unverschämtheit oder die unverschämte Göttlichkeit, nach Schlegelscher Terminologie, dergestalt zum Tone geworden, daß man sich mancherlei poetische Auswüchse erwarten kann, wenn es bei neueren Dichtungen darauf ankommt, einen Effekt, wenigstens, *einen sogenannten* hervorzubringen. (FA 5, 571–72)

It is a useful corrective to the subsequent association of Schiller with the staid theatrical tastes of the bourgeoisie to be reminded by Carl August's comments that he could be considered dangerously daring. The Duke must be thinking back to the playwright's early plays because *Wallenstein* observed a strict decorum, and the recent *Macbeth* adaptation toned down the earthier aspects of Shakespeare's play. Goethe wrote a tactful note to Schiller,[13] who would have known that the impetus came from the Duke, but, according to Genast, the playwright stood firm, though the scene was played only once as Schiller originally wrote it.[14] Thereafter, for lack of conclusive evidence, one assumes that in essentials the version of the scene recorded in the stage manuscripts sent out to other theatres (see below) was also played in Weimar.

---

13 See Goethe's letter to Schiller of 12 June 1800: 'Der kühne Gedancke, eine Communion aufs Theater zu bringen, ist schon ruchbar geworden, und ich werde veranlaßt Sie zu ersuchen diese Funcktion zu umgehen. Ich darf jetzt bekennen daß es mir selbst dabei nicht wohl zu Muthe war, und nun da man schon zum voraus dagegen protestirt, ist es in doppelter Betrachtung nicht räthlich' (NA 38/I, 269).

14 Genast writes: 'Herder besonders söll gegen diese Profanierung der Kirche protestirt haben; dennoch wurde sie dargestellt, aber nur einmal, denn das Publikum selbst erklärte sich dagegen' (Genast, vol. 1, p. 116).

The fact that Schiller wrote with performance clearly in mind from the start of work on *Maria Stuart* saved him the problem of retrospective adaptation, as he wrote to Goethe on 16 August 1799:

> Ich hoffe, daß in dieser Tragödie alles theatralisch seyn soll, ob ich sie gleich für den Zweck der Repræsentation etwas enger zusammen ziehe. Weil es auch *historisch* betrachtet ein reichhaltiger Stoff ist, so habe ich ihn, in historischer Hinsicht, auch etwas reicher behandelt und Motive aufgenommen, die den nachdenkenden und instruierten Leser freuen können, die aber bei der Vorstellung, wo ohnehin der Gegenstand sinnlich dasteht, nicht nöthig und wegen historischer Unkenntniß des großen Haufens auch ohne Interesse sind. Uebrigens ist bei der Arbeit selbst schon auf alles gerechnet, was für den theatralischen Gebrauch wegbleibt, und es ist durchaus keine eigene Mühe dazu nöthig wie beim Wallenstein. (NA 30, 85)

The printed text still takes precedence but he can now prepare for both publics simultaneously.

Three theatre manuscripts of the play, sent out to Hamburg, Leipzig/Dresden and Berlin, show how Schiller put his method of writing simultaneously for the stage and for the book version into practice. All three manuscripts contain virtually the same changes from the book version (published in April 1801).[15] Approximately 100 lines are cut from Act 1, principally from Maria's long exchange with Burleigh about the conduct and legality of her trial. In Act 2 Leicester's counter-argument to Burleigh's and Shrewsbury's concerning Maria's future is reduced. Burleigh's strong speech immediately preceding Elisabeth's monologue, in which he urges reason of state over individual conscience, was cut from the stage manuscripts, but in his letter to Iffland of 19 November 1800, before the Berlin première, Schiller states that the speech had been reinstated in the Weimar acting version and given with great effect. He encloses a copy for Iffland (NA 30, 211).

---

15 The *Nationalausgabe* (9, 340–41) states that it is not certain whether the Berlin manuscript, destroyed in World War 2, was the one sent by Schiller to Iffland or a later one made by the theatre. The changes to the theatre manuscripts, none of which survives, were reconstructed by the editors on the basis of changes preserved by handwritten entries in the book edition in the Cotta archive in the Deutsches Literaturarchiv, Marbach.

The most significant variations from the book version concern the confession and communion scene. In the stage versions Melvil does not reveal himself to be a priest already but rather vows to become one so that he can retrospectively fulfil the spirit of the office he has taken upon himself as Maria's confessor. His words of reassurance to Maria are:

Wenn mich dein Herz dafür erklärt, so bin ich
Für dich ein Priester [...]
Ein Sakrament ist jegliches Bekenntnis,
Das du der ewigen Wahrheit tust. Spricht doch
Im Beichtstuhl selbst der Mensch nur zu dem Menschen,
Es spricht der Sündige den Sünder frei;
Und eitel ist des Priesters Lösewort,
Wenn dich der Gott nicht lost in deinem Busen
[...]   diese Handlung
Hat volle Kraft, sobald du daran glaubst. (NA 9, 352)

Schiller seems to be aiming at a broader, less specifically Catholic vocabulary, and the consequence of the fact that Melvil is not yet a priest is that the words of absolution are omitted, as are the words with which he gives Maria the bread and wine. Thus the adaptation of Christian ritual is attenuated.

The fact that Schiller was unwilling to change the scene until there was incontrovertible evidence that people were offended suggests that he considered it vital to his artistic purpose and to his sense of the stage. Maria is assured through the confession and communion that God has forgiven her and that her death will seal that forgiveness. This belief gives her strength to meet her execution with sovereign composure. Schiller wanted this process to be presented to the audience in visible form. His wish to do so shows that, far from being irreligious, he actually understood the function of ritual as a psychological process for believers as well as recognizing its theatrical value as a method of making psychological realities visible to the observer.

In spite of the controversy Schiller was pleased with the performance. According to Genast the verse speaking was clearer than for *Wallenstein*, the actors having got used to Schiller's rhythms and language.[16] The role of Elisabeth was played by Caroline Jagemann, the young star of the company, an accomplished singer as well as an actress, who became the mistress of Duke Carl August and bore him three children. A native of Weimar, she had trained at Mannheim with Iffland. According to Amalie von Voigt, she brought to the role of the English queen a pride and authority that counterbalanced the character's vacillation and hypocrisy, thus dignifying the queen and creating a more complex contrast with Maria.[17] While Schiller appreciated individual talent, he, like Goethe, was concerned with successful ensemble playing. Warning Körner, who had not yet seen the play, about the guaranteed inferiority of any Leipzig production, he wrote: 'Unsere Gesellschaft ist in jedem Sinne beßer; nicht wegen einzelner hervorragender Talente, sondern wegen der hübschen Haltung und Uebereinstimmung des Ganzen' (NA 30, 168). The Lauchstädt première on 3 July 1800 was a huge success, such that there was lamentation when seats were sold out hours before the start. The orchestra was moved from the pit to the stage to create more space.[18]

Schiller sent the manuscript to Iffland in June 1800, telling him to use his discretion about how to handle the confession scene and making a number of suggestions for casting.[19] The Berlin première took place on 6 January 1801. It was the first performance of *Maria Stuart* not given by the Weimar company. The comparatively long interval between the arrival of the manuscript and the Berlin première may be attributable to the director's wish to save the play for the most profitable part of the year, which, according to his earlier letter concerning *Wallenstein*, was January and February (NA 37/I, 362). The play was well received, though, according to A. W. Schlegel, the production was not in general well cast, apart from the talented Friederike Unzelmann as Maria (see illustration), a role in which she

16   Genast, vol. 1, p. 115.
17   Quoted by Gertrud Rudloff-Hille, *Schiller auf der deutschen Bühne seiner Zeit* (Berlin and Weimar: Aufbau Verlag, 1969), p. 134. Somewhat surprisingly, Amalie von Voigt also claims that the quarrel scene did not work well, with Elisabeth triumphant and Maria humiliated
18   See the *Regisseur* Heinrich Becker's letter to Schiller, 7 July 1800 (NA 38/I, 284–85).
19   See his letter of 22 June 1800 (NA 30, 163–64).

became very popular with Berlin audiences, reprising her success during a *Gastspiel* in Weimar in 1801[20] Schiller had suggested Unzelmann for the role of Elisabeth and Louise Fleck for Maria. His reason for suggesting her for Elisabeth may have had to do with his concern that Elisabeth should be played by a young woman 'welche Ansprüche machen darf, so muß sie von einer Schauspielerin, welche Liebhaberinnen zu spielen pflegt, dargestellt werden' (NA 30, 164). Maria should be about twenty-five and Elisabeth about thirty, he explains, telling Iffland that Caroline Jagemann (in other words, someone young and attractive) had played the role in Weimar. Iffland, whom Schiller would have liked to see as Burleigh or Shrewsbury, opted for the role of Melvil. This choice reassured Schiller that the fifth act would be handled well, while Iffland himself perhaps felt that he would be wise to take control of that potentially controversial part of the performance. *Maria Stuart* became very popular with Berlin audiences and was given forty-seven times during Iffland's directorship.

Die Jungfrau von Orleans

Die Jungfrau von Orleans was Schiller's most popular play on stage during the first two decades of the nineteenth century. He completed his 'romantische Tragödie' only ten months after finishing *Maria Stuart*. It is much more demanding of theatrical resources than his previous play for it has numerous changes of set and a large cast, some of whom must do things such as sword-fighting (and that includes Johanna). Music has a prominent role and is integrated in the plot, for example in Act 4, Scene 1 as an accompaniment to Johanna's monologue, as she reflects on her altered state of mind at the coronation. There are stage effects such as thunderclaps and ghostly apparitions. Metrically, the play is more diverse than *Maria Stuart*, notably through the introduction of trimeter in Johanna's scene (2, 7)

---

20   See Schlegel's letter to Schiller of 5 May 1801 (NA 39/I, 64), in which he mentions that Iffland had stood down as Melvil after a few performances and that Fleck as Leicester was now ill.

199

with Montgomery and a variety of metres with rhyme in Johanna's coronation monologue.

On 18 April 1801 he wrote to Goethe: 'Hier sende ich Ihnen das verlangte Werk, nebst dem Entwurf der Rollenbesetzung. An dem Exemplar fürs Theater sind ohngefehr 6 Blätter weniger' (NA 31, 29). The casting plan is lost but it was obvious that Caroline Jagemann, as the leading young actress, would play the title role. Schiller had been very secretive about the subject of his new work, preferring not to be troubled by unsolicited advice or queries. Thus the play was finished by the time Duke Carl August heard about it. He approached Schiller via the writer's sister-in-law, Caroline von Wolzogen, explaining: 'Das Sujet ist äußerst scabrös, und einem Lächerlichen ausgesetzt, das schwer zu vermeiden sein wird, zumal bei Personen, die das Voltairsche Poëm fast auswendig wissen.'[21] Voltaire's *La Pucelle d'Orléans* (1762), with its scurrilous treatment of the material, is a reminder that Joan of Arc was not at that time the revered figure she became later in the nineteenth and twentieth centuries. The Duke asks Caroline von Wolzogen to pass on to Schiller his wish to see the play before it is published or performed in Weimar. He then goes on:

> So oft und dringend bat ich Schillern, ehe er Theaterstücke unternähme, mir, oder sonst jemandem, der das Theater einigermaßen kennt, die Gegenstände bekannt zu machen, die er behandeln wollte. So gern ich alsdann solche Materien mit ihm abgehandelt, und es würde ihm nützlich gewesen sein; aber alle mein Bitten war vergebens.[22]

The sensitivity betrayed by the tetchiness of this comment was provoked not simply by the subject matter but by the Duke's relationship with Caroline Jagemann. He was known to have fallen in love with her and most people assumed the liaison was already established. Carl August, not without justification, therefore feared that he and Jagemann would be exposed to ribald comment if she appeared in a role in which much is made of her virginity. Having asked for a copy of the work, he quickly changed his mind about the content,

21   *Literarischer Nachlaß der Frau Caroline von Wolzogen*, ed. by D. R. Hase, 2 vols (Leipzig: Breitkopf and Härtel, 1848/49), vol. 1, p. 452
22   *Nachlaß der Frau von Wolzogen*, vol. 1, p. 452.

praising the language, the blend of the sublime and the touching and the treatment of the supernatural: 'denn er hat auch gewußt eine Geschichte [...] dergestalt vergessen zu machen, daß *wir* auch nicht einen Augenblick nur [...] an Voltaires Pucelle dachten.'[23] But having praised the work to the skies, Carl August had to find another reason why it should not be performed, and his argument was that it is a poem not suitable for the limitations of the stage and particularly not for a small stage like Weimar's:

> Leid sollte es mir tun, wenn wir bei Aufführung eines wirklichen Meisterwerkes ungeduldig würden, u. das bloß, weil dieses Werk nicht an seinem rechten Orte steht, und die Wahrheit zu gestehen, Karoline ist mir zu lieb, als daß ich ihr schönes Talent u. Bemühen so zwecklos u. ihr nachteilig hier gezwungen sehen müßte.[24]

In his correspondence with Goethe at that point Schiller took a philosophical view of the setback, thinking of the time and effort the production would cost him, 'den Verlust der guten Stimmung nicht einmal gerechnet' (28 April 1801: NA 31, 32). He had sold it for publication to the Berlin publisher Unger for a large fee, a condition of that fee being that the play should not be performed before publication,[25] and so he was less concerned about income from theatre manuscripts, but later in the summer he wrote to Leopold von Seckendorff:

> Mein neues Stück ist noch gar nicht in Weimar gespielt worden. Verschiedene theatralische Zänkereien und andere verwickelte Verhältniße haben mich in den lezten Monaten des hiesigen Theaterjahrs von dem Schauspielwesen ganz abgezogen. (NA 31, 55)

However mediocre he thought the ensemble to be, it was disappointing not to have the play performed. It was also a disappointment for the Weimar theatre, which was deprived of the world première of a guaranteed success. In November 1801 Schiller hoped a performance might be possible if the Berlin actress Friederike Unzelmann, who had

---

23   *Nachlaß der Frau von Wolzogen*, vol. 1, p. 455.
24   *Nachlaß der Frau von Wolzogen*, vol. 1, pp. 455–56.
25   Unger later retreated from this position and the Leipzig première preceded publication (in October 1801) by about a month; see NA 39/I, 88.

been sorry not to be cast as Johanna in the Berlin production, would make a guest appearance in Weimar, play the role and so solve the Jagemann problem (NA 31, 73). In 1802 another possible solution was mooted: the play could be given at Lauchstädt during the summer season. Because Jagemann was not contracted to play the summer seasons the role would have to be given to another, namely Mad. Vohs, who would then retain it. Carl August did not object, as long as Jagemann was kept out of any preceding rehearsals.[26] That plan also failed and the play was eventually premièred in Weimar on 23 April 1803, during a momentous spring that also saw the premières of *Die Braut von Messina* and Goethe's *Die natürliche Tochter*. By that time it had established itself to great acclaim elsewhere and the Jagemann issue had slipped into the background.

The première of *Die Jungfrau von Orleans* took place therefore not in Weimar but in Leipzig on 11 September 1801. Schiller himself attended the third performance on 17 September. To judge from the report in the *Journal des Luxus und der Moden*, the success of the production was reduced by limited resources that resulted in a failure to realize well the battle and crowd scenes.[27] Schiller himself seems not to have impressed by it, writing to his Leipzig publisher Göschen: 'ich darf hoffen, daß das ruhige Lesen des unverstümmelten Werkes selbst um so reiner auf Sie wirken werde; denn durch die Repräsentation ist freilich vieles, sehr vieles entstellt und herabgestimmt worden' (NA 31, 64). The audience none the less greeted the play and its author with enthusiasm.

The Berlin production is probably the best known of all Iffland's Schiller productions. The première took place on 23 November 1801 and the play was given thirteen times up to the end of 1801, being the last to be performed in the old theatre on the Gendarmenmarkt on 31 December. On 1 January 1802 a new *Nationaltheater* designed by Carl Gotthard Langhans, who also built the Brandenburg Gate, was opened. The production was marked by its emphasis on stage effects,

---

26 Wahl, vol. 1, p. 301.
27 See Julius W. Braun, *Schiller und Goethe im Urtheil ihrer Zeitgenossen. Zeitungskritiken, Berichte und Notizen*, 3 vols (Leipzig: Schlicke, 1882), vol. 1, p. 97.

achieved by employing a large number of extras, lavish costumes and grandiose sets, most notably for the coronation procession. It was a huge success, and by the time Iffland died it had been performed 137 times at the theatre, by a long way the most performed play in this period.[28] The next most performed plays were Kotzebue's *Die Unglücklichen* and *Die deutschen Kleinstädter* with sixty-four performances each. Schiller had suggested Friederike Unzelmann to Iffland as suitable for the title role. Her very petiteness, he argued, was an advantage: 'Die kleine Figur, welche die größte Einwendung dagegen scheint, hat bei Johanna […] nicht so viel zu bedeuten, weil sie nicht durch körperliche Stärke, sondern durch übernatürliche Mittel im Kampf überwindet' (NA 31, 56). Iffland had not been convinced and gave the part to Henriette Meyer, an altogether more statuesque figure. This casting in such an influential production, argues Rudloff-Hille, created a false image of the title figure that was to endure on stage and in the imagination throughout the nineteenth century.[29]

The acclaim was not universal. The political writer and diplomat Friedrich von Gentz (1764–1832) wrote Schiller a detailed letter[30] complaining about the inadequacies of the Berlin production, claiming that Henriette Meyer as Johanna had coped well with the more tender scenes but not with the authoritative and monumental ones. He reported that the acting had been poor, with the exception of Iffland himself, who played Bertrand but stepped down after the first few performances. Gentz also complains that the play had not been saved for the opening of the new theatre, which instead was opened with a performance of Kotzebue's drama *Die Kreuzfahrer*, to general dissatisfaction: 'Auch ist die Indignation, selbst in unserm Prinzipien- und Charakterlosen Publikum, allgemein' (NA 39/I, 162). Given the instant popularity of *Die Jungfrau von Orleans*, Iffland probably estimated rightly that he could make money from it straight away and only increase the takings when the play transferred to the more spacious stage of the new theatre. Indeed a new production was created for it,

---

28 Fetting, *Das Repertoire des Berliner Königlichen Nationaltheaters*, Appendix, p. 70.
29 Rudloff-Hille, p. 143.
30 NA 39/I, 157–63.

the *Journal des Luxus und der Moden* commenting positively on the costumes and sets.[31] Schiller possibly felt that visual effect was over-emphasized in the production, to the detriment of the play's poetic qualities, allegedly saying to Iffland on seeing it on his visit to Berlin in 1804: 'Sie erdrücken mir ja mein Stück mit dem prächtigen Einzug!' (NA 42, 385).[32]

When the play was at last premièred in Weimar, resources were much more limited than in Berlin. Genast recalls the difficulty of persuading the theatre's financial overseer Kirms to provide a cloak with a train lavish enough for the coronation procession:

> Der Krönungsmantel war aber hauptsächlich der Stein des Anstosses; dieser enormen Ausgabe widerstrebte Kirms, und da er Chef über alle Vorräthe der Hofhaltung war, suchte er zu diesem Zweck eine alte blauseidene Gardine hervor. Dagegen protestirten aber Schiller und Goethe auf das bestimmteste, so, dass sich schliesslich der gute Kirms fügen und, wenn auch mit verdrießlichem Gesicht, seine Zustimmung zur Anschaffung eines rothen Krönungsmantels, versteht sich, von unechtem Sammet, geben mußte, der von nun an, wie in früheren Zeiten das Brautkleid einer Grossmutter, von König zu König forterbte. Er wurde das einzige kostbare Stück, welches die weimarische Hoftheatergarderobe aufzuweisen hatte.[33]

Johanna was played by Amalie Miller-Malcolmi. The famous drawing of her in the role by Ferdinand Jagemann, which emphasizes her gentleness, suggests a strong contrast with the more heroic Johanna in the Berlin production. Schiller was heavily involved with the Weimar rehearsals and, as he later told Körner, was satisfied with the result:

> das Stück ist [...] scharmant gegangen und hat einen ganz ungewöhnlichen Erfolg gehabt. Alles ist davon electrisiert worden. Ich wünschte, Ihr hättet es mit angesehen. Denn ob wir gleich keine großen Talente bei unserm Theater haben, so störte doch nichts, und das Ganze kam zum Vorschein. (NA 32, 36)

---

31   See BA 4, 856.
32   Other reported comments by Schiller in a similar vein are recorded in entries 896–98 in NA 42, *Schillers Gespräche*, for example 'Wegen des Rahmens sieht man das Bild kaum!' (896). See also entry 893, p. 384.
33   Genast, vol. 1, p. 140.

In writing *Die Braut von Messina* Schiller departed from the usual practice of his later plays by opting for an invented plot instead of using historical material. The project gave him the opportunity to try out the device of a chorus, an idea he had entertained since the compositional difficulties exposed by *Don Karlos* first made him turn to Greek drama. His plan for *Die Maltheser*, conceived in 1788, was to include a chorus. *Die Braut von Messina* can therefore be seen as the culmination of years of wrestling with the problems of dramatic form and the classical tradition of tragedy, earlier results of which were seen in *Wallenstein* and *Maria Stuart*. After allowing himself a certain epic breadth in *Wallenstein* and in *Die Jungfrau von Orleans* he now wanted to construct a plot of utmost simplicity, writing to Goethe: 'auch ist es eine dankbarere und erfreulichere Aufgabe, einen einfachen Stoff reich und gehaltvoll zu machen, als einen zu reichen oder zu breiten Gegenstand einzuschränken' (NA 31, 157). By using not a single chorus but two choruses he of course departs from the classical model, as he does also from classical metres.

He began writing in earnest in September 1802 and aimed originally to finish in time for the play to be performed for the Duchess's birthday on 30 January. In the event, he finished in February 1803 and the première took place on 19 March. Goethe took responsibility for the production. Reading rehearsals and eight stage rehearsals took four weeks. Before the première Schiller was doubtful about the play's reception on stage, fearing that it overstretched audience and actors:

> Für das Theater möchte es aber keine Speculation seyn und am wenigsten für das eurige, weil man da aufs Poetische gar nicht eingerichtet ist. Die Handlung wird zwar theatralisch genug seyn aber die Ausführung ist durchaus zu lyrisch für den gemeinen Zweck und, ich darf mit gutem Gewißen hinzusetzen, für das Talent gemeiner Schauspieler zu antic. (NA 32, 1)

These words were written to Körner with the Leipzig and Dresden theatres in mind but reflect a general unease about his experiment as a theatrical venture. Nevertheless, a reading of the work requested by the visiting Duke of Meiningen gave him more confidence in its performability. By then he had come to the conclusion that the lines spoken by the chorus would have to be redistributed over five or six individuals, rather than spoken in unison by the whole chorus or by one or other of the two divided choruses. Duke Carl August proposed this distribution, having asked Schiller to send him the manuscript after the reading arranged for the Duke of Meiningen.[34] Carl August was not sympathetic to the experiment, being himself still an adherent of the French neo-classical style, for which Goethe, in spite of his adaptations of Voltaire's *Mahomet* and *Tancred* for Weimar, and Schiller had shown relatively little sympathy. To Goethe the Duke wrote of the chorus: 'Um die lästigen Confidents zu verbannen, ist, dünckt mir, ein viel lästigeres Verbannungs Mittel eingetreten [...] Das Zugleichreden der Coryphéen, oder der Wachtmeisters des Corps habe ich schon gesucht Schillern auszureden' (NA 10, 357).

Genast suggests that the experience of rehearsal strengthened Schiller's doubts about a declamation in unison and also records how difficult the actors found his rhythms:

> Die Trochäen, Daktylen, Spondeen etc. machten den Schauspielern viel zu schaffen. Erst war es die Absicht Schiller's, selbst die größeren Reden des Chors unisono sprechen zu lassen; er überzeugte sich aber sehr bald, daß dadurch eine sehr große Undeutlichkeit fühlbar wurde und daß der strenge Rhythmus durchaus nicht eingehalten werden konnte.[35]

The pains Goethe took over the rehearsal of the chorus are also recorded by the musician Karl Eberwein (1786–1868): 'Schillers Braut von Messina ward mit großem Fleiß einstudirt. Sehr ergötzlich war es, den Geheimrath zu sehen, wie er gleich einem Capellmeister mit der Hand das Tempo und den Rythmus der Chöre marquirte.'[36] Schiller hoped that the chorus would be at least partly accompanied by music and tried to win over the Berlin composer Carl Friedrich Zelter (1758–1832) to the task. Zelter, however, shied away from it, while paying tribute to the care taken at Weimar over proper declamation:

---

34 See his letter to Goethe of 11 February 1803, quoted in NA 10, 357–58.
35 Genast, vol.1, p. 133.
36 See Ernst and Renate Grumach, *Goethe. Begegnungen und Gespräche* (Berlin: de Gruyter, 1965–), vol. 5, p. 322.

Jetzt kann ich nicht deutlich sein, weil ich wirklich noch selber nicht weis, wie sich diese Idee realisiren lassen wird. Aber das neue Genre könte eine Schule werden für die Recitation der Schauspieler [...] Es wäre nur, nach unendlichen Versuchen, auf einem Theater möglich wie das Ihrige ist. (NA 40/I, 35)

Schiller did not pursue the matter.

Goethe's commitment to the production must have encouraged Schiller, who had been downcast during the winter as a result of his friend's withdrawn behaviour (in part the effect of poor health), so much so that he considered leaving Weimar.[37] Yet no play of his brought him closer to Goethe's concept of staging than *Die Braut von Messina* because it demands visual as well as acoustic harmony. The well-known painting by Friedrich Matthäi (see illustration) suggests the symmetry of the arrangement of the two choruses to left and right of the group of main characters in the centre. The gestures of the members of each chorus are unified and contrasting. It is not surprising that *Die Braut von Messina* was staged at about the same time as Goethe was giving instruction to young actors that was later formalized into the *Regeln für Schauspieler* and lays such emphasis on declamation and on harmonious movement.

Both Goethe and Schiller seem to have been pleased with the première. Schiller wrote a letter of sincere appreciation to Genast, the *Wöchner* for the performance.[38] It was eagerly anticipated by the audience. The theatre was full by 4pm. Thirty-two carriages of Jena students arrived and their enthusiastic 'Vivat!' to Schiller after the performance provoked ducal censure. Opinion was very divided about the play's success. As Schiller wrote to Körner, 'Ueber den Chor und das vorwaltend lyrische in dem Stücke sind die Stimmen natürlich sehr getheilt, da noch ein großer Theil des ganzen Deutschen Publicums seine prosaischen Begriff von dem *Natürlichen* in einem Dichterwerk nicht ablegen kann' (NA 32, 25). Of all

---

37   See his letter to Humboldt of 17 February 1803, NA 32, 11–13 (p. 12).

38   See his letter of 20 March 1803: 'Die gestrige Vorstellung ist im Einzelnen und im Ganzen so schön gegangen, daß ich der sämmtlichen Gesellschaft meinen achtungsvollsten Dank bezeugen muß' (NA 32, 23). The *Wöchner* was the actor, one of a team of three, who had responsibility on a weekly rota basis for conducting rehearsals.

Schiller's plays it is the one least performed today. Yet it maintained a firm place in the Weimar repertoire during Goethe's directorship, with a total of twenty-seven performances up to 1817.[39] The pains taken over the verse speaking, combined with an undeniably arresting plot, made it a showcase for the Weimar style and talents, but it was also widely played elsewhere.[40]

The Berlin première on 14 June 1803 was considered a triumph by the exultant Iffland:

> Am 14 und 16 ward die Braut von Meßina mit Würde, Pracht und Bestimtheit gegeben. Gegenfüßler? etliche! Totaleffekt? Der höchste, tiefste, ehrwürdigste! Die Chöre wurden meisterhaft gesprochen und senkten wie ein Wetter sich über das Land! (NA 40/I, 78)

Though Schiller took such extravagance with a pinch of salt, he was gratified by the success. The *Voßische Zeitung* carried a review of the first two performances: 'Die gesprochenen Chöre machten zum Theil eine herrliche Wirkung, nämlich da, wo sie das Schicksal aussprachen, oder eine allgemeine Empfindung.' The leading actors are also commended.[41] Zelter wrote to Goethe testifying to the play's impact and the audience's enthusiasm and expressing his surprise that everyday fare could give way to something so much more elevated:

> Wenn ich bedenke, daß unsere Truppe Jahr aus Jahr ein tag täglich sich mit den sogennanten Hausmannsstücken, mit dem Studium des ordinairen, leichtfaßlichen, familiären Wesens tummeln müssen [...] so gestehe ich meine Verwunderung: wie sie sich so geschickt anzustellen verstehn und Schiller selbst würde nicht mit den einzelnen Teilen unzufrieden sein. (MA 20.1, 39)

---

39 Burkhardt, p. 121.

40 In addition to Weimar and Berlin, NA, 10 mentions productions between 1803 and 1806 in Hamburg, Erfurt, Magdeburg, Kassel, Stuttgart, Leipzig and Dresden (NA 10, 362–63). The play was performed at the Berlin National Theatre 113 times up to 1885 (see Schäffer and Hartmann, p. 11), which indicates a lasting popularity, and at the Vienna Burgtheater 152 times up to 1937; see Minna von Alth (ed. for the Österreichischer Bundestheaterverband), *Burgtheater 1776–1976. Aufführungen und Besetzungen von zweihundert Jahren*, 2 vols (Vienna: Ueberreuter, 1979), vol. 2, p. 59.

41 Reviews of 16 and 18 June 1803: see Klaus Gerlach: Datenbank Berliner Nationaltheater (http://zopeman.bbaw.de/BK/theater).

He reports that the chorus spoke in unison, occasionally given the beat by Iffland as Bohemund: 'Diejenigen Stellen welche glücklich mit dem Takte zutreffen, sind von großer Wirkung' (MA 20.1, 40). The play's success in Berlin was not just a flash in the pan, for there were thirty-six performances during Iffland's time as director, making it the third most performed Schiller play at the *Nationaltheater* after *Die Jungfrau von Orleans* and *Maria Stuart*.[42]

For the printed version of the play Schiller wrote the prefatory essay 'Über den Gebrauch des Chors in der Tragödie'. In fact, an element such as a chorus is easier for a reader to accept than a spectator, so the essay must have been written more as a programmatic statement about performance, in which Schiller could expound the anti-naturalistic approach within a philosophically founded statement of aesthetic theory. But while making strong statements in print in defence of his dramatic experiment, in practice Schiller knew it was time to try something new. Writing to Iffland about *Die Braut von Messina* he first defends lyrical drama but then goes on: 'Uebrigens aber werde ich es vor der Hand dabei bewenden lassen, da Einer allein nun einmal nicht hinreicht, den Krieg mit der ganzen Welt aufzunehmen' (NA 32, 32). In treating the Tell legends he was consciously turning to a more accessible and popular theme and style.

Wilhelm Tell

'Ein rechtes Stück für das *ganze Publikum* verspreche ich Ihnen' (NA 32, 84), he wrote to Iffland on 9 November 1803 of *Wilhelm Tell*. In July of that year Iffland wrote Schiller a long letter explaining his financial and other practical constraints as director of the Berlin theatre and offered him eighty Friedrichsd'or for the exclusive rights for the first three months to stage a play 'von der inneren und äußeren Wirkung des Mädchens von Orleans' (NA 40/I, 99). From an early stage of work Schiller seems to have been committed to giving the play to Iffland for its première, confirming this to the impatient director on 23

---

42   See Fetting, *Das Repertoire des Berliner Königlichen Nationaltheaters*, Appendix, p. 70.

January 1804, when the latter had read an erroneous newspaper report claiming the play would be given its first performance to celebrate the Duchess's birthday in Weimar on 30 January: 'Für Berlin und Sie war das Stück zunächst bestimmt, und soll auch dort zuerst auf die Bühne treten' (NA 32, 103). Iffland's insistent letters through the autumn of 1803 and spring of 1804 forced Schiller not only to keep being precise about his timetable for completion but also to think ahead about the practicalities of staging.

Schiller probably intended *Wilhelm Tell* to be premièred in Berlin for a number of reasons, chief of which was the obligation he felt towards Iffland for the success of the productions of his plays, particularly of *Die Braut von Messina*. The playwright later referred to *Wilhelm Tell* as a 'Seitenschritt' (see below, p. 216), as though he could be accused of pandering to popular taste and was not altogether comfortable with that thought. Iffland's July 1803 letter made Schiller aware of the constraints on him as a man of business:

> Wie ich mich des Ödip, des Tell freue! das werden Sie mir zutrauen. Ödip [wird] für die Auserwählten [sein], Tell für *Alle*. Um das letztere ist es mir zu thun. Nicht bloß als Kaufmann, auch aus anderen Gründen. Ion, Regulus, Coriolan, werden geachtet. Eugenie wird von einer kleinen Zahl angebetet – das Lustspiel sinkt, die Oper – wenn sie nicht das Zauberreich darstellt […] greifft nicht. Das leztere ist selten, das Erstere kostet, wenn nicht mehr, doch so viel, als es trägt. Die Versstücke, welche nicht für das große Volck sind, nehmen im Einlernen mehr als die doppelte Zeit, die ein anderes Stück fordert, die Schauspieler, wenn sie mit Kraft etwas würken sollen, müßen vor- und nachher geschont werden – Hier aber *muß* alle Tage gespielt werden […] Nicht also was ich fühle darf ich wollen […] Da wir bei der Braut von Meßina *nicht* verlohren haben, da dieses Werck *stets* auf dem Repertoir bleiben wird, darf ich um so unbefangener von meiner Lage zu Ihnen reden.(NA 40/I, 98)

The première of *Wilhelm Tell* might therefore be a sort of gesture of thanks to Iffland for the pains he had taken, especially in putting on verse plays, for Berlin acting was much less stylized than Weimar acting and so verse speaking required a particular effort. Of course, the benefits were not one-sided; Iffland knew he had almost guaranteed long-term successes in Schiller's plays. Plays that could stay in the repertoire, draw an audience year upon year and help establish the theatre's reputation were like gold dust. Harnessing the prestige of Goethe and Schiller was also an important part of the cultural politics of Iffland's directorship. A further factor in Schiller's thinking may have been the awareness that *Wilhelm Tell* would stretch the resources of the Weimar theatre to the limit, for the play demands many scene changes, visually striking sets, music, stage effects and a large cast.

In spite of Iffland's strenuous efforts, *Wilhelm Tell* was not in fact premièred in Berlin but at the Weimar theatre. Perhaps Schiller foresaw too much delay in the Berlin production, which would set back the lucrative publication of the work. Possibly he feared problems there with the political resonances of the play and wanted to enjoy the comparative freedom Weimar gave him to have it staged as he wrote it and to try it out for length, which caused a problem in the early performances, before other theatres attempted it. What is instructive is to see the differences between the two productions.

In his *Tag- und Jahreshefte* Goethe tells us that Schiller determined the casting and that both shared in the rehearsal work.[43] In fact, Schiller was unwell for some time during rehearsals and much was left to Goethe. The first reading rehearsal indicated a problem that was still not solved by the première, that of length, for it began at 4pm and ended at 11 and still covered only the first three acts. During rehearsal Goethe also approached Schiller with what he saw as inadequate motivation for the central scene of the play, Gessler's command to Tell to shoot the apple off his son's head. In response, Schiller inserted Walter Tell's innocent boast to the *Landvogt* that his father could shoot an apple from a tree at a hundred paces, so prompting the trial Gessler sets Tell.[44]

The production had to be kept within the modest means of the theatre. Goethe records:

> auch suchten wir in Costüm und Dekoration nur mäßig, wiewohl schicklich und charakteristisch, zu verfahren, wobei, wie immer, mit unsern ökonomischen

43   See also Schiller's letter to Goethe of 19 Feb. 1804 (NA 32, 110).
44   See Goethe's comments to Eckermann, 15 January 1825 (MA 19, 130).

Kräften die Überzeugung zusammentraf, daß man mit allem Äußern mäßig ver-
fahren, hingegen das Innere, Geistige so hoch als möglich steigern müsse.[45]

Although the actors were stretched to cover the many speaking parts,
no-one had to take on more than three minor ones. On 24 March
Schiller wrote to two directors, Jakob Herzfeld in Hamburg and Karl
Schwarz in Breslau, who planned to stage the play. He enclosed in
each a list of suggestions for minor roles that could be played by the
same actor and stressed the importance of the crowd scenes: 'Hier in
Weimar haben wir mit 17. Schauspielern 30 männliche Rollen besezt,
ohne daß es nöthig gewesen wäre, die Hauptrollen zu duplieren [...]
Auf ein geschicktes Arrangement der Volksscenen kommt das Meiste
an' (To Herzfeld, NA 32, 117). To Schwarz he emphasized how important not just the secondary roles are but also small ones such as
Gertrud, Baumgarten, Armgard and Parricida. Tell he describes thus:
'eine edle Simplicität, eine ruhige, gehaltene Kraft ist der Charakter;
mithin wenige, aber bedeutende Gestikulation, ein gelassenes Spiel,
Nachdruck ohne Heftigkeit, durchaus eine schlichte Manneswürde'
(NA 32, 118). Though Tell is clearly the linchpin, the play's effect
depends in Schiller's eyes on ensemble playing and any virtuoso
attention-seeking on the part of the actor playing the title role must be
avoided. The costumes, he suggests, should be medieval and could
include the characteristic Swiss *Pumphose*.

The Weimar première, on 17 March 1804, was a great success,
greater than that of any of Schiller's plays, as he told Körner, adding
modestly: 'Ich fühle, daß ich nach und nach des theatralischen mäch-
tig werde.'[46] Haide as Tell was singled out for praise by the *Zeitung
für die elegante Welt*.[47] It was, however, a very long performance,
lasting five and a half hours. Given that all the seats were occupied by
the middle of the afternoon, this was quite a marathon, and the playwright immediately set to work to make cuts. The play was given with
the controversial Parricida scene and from the first the final act was
held by some to be unnecessary. Schiller agreed to its removal for one

---

45   *Tag- und Jahreshefte*, 1–17 March 1804 (MA 14, 126).
46   Letter of 12 April, 1804, NA 32, 123.
47   Braun, vol. 3, p. 379.

performance in Weimar, in December 1804, not because he believed it was superfluous but because the new wife of Carl August's elder son and heir, Maria Paulowna, was the niece of Csar Paul I of Russia, who had been assassinated in 1801.[48]

From the start the Berlin production was going to be much more lavish than the Weimar one. Iffland was sent the manuscript in March 1804 but delays followed. On the basis of the curtness of his acknowledgement of the manuscript's safe arrival, coupled with the delay in putting the play on, Schmieden has suggested that Iffland wanted to show Schiller his displeasure at the fact that the première had taken place in Weimar after all.[49] Another interpretation is that Iffland had genuine concerns about the political implications and language of the play, which became clearer to him when he had the whole of the manuscript. He sent the secretary of the Berlin theatre, Pauly, to Weimar to discuss various matters concerning the Berlin production, preparing the way with a letter that has a very cloak-and-dagger air: 'Es soll *hier* Niemand wißen, daß und weshalb er geht. Es muß, dünckt mich in *Weimar* Niemand wißen weshalb er dort ist […] Das Uebrige was sich nicht schreiben läßt, durch Herrn Pauli mündlich' (NA 40/I, 196). Iffland's emissary brought a lengthy list of questions, ranging from simple practicalities of staging, such as '*Muß* Stauffachers Haus *sichtbar* seyn' (NA 10, 452), to much more fundamental concerns about the play's possible political resonances.[50] Three passages in particular gave Iffland concern: Stauffacher's Rütli speech beginning 'Nein, eine Grenze hat Tyrannenmacht', Tell's conversation with his son about the contrast of life in the mountains and life in the town (lines 1800–1810) and Attinghausen's dying vision of

---

48   Schiller offered the manuscript of that Weimar performance to Dresden through Körner: 'Kannst Du diese Sache negotieren, versteht sich ohne mich anzubieten, so ist mirs lieb, und ihr entgeht doch wenigstens einer verstümmelten Vorstellung des Stücks.' (Letter of 10 December 1804, NA 32, 173). Though he insisted on the retention of the Parricida scene for Berlin in July, by October the play had appeared in print and so could be freely adapted by any stage.

49   Alfred Schmieden, *Die bühnengerechten Einrichtungen der Schillerschen Dramen für das Königliche Nationaltheater zu Berlin. Erster Teil. Wilhelm Tell* (Berlin: Fleischel, 1906), pp. 14–15.

50   The full list of questions with Schiller's answers is printed in NA 10, 452–60.

future conflict and change (lines 2430–51). Iffland felt that Stauffacher's appeal to 'ewige Rechte' and the right to act upon them in an extreme situation recalled the rhetoric of the French Revolution in such a way as to lay Schiller open to the charge of using the stage to inflame the people:

> diese im hohen, schönen Schwunge dargestellten Menschenrechte, mahnen an eine mißverstandene, die Europa leiden machten. *Will* der Dichter einen Pöbel – wie jede *so* große Volcksmaße ihn hat, zu einem tumultuarischen Aufjauchzen reizen?? Dieses – mit dem was nachkommt – könnte einen Effect machen, den der Dichter nicht will und den ich nicht wünschen kann. (NA 10, 454)

Stauffacher's words certainly do indicate a concept of rights akin to that of the Enlightenment. In other words, Schiller is going beyond the historical framework of the play to a mythical representation of the development of the notion of universal rights. Iffland also stresses the difference between the Weimar and Berlin theatres. In Weimar, a small theatre, every performance is under the proximate eye of the court and this circumstance guarantees decorum in the audience that cannot at all be guaranteed in Berlin: 'Ein Duzend politischer Renomisten können Momente der Widrigkeit veranlaßen, die mit falschem Schein den Stempel einer Aeußerung des Publicums tragen' (NA 10, 459). Schiller was willing to go only so far, writing to the director:

> wenn man einmal ein solches Sujet, wie der Wilhelm Tell ist, gewählt hat, so muß man nothwendig gewisse Saiten berühren, welche nicht jedem gut ins Ohr klingen. Können die Stellen, wie sie jetzt lauten, auf einem Theater nicht gesprochen werden, so kann auf diesem Theater der Tell überhaupt nicht gespielt werden, denn seine ganze Tendenz so unschuldig und rechtlich sie ist müßte Anstoß erregen. (NA 32, 123–24)

He replaced Stauffacher's original lines with:

> Nein, eine Grenze hat Tyrannenmacht,
> Wenn es zum lezten, äusersten gekommen,
> Wenn rohe Willkür alles Recht zertritt,
> Wenn kein Gesetz mehr hilft, dann hilft Natur,
> Das altererbte dürfen wir beschützen
> Gegen Gewalt   (NA 32, 124)

Although the words 'seine ewgen Rechte' are removed, the appeal to nature remains but is linked to tradition ('Das altererbte dürfen wir beschützen'), so arguably Schiller has sacrificed what in Stauffacher's speech seemed to point to a modern concept of rights and emphasized instead the conservative aspects of his standpoint. In the case of Tell's exchange with his son, in which he explains that in the town life of the valley the land belongs to the bishop and the king, no adjustment could be made and the passage was removed. In Attinghausen's speech the lines 'Es bricht die Macht/ Der Könige sich an ihren ewgen Wällen' and 'des Adels Blüthe fällt,/ Es hebt die Freiheit siegend ihre Fahne' were cut. Any mention of kings was dangerous and Schiller complied.[51]

Where he would not compromise was over doubts about Tell's monologue (which Iffland held to be too long) and the Parricida scene (which he felt put Tell in a negative light and was a distraction). In response Schiller made the much-quoted comment:

Parricidas Erscheining ist der Schlußstein des Ganzen. Tells Mordthat wird durch ihn allein moralisch und poetisch aufgelößt. Neben dem ruchlosen Mord aus Impietaet und Ehrsucht steht nunmehr Tells nothgedrungene That, sie erscheint schuldlos in der Zusammenstellung mit einem ihr so ganz unähnlichen Gegenstück, und die Hauptidee des ganzen Stücks wird eben dadurch ausgesprochen, nehmlich: "Das Nothwendige und Rechtliche der Selbsthilfe in einem streng bestimmten Fall." (NA 10, 458)

Given that critical voices after the Weimar première had already questioned the necessity for the Parricida scene, Schiller was clearly convinced that both it and Tell's monologue were integral to the play's meaning and claimed Goethe's support for his view:

Der Casus gehört vor das poetische Forum und darüber kann ich keinen höheren Richter als mein Gefühl erkennen. Auch Goethe ist mit mir überzeugt, daß ohne jenen Monolog und ohne die persönliche Erscheinung des Parricida der Tell sich gar nicht hätte denken lassen. (NA 32, 124)

---

51   Further cuts were lines 1290–1314, 2000–02, 2016–2020, 2119–26, 3035–40, 3059–63 (NA 10, 450).

Schiller was trying in the play to reconcile elements of the popular *Volksstück*, featuring typical aspects of regional life and attitudes in a non-tragic framework, with his own characteristic concern for questions of decision and responsibility. His central figure is forced out of his normal sphere and made to confront moral issues of a complexity to which he is unused. Arguably, Schiller did not find a perfect solution to the problem of blending these ingredients but by including the Parricida scene he ensures that the audience examines the central question of assassination. Iffland had no choice but to accept Schiller's ruling on the monologue and the Parricida scene, and preparations proceeded. As early as 16 January Schiller had approached the composer Zelter to compose some opening music incorporating the sound of cow bells but his letter went astray[52] and so he turned to Bernhard Anselm Weber, musical director at the theatre and older half-brother of the more famous Carl Maria, who took up the suggestion and whose resulting score was much praised. The Berlin première was on 4 July 1804 with Iffland in the title role. Both production and play received mixed reviews. The *Berlinische Nachrichten von Staats- und gelehrten Sachen* was enthusiastic. *Der Freimüthige* praised the monologue, saw the Parricida scene as a postlude and claimed the play was underrehearsed. The *Königlich priviligierte Zeitung* complained that that Tell was not a unified character, that Gessler was too much a villain and that there were only two good scenes, the meeting of Stauffacher, Fürst and Melchtal in Act 1, 4 and the apple shooting scene.[53] The play was nevertheless so popular that it was repeated a further five times during the first fortnight.[54]

Though again gratified by the play's success, in a letter to Wilhelm von Humboldt Schiller writes of *Wilhelm Tell*:

Noch hoffe ich in meinem poetischen Streben keinen Rückschritt gethan zu haben, einen Seitenschritt vielleicht, indem es mir begegnet seyn kann, den materiellen Foderungen der Welt und der Zeit etwas eingeräumt zu haben. Die Werke des dramatischen Dichters werden schneller als alle andre von dem Zeitstrom ergriffen, er kommt selbst wider Willen mit der großen Masse in eine

---

52   See NA 40/II, 266.
53   For all these reviews see Braun, vol. 3, pp. 380–91.
54   Gero von Wilpert, *Schiller-Chronik* (Stuttgart: Kröner, 1958), 302.

vielseitige Berührung, bei der man nicht immer rein bleibt. Anfangs gefällt es, den Herrscher zu machen über die Gemüther, aber welchem Herrscher begegnet es nicht, daß er auch wieder der Diener seiner Diener wird, um seine Herrschaft zu behaupten. Und so kann es leicht geschehen seyn, daß ich, indem ich die deutschen Bühnen mit dem Geräusch meiner Stücke erfüllte, auch von den deutschen Bühnen etwas angenommen haben. (NA 32, 206)

This comment sums up the enduring conflict Schiller felt between poetic truth on the one hand and the demands of theatrical effectiveness and public success on the other. Certainly his next project, the unfinished *Demetrius*, has an uncompromisingly tragic plot, so there is no doubt that when he died Schiller was returning to the genre in which he excelled. The extant scenes show his characteristic flair for intense dialogue and well-orchestrated public show.

The work of adaptation

Goethe did not regard the Weimar theatre primarily as an opportunity to see his own existing plays performed or to write new ones for immediate staging. His invitation to Schiller to adapt *Egmont* was thus for him, at that point in the theatre's history, an unusual move. When the theatre experiment with Schiller got under way with *Wallenstein*, however, both men acutely felt the lack of plays that would help the ensemble to develop a distinctive style. In particular they lacked verse plays, for one of the greatest challenges facing the Weimar company was the improvement of their verse speaking.

Encouraged perhaps by the evidence of classical influence in *Wallenstein*, Duke Carl August suggested to Goethe a performance of Voltaire's *Mahomet* for the Duchess's birthday on 30 January 1800. Goethe produced a blank verse translation, publishing some scenes in his art journal *Die Propyläen* as a way of preparing the audience for the performance. In his preface he expresses the hope that actors would in future overcome their fear of verse drama and through it achieve a more measured and restrained style: 'Um eine solche

Epoche beschleunigen zu helfen, den Schauspieler zu einem wört-
lichen Memorieren, zu einem gemeßnen Vortrag, zu einer gehaltnen
Aktion zu veranlassen, ist diese Bearbeitung des Voltairischen
Mahomets unternommen worden.[55] He was aware that a revival of
French neo-classical drama would be controversial in Weimar. Carl
August and members of the court aristocracy had been educated to
appreciate French taste, but those who welcomed German writers'
emancipation from a sense of cultural inferiority and the dominance of
French classical norms were likely to be sceptical about and even
hostile to the reintroduction (admittedly in blank verse rather than in
alexandrines) of the arch-representative of an outmoded style. Schiller
himself felt obliged to forestall criticism by writing a poem for
declamation before the performance, in which he emphasized that the
production did not herald the reimposition of a formal strait-jacket:

> Nicht Muster zwar darf uns der Franke werden,
> Aus seiner Kunst spricht kein lebend'ger Geist,
> Des falschen Anstands prunkende Gebärden
> Verschmäht der Sinn, *der* nur das wahre preißt,
> Ein Führer nur zum Bessern soll er werden,
> Er komme wie ein abgeschied'ner Geist,
> Zu reinigen die oft entweihte Scene
> Zum würd'gen Sitz der alten Melpomene. (NA 2/I, 406)

'An Goethe, als er den Mahomet von Voltaire auf die Bühne brachte'
was not in the end recited that evening, probably because of fears that
Carl August might find the anti-court sentiment offensive, for Schiller
expressly links the French classical tradition to the absolutism of the
ancien régime. Goethe's blank verse version of *Tancred* followed in
January 1801. Neither enjoyed great success but both remained in the
repertoire for a number of years none the less.

In May 1800 one of Schiller's most durable adaptations, that of
Shakespeare's *Macbeth*, was premièred and it enjoyed considerable

---

55   'Einige Scenen aus Mahomet' (MA 6.2, 692). For further detail see my essay
      'Voltaire's *Mahomet* and the Repertoire of the Weimar Court Theatre' in
      Nachdenklicher Leichtsinn. Aufsätze zu Goethe und Goetherezeption, ed. by
      Heike Bartel and Brian Keith-Smith (Lewiston and Lampeter: Mellen, 2000),
      pp. 155–67.

success for several decades in Weimar and beyond, replacing the versions (Bürger's and Wagner's) most commonly used up to that point. Only after the appearance of the complete Schlegel–Tieck Shakespeare translations in 1839–40 did Dorothea Tieck's version supplant Schiller's.[56] His priority was a version that would be compact, suited to performance and easily comprehensible to the audience. He renders the whole play into blank verse, even the prose scenes. *Macbeth* had been much in his mind as he pondered the principles of tragedy during the early stages of work on *Wallenstein*. Paulin calls the translation 'a re-enactment of his agonizing over *Wallenstein*', for both Macbeth and Wallenstein bring about their own downfall through ambition and yet are weakened and misled by their belief in portents, which makes their transgressions more humanly understandable. This wish to emphasize the power of Fate makes him turn the witches into figures more reminiscent of the classical Eumenides.[57] Schiller's English was not adequate to allow him to engage deeply with the original and thus his version, as Paulin says, is less concerned with poetic language than with the underlying dramatic dynamic.[58] In addition to bringing a more classicized Shakespeare to the Weimar audience it may well have served the playwright as a useful compositional exercise, bridging the gap between *Wallenstein* and the start of work on his next drama project, *Maria Stuart*, which he was determined to treat in compact form and not in three parts like *Wallenstein*.

Unlike Schiller's other adaptations, *Macbeth* was not at first accepted by Iffland for the Berlin stage, as he considered it impractical to expect the company to learn a verse version when a prose version was already established in the repertoire.[59] The Berlin première of Schiller's version did not take place until 11 December 1809. In Joseph von Eichendorff's recollection, the urgency with which it was awaited and the dangerous crush outside the theatre's doors matched

---

56 For the reception of Schiller's translation, see FA 9, 880.
57 Roger Paulin, *The Critical Reception of Shakespeare in Germany 1682–1914. Native Literature and Foreign Genius* (Hildesheim, Zurich, New York: Olms, 2003), p. 246.
58 Paulin, p. 246.
59 See his letter to Schiller of 20 May 1800 (NA 38/I, 261).

the horror inside aroused by the appearance of the witches, an indication that Iffland did not want to lose the chance of creating a spectacle.[60]

Produced at Goethe's request, Schiller's adaptation of Lessing's *Nathan der Weise* was instrumental in bringing that play into the repertoire at many theatres. Up to that point only *Emilia Galotti* and *Minna von Barnhelm* were regularly, if not very frequently, played.[61] Doebbelin had premièred it in Berlin in 1783 but the play had not established itself. The actor, director and playwright Friedrich Ludwig Schmidt recalls attempting it at the Magdeburg theatre precisely as a change from Schiller:

> Im Gegensatz zu Schillers schwerterklirrenden, geharnischten Gestalten wagte ich es, am 27. Juli 1801 ein Frieden in jedem Worte athmendes Drama auf die Bühne zu bringen, nämlich Lessing's, bis dahin erst auf einem einzigen Theater aufgeführten *Nathan*.[62]

Schiller's version, first performed on 28 November 1801, brought the play into wider circulation: 'In dieser Form zunächst (und mit späteren vielfachen Abwandlungen) kann sich Lessings Drama auf dem Theater behaupten.'[63]

It was Goethe again who asked Schiller in 1802 to adapt his *Iphigenie auf Tauris* for the stage. The adaptation is not extant but we know that Schiller was concerned about the lack of visible action and the consequent lack of a counterbalance to the weight of moral argu-

---

60   'schon um 4 Uhr ins Schauspielhaus [...] Hier im Vorsaale eine Stunde lang, Kopf an Kopf gedrängt, gestanden. Poltern an die Thüre. Als sie endlich um 5 Uhr eröffnet wurde, schreckliche, mit Lebensgefahr verknüpftes Drängen. Todesgeschrey der Frauenzimmer [...] Bis ins innerste Mark grauenhafter Anblick der 3 Hexen mit ihren grauen Kitteln, langen dürren Fingern, gespenstischen Stellungen u. wild verworrenen rothen Haaren' in *Sämtliche Werke des Freiherrn Joseph von Eichendorff*, ed. by Wilhelm Kosch and August Sauer, 22 vols (Regensburg: Habbel, 1908–86), vol. 11: *Tagebücher*, pp. 249–50.

61   Dalberg had considered staging *Nathan der Weise* in Mannheim soon after its publication. See p. 101.

62   Friedrich Ludwig Schmidt, *Denkwürdigkeiten*, ed. by Hermann Uhde, 2nd edn, 2 vols (Stuttgart: Cotta, 1878), vol. 1, p. 84.

63   FA 9, 1156.

ment. He particularly felt that Orest's agony, in the absence of visible Furies, was too extended and that Thoas and the Taureans disappear for too long from the stage. Goethe clearly resisted any such radical changes to the work; Genast recalls that Schiller hoped until shortly before the first performance that he would get his way over the Furies, but Goethe stood firm.[64] The discussion is further evidence of the radically different concepts the two men had of how stage drama works as an aesthetic experience (see Chapter 5, p. 174) but also shows how by this moment in their collaboration they had found ways of negotiating compromises.

The last translation/adaptation Schiller completed was that of Racine's *Phèdre*, again into blank verse, during the winter of 1804/05, a season when, by his own admission, he found it difficult to find inspiration for his own work. His reading knowledge of French was good and his translation precise, though Carl August made numerous suggestions for improvements in versification. *Phädra* was performed five times in Weimar in 1805, then revived occasionally from 1809 onwards. The translation enjoyed considerable success at other theatres and was widely played.[65] In Berlin it became a very useful item for Iffland during the French occupation of the city (October 1806 to December 1808), when he had to try to accommodate French taste in order to ensure the theatre's survival. In his final months Schiller also advised Heinrich Voss, the young classical scholar, who was tutor to Goethe's son August, on a translation of Shakespeare's *Othello*. He did not, however, live to see it performed.[66]

Schiller added to the comic repertoire with two translations of comedies by the popular French writer Louis Benoît Picard (1769–1828), an actor and theatre director in Paris, where both *Encore des Ménechmes* (*Der Neffe als Onkel*, 1791) and *Médiocre et rampant ou le moyen de parvenir* (*Der Parasit oder die Kunst, sein Glück zu machen*, 1797) had been successful. Schiller embarked on both

---

64   Genast, vol. 1, p. 127-28.
65   See FA 9, 1155. It was, for example, one of the bedrocks of Racine reception in the first half of the nineteenth century at the Burgtheater in Vienna; see Alth, vol. 1, p. 106 and 248.
66   The première was on 8 June 1805.

translations after completing work on *Die Braut von Messina*. Neither remained long in the Weimar repertoire after they were first given in 1803. *Der Parasit*, which involves satire on contemporary manners, was more successful elsewhere than the simpler comedy of mistaken identity of *Der Neffe als Onkel*. Beginning with Berlin, where Iffland played the title role, it remained for at least twenty years in the repertoire, the *Frankfurter Ausgabe* recording a performance in Hamburg in 1832.[67] A much bigger task was the adaptation of Carlo Gozzi's *Turandot* (1762), a tragi-comedy, the occasion for which was the search for greater variety of comedy in the Weimar repertoire. It also provided another opportunity to experiment with masks after their revival in a classical context for the staging of Einsiedel's translation of Terence's *Die Brüder*. Though widely played and offering the opportunity for visual display by virtue of its Chinese setting, the work was never very popular. Iffland commented to Kirms: 'Schiller mußte kein Stück aufnehmen, wo Schinder, Tollheit, Pracht, Dummheit, Wizzelei und pöbelhafte Natur den Wettkampf bestehen.'[68]

Taken together with his own plays, the translations and adaptations form a considerable corpus of work, almost all of which went on being performed for some three decades and boosted the number of playable works from the international repertoire. More importantly, perhaps, most of these adaptations were in verse. What had originated in part as a training exercise for the Weimar actors had succeeded, along with Schiller's later plays, in making verse drama accepted on the German stage.

---

67   FA 9, 1101.
68   Quoted by Ludwig Geiger, 'Schauspielerbriefe. 23 Briefe A.W. Ifflands und zwar 21 an Goethe und Kirms, je 1 an H.A.O. Reichard und G. Forster. 2 Briefe von Friederike Unzelmann-Bethmann an Goethe', *Goethe-Jahrbuch* 26 (1905), 51–92 (p. 60).

Chapter Seven
Iffland and Berlin (1796–1814)

It might be supposed that in moving to Berlin Iffland was arriving in a great theatre centre with a long tradition. However dazzling the theatre world in Berlin was to become in the nineteenth and twentieth centuries, in 1796 the Prussian capital, which had about 160,000 inhabitants, was not a leading theatre city. In fact, at the time he arrived the still youthful *Königliches Nationaltheater*, founded in 1786, had failed to establish a significant reputation or a secure financial and administrative foundation.

One reason for the tardy development of German-language theatre in Berlin was lack of support from the Francophile monarch, Friedrich II (Frederick the Great, 1712–86), whose generous subsidies went to French-language theatre enjoyed primarily by court and aristocratic circles but also by the Huguenot population that had found a home in Prussia at the end of the previous century.[1] The most successful commercial theatre was that in the Behrenstrasse, created by the *Prinzipal* Franz Schuch the Younger. After his death it was sold to Gottfried Heinrich Koch[2] and after Koch's death in 1775 to Carl Theophil Doebbelin (1727–93). Doebbelin's vigorous and artistically ambitious approach to building up his company's strength

---

1   For a compact but detailed overview of the history of Berlin theatre, see Ruth Freydank, *Theater in Berlin* (Berlin: Henschelverlag, 1988); on Doebbelin see pp. 101–21, also Richard Daunicht, 'Von Doebbelin zu Iffland. Das Berliner Nationaltheater, 1786 bis 1814', *Theater der Zeit*, 11 (1956), 7–16. Other informative studies covering this period are Gerhard Wahnrau, *Berlin, Stadt der Theater* (Berlin: Henschelverlag, 1957), pp. 99–186, and Rudolf Genée, *Hundert Jahre des Königlichen Schauspiels in Berlin 1786–1886* (Berlin: Hofmann, 1886), pp 1–22;; for the pre-Iffland period, see Albert Emil Brachvogel's *Geschichte des Berliner Theaters*, 2 vols (Berlin: Jankc, 1877, 1878).

2   This was the same Koch, discussed in the Introduction, who collaborated with Hiller and Weisse to introduce German *Musiktheater* in Leipzig. in the 1750s and 1760s and who had played at the Weimar court in the 1760s.

had, by the mid-1770s, secured him a pre-eminent position in Berlin commercial theatre. He staged the Berlin première of Lessing's *Minna von Barnhelm* in 1768 and that of *Nathan der Weise* in 1783, and played works by Shakespeare and the young Schiller with great success. His repertoire comprised an ambitious mixture of plays, ballet and *Musiktheater*. With around thirty premières a year, however, and such an expensive range of productions to sustain, he was already losing his artistic reputation and financial viability when in 1786 Friedrich II died and the *Prinzipal* was able to persuade his successor, Friedrich Wilhelm II, to follow the lead given by several princes and prominent cities and create a national theatre. Doebbelin was given a subvention of 12,000 Talers, the promise of an annual subsidy and offered the Französisches Komödienhaus with all its equipment as its home. Built in 1774, the theatre, situated on the Gendarmenmarkt, was occupied until 1778 by the French court players but since then, the time of the War of the Bavarian Succession, in which Prussia, as ever, was a major player, it had not been in use as a theatre.[3]

In spite of wanting a national theatre and hoping for improvements in the standard and range of performances as a result, the King was not prepared to give it serious financial help. The royal subsidy dropped in the second year to 5,400 Talers a year and remained at that level into the early years of the next century. Doebbelin soon felt the effects of an alliance with the court when the King, concerned to hasten improvements and exercise some control, made him share authority as part of a court-appointed directorate with the playwright, academic and royal tutor Johann Jakob Engel, and the academic and poet Karl Wilhelm Ramler (1725–98), who acted as dramaturge. Finances were dealt with by a court official (and member of the aristocracy), Karl Ludwig von Beyer. Doebbelin, used as a *Prinzipal* to autonomy, was unhappy about this arrangement, while Engel and Ramler, who, in spite of the fact that the former had published a

---

3   On the succession of theatre buildings erected on the Gendarmenmarkt between 1774 and 1821 – the Französisches Komödienhaus, the Langhans theatre and then the Schinkel theatre – see Matthes, '*Der allgemeinen Vereinigung gewidmet*', pp. 45–54.

treatise on acting (*Ideen zu einer Mimik* in two volumes appeared in 1785/86), were primarily literary men, had little practical experience of theatre and consequently little ability to impress their views on the actors. Doebbelin lasted less than a year before he was forced to stand down as director. Because the legal position with regard to the ownership of the theatre and its effects had never been properly clarified, he was obliged to go to court to sue for his rightful share, which he eventually received. Engel was unhappy in his post, suffering interference and financial constraints from the court as well as being aware of rumours that he had forced Doebbelin out. As early as 1790 he had asked for leave to resign. His resignation was finally accepted in 1794, when the King was displeased that, having requested several times that the theatre put on Mozart's hugely popular *Die Zauberflöte*, it was finally performed in his absence. Engel was granted no pension and had to leave Berlin. Ramler continued until Iffland's appointment in 1796, with the aid of the leading actor Ferdinand Fleck, who had been *Regisseur* since 1790.[4]

By the time Iffland was appointed, the lack of clear leadership and authority that would bridge the gap between the company and the court was apparent. What was needed was a single figure with the experience and status to give the enterprise cohesiveness. This solution had been clear for some years and as early as 1790 Iffland was approached by Berlin. His letter of appointment from the King in December 1796 states explicitly that the new director was to have sole authority:

> Überzeugt, daß jede Theilung der eigentlichen Direction nicht anders als durch Mangel an Einheit in Sistem und Ausführung, den Fortgang des Ganzen hemmen könne, vertraue ich dieselbe lediglich Euch an.[...] Ihr allein seid Director des Nationalschauspiels.[5]

---

4   Johann Valentin Teichmann stresses the extent to which the real burden fell on this much-admired actor. See Teichmann, *Literarischer Nachlaß*, ed. by Franz Dingelstedt (Stuttgart: Cotta, 1863), p. 67.

5   Copy of Cabinets-Ordre, 16 December 1796: Geheimes Staatsarchiv Preußischer Kulturbesitz (GStA PK), I. HA Rep. 36: Geheimer Rat Hof- und Güterverwaltung, Nr. 2547.

The letter, indicating the King's concern about mounting costs, stresses the need to exercise financial control and to cost productions carefully in advance. Iffland is enjoined to maintain both German-language opera and drama and to take full advantage of co-operation with the experienced *Regisseur* Fleck.[6] Given that by the mid-1790s annual outgoings stood at about 54,000 Talers, the royal subsidy of 5,400 Talers was clearly small, which meant that commercial success was imperative.[7]

Iffland quickly had to assert his place at the top of the hierarchy for, as soon as he was appointed, Privy Councillor von Warsing, who had replaced Beyer as the court appointee and member of the theatre directorate with financial responsibility, indicated that he did not accept his subordination to the new director. A member of the nobility, he may have looked askance at the appointment of a commoner and practical man of the theatre to the post. Confident of his royal mandate, Iffland made his position clear to von Warsing:

> Ich erkenne keine Mitdirektion, keine Ökonomie-Direktion an, alle Ressorts vereinigen sich in meiner Führung zum ehrlichen Zweck des zu hebenden Ganzen, denn die königliche Ordre sagt: Ihr seid allein Direktor.[8]

Warsing retained responsibility for some aspects of the upkeep of the building, proceeds of ticket sales, policing and season tickets, but he retained only half the salary he was paid as joint director under the old regime and thus, to his mortification, the new chain of command was brought home to him.

---

6 'Es dürfen weder besonders die Opern, noch auch besonders die Schauspiele Eurer Aufmerksamkeit ausschließlicher Gegenstand werden. Ihr habt vielmehr durch gleiche Rücksicht auf beide verwandte Künste, die Erhaltung des Ganzen zu bewirken zu suchen [...] Ihr entwerft das Repertoir; der Regisseur macht es aber bekannt und ihr sezt es nicht eher fest, als mit seiner Überzeugung': Copy of Cabinets-Ordre, 16 December 1796: GStA PK, I. HA Rep. 36. Nr. 2547.

7 For Iffland's analysis of the financial situation he had inherited see Louis Schneider, 'Iffland als Direktor des Berliner Theaters' *Almanach für Freunde der Schauspielkunst* (1853), Part 2, pp. 71–110 (pp. 73–80). Part 1 appeared in *Almanach für Freunde der Schauspielkunst* for 1852, pp. 76–109, and Part 3 in the same journal in 1854, pp. 126–78.

8 Schneider 1, p. 86.

The words 'des zu hebenden Ganzen' make it clear that Iffland understood his task as being to create a Royal National Theatre for Berlin more worthy of that title. What then were the problems that needed to be rectified? As at many theatres, they were a combination of financial, artistic and professional. Several financial problems that undermined efforts to keep costs in check were identified by Iffland in a revealing draft letter to the court. One is the huge rise in non-specific costs (as distinct from specific costs such as salaries and pensions), which suggests a lack of budgetary restraint. Another is the frequent granting of benefit performances (where the box-office takings go to a specified member of the company), not as an exception or to reward leading individuals but as kind of regular salary boost accorded to and expected by even quite junior and secondary members of the company on virtually a rota basis. Another is the loss to the box-office through the liberal granting of large numbers of free tickets to members of the company and the orchestra. Yet another is the huge rise in bills for costumes and sets, which is indicative of audiences' love of showiness and spectacle; this tendency is distorting the repertoire as a whole, which Iffland sums up in the following comment:

> Der Geschmack des Publikums ist mit einer Gattung Gewalt zu den Operetten der geringen Art verleitet.
> Die *wahre* Musik ist verdrängt, und indem das eigentliche Schauspiel fast ganz vernachläßigt, oder nur nebenbei behandelt wird, ist von beiden Seiten ein solcher Hang, nur Flitter geben, und nur Flitter empfangen zu wollen, eingegriffen, daß es bedenkliche Folgen erwarten läßt, die zum Theil schon sehr sichtbar sind.[9]

If we look at the premières recorded for the six years leading up to Iffland's appointment, his analysis is perhaps not quite accurate.[10] Each year something between 25% and 30% of new productions fall under the heading of *Musiktheater*, though by no means all could be described as 'Operetten der geringen Art'. Mozart's *Così fan tutte*, *Die Zauberflöte* and *Don Giovanni* all came into the repertoire in this period. Some serious operas such as Gluck's *Iphigenia in Tauris* and

---

9   Schneider 2, pp. 75–76.
10   See Schäffer and Hartmann, pp. 102–06.

Grétry's *Le Mariage samnite* (*Die Samnitische Vermählungsfeier*) were introduced, as well as older favourites from the *Musiktheater* repertoire elsewhere such as Weisse's and Hiller's *Die Jagd* and Audinot's *Der Faßbinder*. What is accurate about Iffland's comment is the neglect of spoken drama, as evidenced by the large number of short comedies, many of which were very short-lived, the comparative lack of serious drama and the almost complete absence of tragedy. As at most other theatres, the two most performed writers of *Schauspiele* in those six years are himself and Kotzebue, with other relatively successful contemporary dramatists such as Johann Gottfried Lucas Hagemeister (1762–1806), Christian Heinrich Spiess (1755–99) and Louis Sébastien Mercier in translation also featuring. Shakespeare premières are virtually absent.

Professionally and artistically Iffland saw long-established examples of poor practice. The way that the old conventions of the *Rollenfach* were applied and adhered to meant that certain actors had a virtual monopoly of certain types of role, while others were underemployed. This imbalance was exacerbated by the fact that the theatre was open almost every night of the year, which led to a punishing regime that exhausted many members of the company and orchestra and depressed standards. Iffland's judgment is:

> Die Direktion, indem sie immer nur einen und denselben mit Recht beliebten, kleinen Cirkel des Personals, durch zugemuthete Lasten überspannte, that stillschweigend auf alle Kunstforderung selbst Verzicht, da sie in ihrer Behandlungsweise einen Fabrik-Gang einführte und nur auf das Meistgelieferte, nicht auf das Bestgelieferte sah.[11]

The relentlessness of the schedule meant that younger talents could not be effectively trained. A compensation for the poor standard of performances and often poor quality of the works performed was the showiness of the costumes and expenses of staging, the former not only at times endangering the artistic coherence of the production but also costing the actors (and more particularly the actresses) additional expense. To add to these backstage problems were the difficulties presented by the building and by the audiences. The house was so

---

11   Schneider 2, p. 76.

constructed that actors in costume had to make their way through the public areas in order to get to the stage. Unruliness among sections of the audience was commonplace. Army officers in particular were used to making their reactions to the performances known.[12] Often there were many additional people in the building who were not part of the audience proper – children, servants, prostitutes – whose presence caused continuous disturbances. In spite of, and indeed in part because of, these additional people, the income from the sale of seats was depressed by the number of free tickets claimed by members of the company and orchestra.

Iffland therefore had a daunting task ahead of him when he took over as director. Within a year he was serving a new master; Friedrich Wilhelm II died in November 1797 and was succeeded by his son, Friedrich Wilhelm III, a man utterly different in his tastes and personality.[13] The former was outgoing, affable and a lover of women, the latter reserved, quiet and a model of respectability. Whereas the deceased king had been engaged enough for the arts to set up the *Nationaltheater* (though without placing it on a secure financial or managerial footing), his son was not very interested in it. Given the turmoil of Prussia in the first decade of the nineteenth century, with military defeat, occupation and the removal of the royal family and court from Berlin to Königsberg, he certainly had much bigger problems to deal with. On the positive side, rather than interfering, he accepted that the theatre existed and allowed it to struggle along on its small subvention. Thus Iffland was generally free from unwelcome interventions from above, even if he was always bound to seek royal approval for many routine matters (for example benefit performances and *Gastspiele*). The most important issue that arose between Iffland

---

12   See, for example, Genée, pp. 57–58. For an extensive analysis of the composition of the audience see Rudolf Weil, *Das Berliner Theaterpublikum unter A. W. Ifflands Direktion (1796 bis 1814). Ein Beitrag zur Methodologie der Theaterwissenschaft* (Berlin: Selbstverlag der Gesellschaft für Theatergeschichte, 1932). See also Fetting, *Das Repertoire des Berliner Königlichen Nationaltheaters*, pp. 205–20.

13   On the contrast between the monarchs see James Sheehan, *German History 1770–1866*, The Oxford History of Modern Europe (Oxford: OUP, 1989), pp. 291–94.

and the court was the building of the new theatre to replace the old *Französisches Komödienhaus*, and for that project he was able to secure the court's approval. Iffland saw immediately on taking up his post that a new building was essential. The new theatre, designed by Carl Langhans the Elder and nicknamed 'Der Koffer' on account of its unusual long and high roof, opened on 1 January 1802, the old theatre having been kept in use during its construction right up to 31 December 1801, so that no income was lost as a result of a period of closure.

One of the reasons why the King was prepared to consent to the building of the new theatre may have been that Iffland had overseen a slowing down in the rise of the theatre's indebtedness.[14] Never able to live within his means in his private sphere, the new director nevertheless saw clearly that there was a need to increase the theatre's revenue and control unnecessary expenditure. He attempted this in the most humane way possible, namely by resisting the most obvious expedient of dismissing artistically weaker members of the company, who, he was aware, would have difficulty finding new engagements at a time when theatre life was being disrupted in many places by the wars. The only answer was to cut back on inessentials: 'Sollen Menschen nicht leiden, so leide der leblose Luxus!'[15]

In addition to various cost-cutting measures, Iffland states his intention to increase the theatre's appeal by reviewing the repertoire with the object, 'so viel als die Umstände verstatten, Abwechselung in das Repertoir zu bringen, und die Einseitigkeit der Rollenvertheilung zu verhüten suchen.'[16] At an early stage he recognized that in order to maintain the theatre's popularity he had to ensure its appeal to a wide range of people and satisfy the desire for more serious plays and for the newest literary products as well as for light entertainment, for, as shown above, it had been light entertainment in the form of comedies and comic operas that had predominated in the earlier 1790s. In order

---

14   See Günther Bellmann, *Schauspielhausgeschichten. 250 Jahre Theater und Musik auf dem Berliner Gendarmenmarkt* (Berlin: Links, 1993), p. 35. Wahnrau (p. 243) points out that Iffland went into debt with the city of Berlin to help finance the new theatre in the absence of sufficient support from the King.

15   Schneider 2, p. 77.

16   Schneider 2, p. 81.

to provide that increased variety where there could be no increase in the size of the company Iffland had to insist on a more equitable and flexible distribution of roles. In a letter of 1798 to the actor Karl Wilhelm Ferdinand Unzelmann he sums up his attitude:

> Die Rollen-Monopolia, womit alle Theile belastet waren, haben ein Ende, es ist also niemand mit Arbeit überladen und Jedermann hat Zeit und Muße zu leben, zu lernen und froh zu sein. Das verlange ich und halte es und setze es durch. Aber Partheysucht kenne ich nicht![17]

This emphasis on encouraging actors to see themselves as part of the ensemble is typical of Iffland. He himself was highly flexible in the roles he took on, even if he was not always equally successful in them. The dominance of the *Rollenfach* had to be challenged, not only if a theatre were to maximize its resources but also if the actor were to move towards a greater artistry and a more conscious development of that blend of the typical and the individual that lay at the heart of Iffland's conception of acting.

As when he was *Regisseur* in Mannheim, Iffland aimed to treat all members of the company as professionals deserving respect for the sake of the honour of the actor's calling. Striking is the amount of time and effort he was prepared to put into resolving problems with members of the company and the voluminous correspondence that policy entailed.[18] Yet he was not universally admired in the company. In a letter dated 11 June 1804 a number of the actors wrote to the King to complain about, amongst other things, his absences on *Gastspielreisen*, his alleged favouritism, his poor financial management, his failure to accept suitable new plays and promotion of his own, and his homosexuality.[19] They suggested that the King rein in his freedom of action by setting a steering committee above him. The King was clearly not inclined to act on these accusations or to return to the earlier days of divided responsibility, no doubt because Iffland had been very successful in raising the profile of the National Theatre.

---

17   Schneider 2, p. 106.
18   Schneider, particularly Parts 2 and 3, publishes a large amount of such correspondence relating to the early Berlin years.
19   GStA PK, I. HA Rep. 36, Nr. 2415.

The development of the Berlin repertoire

Satisfying the Berlin public was always a challenging task and from the start Iffland was a controversial figure. His acting was the least controversial part of his activities and, although he did not please in every role, he continued to demonstrate his skill and to act with his company until the end of his career, being happy to take small parts, such as Melvil in *Maria Stuart*, but make sure they were acted well.[20] Given that the negligent playing of secondary roles was a constant criticism in reviews of performances of all theatres at the time, Iffland was setting an important example, particularly to younger actors. His various guest performances at other theatres, apart from satisfying a restlessness he had shown from an early stage, had the effect of bringing to those theatres some of the more serious plays, including Schiller's, that had been successful in Berlin and so extending its reputation and influence, and Schiller's renown as a writer for the stage.

As director of the Berlin National Theatre Iffland was more controversial. His devotion to the King sometimes made the theatre the scene of shows of patriotism, such as the famous performance of *Wallensteins Lager* on 16 October 1805, the eve of the Prussian army's new, and in the event disastrous, campaign against France:

> Am Ende des Reiterliedes stimmte das Orchester ein neues Lied, das 'Lob des Krieges', an, wovon man viele hundert Abdrücke vertheilt hatte. Es ward daher vom ganzen Hause gesungen; hierauf aber mit noch allgemeiner Theilnahme das Volkslied: 'Heil dir im Siegerkranz' angestimmt. Ein stürmisches Jubeln, das immer wieder von neuem anfing: es lebe der König! und dann: es lebe die Armee! schloß diese patriotische Feyer.[21]

---

20   The writer and *salonnière* Henriette Herz comments on Iffland's tendency towards naturalness: 'Iffland, der schon etwas von dieser Unart hatte, galt auch trotz seines trefflichen Spiels bei allen Leuten von Geschmack in dieser Beziehung für einen Manieristen, namentlich der so ganz unverkünstelte Fleck mit seinem wahrhaft wunderbaren Naturell neben ihm stand': *Henriette Herz in Erinnerungen, Briefen und Zeugnissen*, ed. by Rainer Schmitz (Leipzig and Weimar: Kiepenheuer, 1984), p. 52.

21   *Neuestes Allerlei oder Leipziger Fama*, 43. Stück, 1805, p. 680, quoted according to Fambach, Abt. A, 38.

The use of *Wallensteins Lager* for patriotic purposes was repeated in other German cities such as Königsberg, Breslau and Leipzig. Iffland's lavish production of *Die Jungfrau von Orleans* aroused negative comment not merely because of its use of spectacle but also because in Berlin the patriotic resonance of some of the lines, albeit the play concerns a French heroine, stirred the audience. By the same token, Iffland was careful to avoid material that might suggest any critical response to established authority, hence his decision not to perform *Wallensteins Lager* in 1799 and his anxiety in 1804 about *Wilhelm Tell*.

It was primarily in Berlin, however, that he became a target of criticism for a new reason, namely his dramas and their effect on public taste. Although never warmly received in their published form by critics in the 1780s and early 90s, his plays as theatre had been regarded as morally worthy and thus elevating for the audience. In Berlin voices were soon heard that condemned his influence on the theatre. One voice was that of the famous *salonnière* Rahel Levin, later Varnhagen von Ense, of whom her husband Karl wrote:

Namentlich klagte sie, daß Iffland, abgerechnet sein großes persönliches Talent, [...] durch sein wachsendes Ansehen und Einwirken die Bühne und Schauspielkunst in Berlin auf weithinaus zugrunde richte, ins Gemeine und Manierierte hinabziehe, und der leitenden Behörde wie selbst dem Publikum die falschesten Maximen und Urteile einflöße und verhärte.[22]

In his *Vorlesungen über die dramatische Kunst und Literatur* of 1808 August Wilhelm Schlegel (1767–1845), the Berlin Romantic critic, gave a damning appraisal of the development of German theatre from the end of the eighteenth century to the time of writing, laying particular blame on Iffland and Kotzebue (without actually naming them) for contributing to a decline in taste:

Das Repertorium unserer Schaubühne bietet daher in seinem armseligen Reichtum ein buntes Allerlei dar, von Ritterstücken, Familiengemälden und rührenden Dramen, welche nur selten mit Werken in größerem und gebildetem Stil von Shakespeare oder Schiller abwechseln. Dazwischen können wir die Über-

---

22   Karl Varnhagen von Ense, *Denkwürdigkeiten des eigenen Lebens*, ed. by Joachim Kühn, 2 vols (Berlin: Wegweiser Verlag, 1922), vol. 1, p. 267.

setzungen und Bearbeitungen der fremden Neuigkeiten, besonders der franzö-
sischen Nachspiele und Operetten, nicht entbehren. Bei dem geringen Wert des
einzelnen lenkt sich die Schaulust bloß auf den flüchtigen Reiz der Neuheit, zu
großem Nachteil der Schauspielkunst, da eine Menge unbedeutender Rollen
übereilt eingelernt werden müssen, um sogleich wieder vergessen zu werden.[23]

Schlegel thoroughly chastises Iffland and Kotzebue for pursuing only
immediate popularity and success. He also criticizes the concept of the
national theatre, accusing such theatres of featherbedding the actors,
who become neglectful of standards.

Schlegel was writing at a difficult time for the Berlin theatre,
namely during the French occupation, which, as will be discussed later
in this chapter, led to a decline of serious drama in the repertoire, but
his critical attitude to Iffland predates the occupation. Another member of the Berlin Romantic circle, Ludwig Tieck (1773–1853), writing
in 1828, looked back on the Iffland years and concurred with the
accusation that he and Kotzebue had dragged down public taste,
claiming that in the 1780s he had seen a wider selection of plays of
literary merit in Berlin than later and that the emergence of the
Familiengemälde and the sentimental play (marked by the success of
Die Jäger and *Die Mündel*) pushed this broader repertoire out:

> Nach und nach aber ward die Vorliebe für diese kleinlichen Gemälde des häus-
> lichen Familienlebens überwiegend; das Publikum gewöhnte sich an diese
> Manier und übersah bald die Uebertreibung, die Unnatur und das Häßliche, was
> sich unvermerkt einschlich, weil der Dichter, statt zu schildern, immer mehr
> lehren und bessern wollte.[24]

In 1797 Tieck wrote his play within a play about the theatre, *Der gestiefelte Kater*, satirizing contemporary personalities and tastes. In his
preface of 1828 he recalls coming upon Böttiger's account of Iffland's
performances in his *Gastspiel* in Weimar in 1796 (written apparently
without the latter's encouragement or approval) and being amazed

---

23   A. W. Schlegel, *Kritische Schriften und Briefe*, ed. by Edgar Lohner, 7 vols
      (Stuttgart: Kohlhammer, 1962–74), vol. 6, *Vorlesungen über dramatische Kunst
      und Literatur*, pp. 286–87.
24   'Vorbericht' in *Ludwig Tieck's Schriften* (Berlin: Reimer, 1828), vol. 1, p. xiii.

that these acting techniques were held to represent art.[25] Böttiger is satirized as the character Bötticher in Tieck's play and Iffland himself as the principal actor playing Puss in Boots. The audience to the dramatized fairy tale tell the writer they want 'Familiengeschichten', 'Lebensrettungen, Sittlichkeit und deutsche Gesinnung', 'Religiös erhebende, wohltuende geheime Gesellschaften!' 'Hussiten und Kinder' – a mixture of the sensational and the moralistic.[26] Tieck saw Iffland's acting as a manifestation of the sentimentality and contrivance he criticized in his plays.[27]

Leaving aside the Romantics' uncompromising insistence on the purity of an art theatre, a purity that a practical theatre man such as Iffland, even if he had been in sympathy with it, simply could not afford, the accusation one might infer from the criticisms of Tieck and Schlegel is that Iffland used the Berlin theatre to promote his and Kotzebue's plays.[28] Tieck wrote *Der gestiefelte Kater* at the height of Iffland's popularity as a playwright, but the seventeen years of the latter's directorship of the Berlin theatre present a more varied picture, which the older Tieck could have taken into account when looking back, but did not. There is no doubt that Iffland put on his own plays

---

25 *Entwickelung des Ifflandischen Spiels in vierzehn Darstellungen auf dem Weimarischen Hoftheater im Aprillmonath 1796* (Leipzig: Göschen, 1796).

26 Ludwig Tieck, *Schriften*, ed. by Manfred Frank and others, 12 vols (Frankfurt am Main: Deutscher Klassiker Verlag), vol. 6: *Phantasus*, p. 496.

27 'Vorbericht', p. xvii. Iffland exacted a small revenge on Tieck when the Berlin theatre staged Heinrich Beck's comedy *Das Chamäleon* in 1800. Tieck, who regarded himself and Schlegel as the butt of Beck's satire in the figure of Schulberg, complained to Iffland and tried to insist on the role being changed but Iffland refused with uncharacteristic forthrightness. For the correspondence on this matter, see Teichmann, pp. 275–85. Schlegel kept his distance, probably wishing to avoid a rupture with Iffland, who went on to stage his play *Ion* in 1802.

28 Comparatively recently the same view was expressed: 'In der Spielplangestaltung bevorzugte Iffland bürgerliche Dramen. Er ließ vor allem Kotzebues und seine eigenen Stücke aufführen, die dem Geschmack der meisten Berliner Theaterbesucher entsprachen.' See Georg Reichard, *August Wilhelm Schlegels 'Ion'. Das Schauspiel und die Aufführungen unter der Leitung von Goethe und Iffland* (Bonn: Bouvier, 1987), p. 199. Reichard concedes: 'Iffland bemühte sich aber auch um die Werke der Klassiker'. I argue that one must take a more differentiated view of the repertoire.

and those of Kotzebue in large numbers, but that policy he shared with every theatre in Germany at the time, including the Weimar Court Theatre. One should also remember that a substantial part of the repertoire of spoken drama everywhere was composed of short comedies, many of which were naturally set in a contemporary milieu, and also that another substantial part of the repertoire consisted of *Singspiele* and *Operetten*, again often short and comic and similarly set in a contemporary milieu. We therefore have to look at change and balance in the repertoire in order to evaluate his policy in building it up, using not only his and Kotzebue's plays but also Schiller's.

As mentioned in the first section of this chapter, the repertoire Iffland inherited in Berlin, though not entirely supporting his claim that it was dominated by 'Operetten der geringen Art', does show a neglect of spoken drama, such that short comedies had almost pushed out serious drama. Tieck recollects that in his youth in the 1780s he saw a mixed repertoire:

> In meiner frühen Jugend sah man in Berlin, neben manchen schwachen und unbedeutenden Versuchen deutscher Dichtkunst, viele französische Dramen und Lustspiele, die früheren Tragödien Schillers sehr häufig; eben so viele Werke Shakespears, die, wenn auch in der Umarbeitung entstellt, das Gepräge der Großheit behalten hatten. Andre englische Trauerspiele, wie Athelstan, Ethelwolf und ähnliche, wurden mit Beifall gegeben, so wie die gemilderten Comödien des Farghuar [*sic*] und Congreve. Emilie Galotti und Minna von Barnhelm erhielten sich ihre Verehrer, so wie Gotters fein ausgeführte Umarbeitungen.[29]

Certainly the period from the creation of the National Theatre in 1786 to the early 1790s shows a more challenging repertoire than the early to mid-1790s. Among the premières of those first years are those of seven Shakespeare plays (*Coriolanus, Othello, Hamlet, Macbeth, The Merchant of Venice, King Lear* and *Measure for Measure*).[30] All of Schiller's early plays were staged, including *Don Karlos*,[31] Lessing's *Minna von Barnhelm* and *Emilia Galotti* and Goethe's *Clavigo, Die*

---

29 'Vorbericht', xiii–iv.
30 See Schäffer and Hartmann, pp. 98–103. Freydank (p. 122) records that it was the King who requested Shakespeare.
31 According to Wahnrau (pp. 212–13) it was not a success because it was badly cast and the audience was not ready for its content.

Geschwister and *Claudine von Villa Bella*. Racine's *Athalie* was also given. During the years 1791–96 there seems to have been a decline in emphasis on serious drama. One exception was the actor Fleck's request in 1792 to put on a new production of Schiller's *Fiesko* as his benefit performance.[32] Works of literary quality were either not given at all (Goethe's *Egmont* was one such omission) or only when guest performers requested them.[33] Engel had asked for leave to resign as early as 1790, frustrated by the unsatisfactory support from the court with its indecisive king and the intrigues of his courtiers. Following the popular taste of the time was probably the safest option. By the early 1790s both Iffland and Kotzebue had numerous plays to their credit that were guaranteed to please audiences.

It would be wrong, however, to see Iffland as continuing this trend. In his important, and sadly unpublished, doctoral dissertation, Hugo Fetting demonstrates on the basis of precise numerical and statistical analysis that Iffland did successfully pursue his early policy of bringing variety into the repertoire, thus making it appeal to a broad section of potential theatre-goers and opening up the possibility of introducing works of a more challenging nature, including serious drama and tragedy. By virtue of his inclusion of such serious drama, Fetting sees in Iffland a certain pedagogic impulse, a belief in the possibility and indeed duty of theatre to educate and elevate as well as to entertain.[34] An additional motive must have been that he knew that such a repertoire would help to put Berlin in the forefront of the German-speaking theatre world. But where to find actable serious drama that would satisfy a demanding and literate public and yet not alienate those who looked primarily for entertainment?

In his first season in Berlin, the new director, as one might expect, introduced a number of works that had proved their popularity in Mannheim: Beck's *Die Schachmaschine*, *Der verstellte Kranke* (from Goldoni's *La finta ammalata*), Gotter's *Der argwöhnische Ehemann* (Gotter was already popular in Berlin), and Iffland's own

---

32   Freydank, p. 125 and Wahnrau, p. 213. Wahnrau comments that it was a great personal success for Fleck but not for the play.

33   Freydank, p. 124.

34   Fetting, *Das Repertoire des Berliner Königlichen Nationaltheaters*, p. 179.

adaptation of Thomas Otway's tragedy *Venice Preserv'd* (*Das gerettete Venedig*). Musical works were Benda's monodrama *Pygmalion*, after Rousseau, and Dezède's *Töffel und Dortchen* (originally *Blaise et Babet*). There was a production of *Richard III* after Shakespeare and Weisse (whose changes were, admittedly, drastic). Iffland introduced three of his own recent plays (*Das Gewissen*, *Leichter Sinn* and *Die Erinnerung*) and four of Kotzebue's.

In 1799 *Die Piccolomini* and *Wallensteins Tod* came into the repertoire. As already noted, Iffland was anxious to lose no time in obtaining a theatre manuscript. The reasons may be obvious, but it is perhaps nevertheless worth asking why Iffland wanted to put Schiller on so urgently. His plays had not formed a significant part of the Mannheim repertoire in Iffland's later years there, any more than they had done in the 1780s. A glance at the Berlin premières of 1798 reinforces the impression made by 1797. In a situation where Iffland wanted to build up spoken theatre there was a shortage of plays to provide the necessary range, above all a shortage of actable serious plays. In 1798 Kotzebue provided three more *Schauspiele* (*Graf Benjowsky*, *Die Corsen* and *Das Schreibepult*) and one comedy (*Das Epigramm*), while Iffland supplied three *Schauspiele* (*Der Veteran*, *Der Mann von Wort* and *Selbstbeherrschung*) and one comedy (*Der Fremde*). A *Sittengemälde* entitled *Richelieu's Jugend*, from the French, was given but repeated only once and Cumberland's popular *The Jew* (*Der Jude*) started a run of 29 performances up to 1814. The only other *Schauspiel* was Ziegler's *Der Lorbeerkranz* and all the other plays were comedies or farces.

The following year saw, in addition to Schiller's new works, the premières of Gotter's version of Voltaire's *Mérope*, Eschenburg's new adaptation of Voltaire's *Zaïre*, Iffland's new version of his first play *Albert von Thurneisen*, a tragedy, and the first performance of August Wilhelm Schlegel's new blank verse translation of *Hamlet*. The following year an adaptation of Voltaire's *Alzire* was given and in 1801 Schiller's *Maria Stuart* and *Die Jungfrau von Orleans* as well as Goethe's *Egmont* in Schiller's adaptation and Goethe's blank verse translation of Voltaire's *Tancred*. Thus the addition of tragic drama appears to be a deliberate policy to strengthen and broaden the range of spoken drama and provide some counterbalance to the large number of comedies. Iffland knew that although Schiller had not written any drama since *Don Karlos* he was unsurpassed as a contemporary writer of tragedy and, presumably, that his early plays, though not big box office, were nevertheless maintaining their place in many repertoires. Iffland was not, of course, alone in recognizing this and Schiller himself was quick to realize that he could now expect to make considerable sums from theatre manuscripts of his new and as yet unpublished plays.

Added to the need for actable serious plays of quality was Iffland's recognition of the prestige of Schiller and Weimar, which could add lustre to his own theatre and repertoire. There was never any attempt in Berlin to copy the Weimar style, as that distinctive style began to emerge after the *Wallenstein* premières. Iffland continued to cultivate among the company his own preference for psychologically nuanced playing and a realistic more than an idealized style. He did, however, share at least three important artistic aims as a theatre director with Goethe. One was a concern for clear enunciation.[35] The 0second aim was to transcend the limitations of the traditional *Rollenfach*. Iffland's own ability to lose his individuality and immerse himself in the role and bring it to life was the quality Goethe had particularly admired when Iffland played in Weimar. Goethe's efforts to force the Weimar company to show greater flexibility in the range of roles they were willing to attempt were matched by Iffland's conviction that the old *Rollenfach* tended to debase acting by reducing it to the portrayal of a few stock types. Both from an artistic and from a managerial point of view it was desirable to cultivate greater versatility so that actors faced new challenges and directors could cope better with a broad repertoire and with changes of personnel.

A third shared aim was to establish a repertoire of plays, old and new, that would be a lasting support to the theatre. Writing to Dalberg in 1784, as noted in chapter 2 (see pp. 93), Iffland had pleaded for a place to be given to '[die] guten alten Stücke' and thus that the theatre resist the public's call for constant novelty. In Berlin, where the public

---

35   On this subject, see below, pp. 252–53 on Iffland's circular to the Berlin
      company during the French occupation.

was larger and more varied than in Mannheim, Iffland was still forced to guarantee a stream of premières, particularly of short comedies and *Singspiele*, and yet he seems to have been determined to consolidate. Schiller helped him to do that by providing the serious plays that the public, and particularly the educated public, would come to see. If he had to employ spectacle as part of the bait to secure a wider audience, as in his production of *Die Jungfrau von Orleans*, the expense was easily covered by the enduring popularity of the work. Reviewing the repertoire and defending his policy in shaping it in 1811, he wrote: 'Man vereint sich, die Darstellungen der guten Stücke und der guten alten Stücke mit erneutem Eifer, mit besonderem Studium und Sorgfalt zu geben.'[36] He stresses the need for directors to search for quality work and then to perform it well: 'Kein Sorgfalt und kein billiger Aufwand darf vermißt werden, um ein wahrhaft poetisches Werk mit Würde und Glanz erscheinen zu lassen.'[37] There can thus be no justification for accusing Iffland of using the theatre to promote his, Kotzebue's and Schröder's types of drama to the detriment of other, more literary plays. Rather, such plays had their place in ensuring that the repertoire contained the necessary variety to appeal to a wide spectrum.

It has often been commented that Iffland was hostile to the speaking of verse, and it is true that some members of the Berlin company, as was the case in Weimar, had great difficulties with it. The writer and later director of the Brunswick theatre, Ernst August Klingemann (1777–1831) is on record as having complained about how Iffland himself mangled the speaking of verse, destroying its rhythms by an attempt at naturalness.[38] Teichmann quotes anonymously from a letter written by a member of the Berlin company in 1811: 'ferner liebt er die dramatische Poesie so wenig, daß er seinen Schülern einprägt, die Verse nicht hören zu lassen, sondern sie wie Prosa vorzutragen, was ihnen denn auch trefflich prosaisch gelingt.'[39] Schiller's

---

36 'Über die Verhältnisse der Direktionen, bei Auswahl der Vorstellungen für die Bühne', *Almanach fürs Theater 1811* (Berlin: Saalfeld, 1811), pp. 83–113 (p. 102).
37 'Über die Verhältnisse', p. 101.
38 See Friedrich Ludwig Schmidt, *Denkwürdigkeiten*, vol. 1, p. 177.
39 Teichmann, p. 103.

comment on Friederike Unzelmann's excessive naturalness of speech in the title role in *Maria Stuart* ('Das ist Ifflands Schule')[40] is also often cited. Yet, as Genée rightly says, by the time Iffland came to Berlin Unzelmann was an established and experienced actress whose style was not going to be readily influenced. Of Iffland he says:

> Iffland hatte [...] das ganz richtige Gefühl, daß, wenn ein Drama in Versen geschrieben ist, die Verse auch im Vortrag gehört werden müßten, und er hatte mit einzelnen Schauspielern, denen das Sprechen der Verse noch viel Noth machte, große Schwierigkeiten. Aber er wollte den Vers nicht als solchen deklamiren lassen, sondern ihn als natürliche Rede behandeln, bei welcher der Rhythmus nur etwas Zufälliges ist.[41]

The fact that, in addition to pressing Schiller for his plays, Iffland was the first director to stage *Hamlet* in Schlegel's blank verse translation must be an indication that he recognized the appropriateness of verse for high tragedy, though he clearly did not want to devote the energy to the development of verse speaking that Goethe did. For him it was not an end in itself, nor did he see verse drama as implying the need for a more stylized type of acting.

In addition to staging new works by Schiller and works old and new by Goethe, Iffland put on almost all the adaptations the two writers prepared for the Weimar theatre.[42] One of the first after the première of *Wallenstein* was Goethe's *Egmont* in Schiller's adaptation, which had not been repeated in Weimar since Iffland's first *Gastspiel* there in 1796 and had not been widely taken up. It may well

---

40   Letter to Körner, 23 Sept. 1801 (NA 31, 59).

41   Genée, p. 63.

42   These were: Schiller's translations/adaptations of *Egmont*, Lessing's *Nathan der Weise*, Gozzi's *Turandot*, Racine's *Phädra* and Picard's *Der Parasit* (played in Berlin under its subtitle *Die Kunst, sein Glück zu machen*); Goethe's *Die natürliche Tochter* and *Torquato Tasso* and his translations/adaptations of Voltaire's *Mahomet* and *Tancred*. *Macbeth* was introduced successfully in 1809 (see p. 219). Later, in 1812, Iffland bought Goethe's adaptation of *Romeo and Juliet*. On the relations between the two theatres see Werner Frick, 'Klassische Präsenzen. Die Weimarer Dramatik und das Berliner Nationaltheater unter Iffland und Graf Brühl', in Ernst Osterkamp (ed.), *Wechselwirkungen. Kunst und Wissenschaft in Berlin und Weimar im Zeichen Goethes* (Bern, Berlin, Frankfurt am Main: Lang, 2003), pp. 231–66.

have recommended itself to Iffland as a compact play, already adapted for the stage. In Friedrich Beschort he had a suitable actor to play the title role, while he took the role of Oranien. Klärchen was played by Friederike Unzelmann. The *Zeitung für die elegante Welt* expressed regret that Iffland had not stuck even to the adaptation's unfortunate changes to the original but had trimmed it further so that it would not give offence to the Prussian authorities (presumably through its allusions to freedom).[43] The journal *Kronos* carried a review that, while blaming the play's unenthusiastic reception on the actors playing the secondary roles and on the public's lack of receptiveness, went on to complain about those who had destroyed that receptiveness:

> Wer hat es [das Publikum] verwöhnt? Wer hat die Montfaucons, die Octavien, die Schwestern von Prag, die Sonntagskinder und wie diese Dinge alle heißen, wer hat sie gekocht und aufgetischt? Man pflegt Speisen, die ungenießbar zu werden drohen, zu mariniren, und wie kann der, welcher seine Gäste an solche Kost verwöhnte, verlangen, daß ihnen die reife Frucht aus der Hand der Natur behage.[44]

This quotation, admittedly more anti-Kotzebue than anti–Iffland, is characteristic of Romantic polemic of the kind quoted earlier in this chapter from A. W. Schlegel and Tieck and illustrates a failure to understand that no theatre could maintain itself without a mixed repertoire.

A comparison of the Berlin repertoire of 1803 with that of Weimar in the same year is revealing.[45] This was a year when the Weimar experiment was at its height. In Weimar plays by Iffland and

---

43   *Zeitung für die elegante Welt*, 16 June 1801 (72. Stück).
44   Quoted in Teichmann, p. 67. *Johanna von Montfaucon* and *Octavia* were plays by Kotzebue; *Die Schwestern von Prag* and *Das neue Sonntagskind* were *Singspiele* by Wenzel Müller.
45   For Berlin I have reconstructed the repertoire using the information on performances given in Klaus Gerlach's database Datenbank Berliner National-theater (http://zopeman.bbaw.de/BK/theater) and supplemented this information with data from the Sammlung Oscar Fambach. The list of performances is probably not quite complete, as for some dates there is no information, but these omissions are likely to be no more than 3–5% of the total and do not prevent rough percentage comparisons from having some indicative value.

Kotzebue were given a total of 38 times out of the 158 performances falling under the heading of spoken theatre, in other words 24% of that total. In Berlin in 1803 the total for Iffland and Kotzebue performances was 90 out of 307 of spoken theatre, which is 29%. Given, however, that the Berlin theatre played almost every night of the year and put on twice as many plays in 1803 as the Weimar theatre, and that the Weimar theatre had a much larger proportion of its costs covered by court subsidy than Berlin and was therefore less dominated by the need for commercial success, the percentage difference between the two is not striking. At the Mannheim National Theatre in the same year, 106 performances of spoken drama (the theatre was open three nights a week) included 40 by Iffland and Kotzebue, which is c. 38%.[46] There Schiller was given three times, Lessing twice and Goethe not at all. In Weimar works by Goethe and Schiller were given 42 times, taking up over 26% of the spoken drama performances for the year. In Berlin Goethe and Schiller performances totalled 43, in other words 14% of spoken theatre, but with 36 of those performances being of works by Schiller the number of performances of his plays is almost double that of performances of Iffland's own (19) in that year.

The difference between the the Weimar and Berlin statistics for Goethe and Schiller combined is partly accounted for by Goethe. In Weimar works by Goethe were given 12 times out of 158 performances (8%) and in Berlin only 7 times out of 307 performances or 2.3%. Although the Berlin Romantics were strong admirers of Goethe and took a distanced view of Schiller, their partisanship was not sufficient to guarantee a following for Goethe's plays.[47] It should also be remembered that the Weimar ensemble played a summer season each year in Lauchstädt and usually in another venue, frequently Rudolstadt. Almost no premières were given during these two months from mid-June to mid-August, another reason therefore why there was less pressure for constant novelty in Weimar than in Berlin.

Fetting has provided a wealth of statistical analysis spanning the whole period of Iffland's time in Berlin. Over all, 60.2% of all perfor-

---

46   The calculation is based on the repertoire in Walter, vol. 2, pp. 373–77.
47   Those performed that year were *Iphigenie auf Tauris*, *Clavigo* and *Die natürliche Tochter*.

mances were spoken drama, 34.2% *Musiktheater* and 5.6% ballet. The musical works were performed on average more frequently, which indeed they had to be if they were to recoup the higher costs of staging. Average performance figures for individual works were as follows:

Spoken drama	11 performances
Musiktheater	15
Ballet	10

Iffland regarded three performances as the break-even point for a production.[48] In the light of these averages Schiller's plays were extremely successful. His statistics over all are: 13 works totalling 430 performances, giving an average of 33 performances per play. For individual plays the figures are:

Die Jungfrau von Orleans	137
Maria Stuart	47
Wilhelm Tell	39
Die Braut von Messina	36
Wallensteins Tod	33
Die Räuber	31
Don Karlos	29
Kabale und Liebe	19
Die Piccolomini	16
Wallenstein Lager	16
Fiesko	12
Turandot (after Gozzi)	8
Der Parasit (after Picard)	7[49]

Kotzebue was the most performed playwright with 1226 performances of 86 works. This makes his average between 14 and 15 per play. Schiller was the second most performed playwright, though with a much higher average number of performances per play, and in third place is Iffland, with 380 performances of 41 works, giving an average per work of 9.5 performances, which is slightly below the theatre's average for spoken drama. If one takes out *Die Jungfrau von Orleans* and the Gozzi and Picard adaptations from Schiller's

---

48 Fetting, *Das Repertoire des Berliner Königlichen Nationaltheaters*, pp. 86–87.
49 Fetting, *Das Repertoire des Berliner Königlichen Nationaltheaters*, Appendix, pp. 70–78.

statistics, the total comes to 278 performances of 10 plays, an average of almost 28. Many plays by Kotzebue and particularly Iffland were performed three times or less. Fetting lists 15 such for Kotzebue and 18 for Iffland. For Iffland this is quite a significant figure, for it indicates that almost half of his plays were either not very successful in Berlin or were older plays that were no longer popular. *Verbrechen aus Ehrsucht* is an example of a play that clearly fell away in popularity, being performed only three times under Iffland's directorship, even though it remained in the repertoire, according to Schäffer and Hartmann, until 1830, having been performed twenty-two times since 1787.[50] *Die Jäger* and *Die Hagestolzen*, by contrast, continued to be played, both remaining in the repertoire into the 1880s.[51] Of the plays Iffland wrote in his Berlin years several were performed four or five times in all but only in the year of their première. Examples are *Das Gewissen* (1797), *Der Mann von Wort* (1798), *Das Erbteil des Vaters* (1800), *Die Höhen* (1800), *Seelenwanderung* (1800). These findings lend support to the evidence of the Weimar repertoire, which shows the striking decline in popularity of Iffland's plays as the new century got under way. More successful were *Die Erinnerung* (1797), *Die Selbstbeherrschung* (1798) and *Das Vaterhaus* (1800), a continuation of *Die Jäger*, all of which enjoyed more than 20 performances in Berlin in Iffland's lifetime.

With 137 performances up to Iffland's death, the most performed play at the Berlin theatre was *Die Jungfrau von Orleans*. In joint second position and a long way behind with 64 performances each were two plays by Kotzebue, *Die deutschen Kleinstädter* and the one-act comedy *Die Unglücklichen*. An important factor in the play's success was the spectacle and pageantry. In the *Almanach fürs Theater* of 1811 Iffland lists the extras needed to mount his version of the coronation procession, justifying this lavishness from Schiller's own stage directions. The figure comes to 297.[52] He mentions other

---

50   Schäffer and Hartmann, p. 87.
51   Schäffer and Hartmann, pp. 44 and 39.
52   'Verhältnisse der gegenwärtigen Theaterdirectionen, im Vergleich mit denen, worin die Directionen der Theater vormals sich befunden haben', *Almanach fürs Theater 1811* (Berlin: Saalfeld, 1811), pp. 38–83 (p. 69).

plays that are known to be costly – *Wilhelm Tell*, Collin's *Regulus,* Zacharias Werner's *Die Weihe der Kraft* – but maintains that, for a play to be put on with suitable dignity, the necessary personnel, appropriately dressed, must be available.[53] One suspects that Iffland is answering his critics here. He uses an artistic argument to justify a pragmatic decision to win an audience broader than the intellectual elite for Schiller's play. His attitude also bespeaks the confidence of someone who by 1811 knew he was in charge of one of Germany's leading theatres. It would, however, be wrong to conclude that spectacle or patriotic emphasis accounted for the success of Iffland's Schiller productions. The example of *Die Braut von Messina*, the success of which Schiller himself was surprised by, is remarkable. Curiosity was bound to guarantee an audience for a few performances of the play but with a total of 36, stretching over several years, the play simply must have been popular with audiences. It was the 21st most performed play over all in the spoken repertoire in Iffland's time, even though it did not come in until 1803.

In that year in Berlin the emerging German playwrights of the classical repertoire were supplemented by renowned dramatists and plays, serious and comic, from the international repertoire: Holberg, Goldoni, Sheridan, Goldsmith, Beaumarchais, Molière, Cumberland, Voltaire. Shakespeare was present only in Gotter's and Reichardt's adaptation of *The Tempest* as a *Singspiel* with the title *Die Geister-insel*. One of the effects of the prolific outputs of Iffland and Kotzebue was a consequent decline in the need for rapidly translated adaptations of foreign works, in particular French comedies. Thus the foreign works performed tended increasingly to be those that had acquired a certain status in the repertoire generally, as the list of names above indicates. It was the *Musiktheater* repertoire that maintained a stronger international flavour, as one would expect. Like Goethe, Iffland was a strong promoter of Mozart and Gluck, *Die Zauberflöte* being the most performed opera in Berlin during his period. French (Dalayrac and Méhul) and Italian (Cimarosa, Salieri, Paisiello) composers were also highly popular, as they were at most German theatres.

---

53   'Verhältnisse', pp. 70–73.

Schiller's Berlin visit

Iffland's regard for Schiller and appreciation of his value as a col-
laborator were demonstrated by his eagerness to win the playwright
for the Berlin theatre. He had kept faith with Schiller after the success
of *Die Jungfrau von Orleans* by putting great effort into the première
of *Die Braut von Messina* and was rewarded by the considerable stage
success mentioned above but also by a grateful Schiller's promise to
write a play 'fürs ganze Publikum', namely *Wilhelm Tell*. During the
visit of Pauly, the Berlin theatre's secretary, to Weimar in 1804 to
discuss Iffland's numerous queries about the *Wilhelm Tell* production,
the question of a closer collaboration or even a move by Schiller to
Berlin was probably broached, for at the end of that same month the
playwright and his wife set off on a journey to the Prussian capital.[54]
To honour the sudden visit Iffland arranged a series of performances
of Schiller's plays, culminating in *Wallensteins Tod* with Iffland
himself in the title role. The Schillers were received by Queen Luise
and on 17 May, at the end of the visit, Schiller had a meeting with the
court official Carl Friedrich Beyme, presumably to discuss the conditions for a possible move. Iffland sent a memorandum to Beyme in
preparation for the meeting, letting him know that Schiller had expressed a wish to remain in Berlin, at least for a few years: 'Ob es
nicht zu bewirken seyn möchte, daß er als Academicien mit einem Ge-
halt, nach der Kenntniß, die er nun vom Berliner Publikum erhalten
habe, und noch erhalten werde, für das National-Theater arbeiten
könne?'(NA 32, 479). Schiller left Berlin with the prospect of a salary
of 3000 Talers, the same as Iffland's starting salary in Berlin, which
was clearly a dramatic improvement in income by comparison with
the 400 Talers he received from Duke Carl August.

---

54   See Michael Bienert, *Schiller in Berlin oder Das rege Leben einer großen
      Stadt*, Marbacher Magazin, 106 (Marbach am Neckar: Deutsche Schillergesell-
      schaft, 2004), p. 37. On the visit see also Hugo Holstein, 'Zu Schillers Reise
      nach Berlin' in Max Koch (ed.), *Studien zur vergleichenden Literaturgeschichte*
      4/4 (1904), 471–74.

Probably the most important factor that led to Schiller's considering this surprising move – surprising because his health was so precarious – was concern over the future of his family. He already had three children and Charlotte Schiller gave birth to a fourth, their second daughter, Emilie, in July of that year. Given his expectation of an early death, his aim was to put aside sufficient funds to ensure that they would enjoy some independence as adults. In Berlin he would earn a salary amounting to almost twice the sum he earned from his writing. He also expressed to his brother-in-law Wilhelm von Wolzogen the wish to experience a more metropolitan atmosphere:

> Ich habe ein Bedürfnis gefühlt, mich in einer fremden und größeren Stadt zu bewegen. Einmal ist es ja meine Bestimmung, für eine größere Welt zu schreiben, und ich sehe mich hier in so engen Verhältnißen, daß es ein Wunder ist, wie ich nur einiger maaßen etwas leisten kann, das für die größere Welt ist. (NA 32, 142)

Clearly torn, he approached Carl August with the request that his pension be raised to 800 Talers, with the prospect of a further increase to 1000 Talers, emphasizing that his family's future made the Berlin offer difficult to refuse. Carl August immediately responded positively and encouraged Schiller to see if he could reach an agreement with Berlin over a partial commitment rather than a complete move. Shortly after, on 18 June, Schiller wrote to Beyme proposing a partial move for several months of the year, justifying it on artistic grounds: 'denn aus der größeren Welt schöpft zwar der Dichter seinen Stoff, aber in der Abgezogenheit und Stille muß er ihn verarbeiten' (NA 32, 143). 2000 Talers a year would put him in a position to live for the requisite time in Berlin. A partial move was clearly not sufficient for the Prussian government and the letter went unanswered, the original bearing the note 'Ad A[ct]a. bis sich Gelegenheit findet. 1805' (NA 32, 486).

It is remarkable, given Schiller's state of health, that he should have contemplated a move. Apart from his concern for his family, it is also explicable as another expression of his temperamental restlessness and need for new challenges. To be present in the capital of the most powerful German state and to have a series of his plays performed at one of the most prestigious theatres in the German-speaking world made a strong impression on one whose practical possibilities of travel were so limited and who had relied so much in later years on second-hand reports for a sense of his rising significance as a stage writer. His death on 9 May the following year, less than a year after his interview with Beyme, left Charlotte Schiller with the task of securing her children's future. She wrote to Iffland to ask if he could arrange benefit performances for them of her husband's plays: 'Durch Ihren Einfluß hat Schiller zum ersten Mal in Berlin das belohnende Gefühl genoßen, für eine Nation gearbeitet zu haben.'[55] After some delay on the part of the Prussian king[56] a performance of *Die Braut von Messina* on 10 May 1806 brought in 2233 Talers, made up by the King to 3003 and sent along with four gold medallions from the royal children. Iffland was also active in encouraging further benefit performances in Germany, for example, by amateur groups.[57]

The French occupation and after

By 1806 Iffland could credit himself with considerable achievements in building up the reputation of the Berlin National Theatre and securing a new and much more suitable building for it. As in Mannheim, war was to disrupt his work and bring new anxieties. On 14 October the Prussian army, drawn once more into attempts, this time led by Britain, Russia and Austria, to resist Napoleon's territorial ambitions, was utterly defeated at the battle of Jena/Auerstedt. On 27 October Napoleon himself appeared in Berlin and there followed just over two years of French occupation of the city, lasting until December 1808.

---

55 Letter to Iffland, 20. 6. 1805. In: Marbacher Schiller-Buch II, ed. by Otto Güntter (Stuttgart: Cotta, 1907), p. 403.

56 See Bienert, p. 71.

57 See 'Vorschlag an die Liebhabertheater in Deutschland, zu Schillers Gedächtniß', *Almanach fürs Theater 1807* (Berlin: Oehmigke jun., 1807), pp. 219–27. In addition to professional theatres, the suggestion was acted upon by the group in Drebkau in Niederlausitz and brought in 220 Talers, as reported in 'Schillers Todtenfeier', *Almanach fürs Theater 1812* (Berlin: Duncker & Humblot, 1812), pp. 241–45.

The King fled eastwards with his court and administration to Königsberg and many members of the Prussian aristocracy abandoned the city. During the occupation the royal subsidy to the theatre, relatively small though it was, was not paid. Iffland was conscious that the French occupying powers might decide to replace his company with a French one. In addition, the military defeat of Prussia was not simply a setback, it was a humiliating collapse that made the remaining Berliners disinclined to go out to the theatre. Moreover, many of its most regular supporters, namely army officers on the one hand and the wealthy and leisured part of the population on the other, had gone.

Concerned about the theatre's rapid decline, Iffland sent every member of the company a circular, which although undated was probably written some months into the occupation.[58] He reminds the company that many other theatres regularly end the contracts of the actors in order to ensure the supply of new blood, whereas his policy has been to give his company continued employment so that, freed from anxiety, they can devote themselves to their art and the ensemble can grow together. He suggests that, while some members show suitable conscientiousness and professionalism, others are taking advantage of the security to become slovenly in learning their parts, in prompt attendance at rehearsals, in enunciation and audibility, and in careful movement on stage. The playing of secondary roles is particularly neglected. While he welcomes the fact that actors now have the opportunity to become respectable members of society, some are putting their outside concerns before their commitment to the theatre. He reminds them that their task is to give pleasure and distraction to those who are suffering through the war, especially given that they themselves are exposed to much less disruption as a result of hostilities than actors in many other companies. Then Iffland comes to the French-speaking members of the audience:

> Die möglichste Anstrengung sollte um so mehr jetzt von dem eignen Ehrgefühl erwartet werden, da wir jetzt größtentheils vor einem fremden Publikum spie-

---

58 'Circular an die Mitglieder der Berliner Bühne', published in Carl Duncker (ed.), *Iffland in seinen Schriften als Künstler, Lehrer und Director der Berliner Bühne* (Berlin: Duncker und Humblot, 1859), pp. 111–29.

len, welches bei sich zu Hause, einer sehr sorgfältigen Bühne, der größten Pünktlichkeit der Darstellungen, gewöhnt ist.

Da dieses Publikum, ungeachtet es in der großen Mehrheit unserer Sprache nicht kundig ist, gleichwohl die Rücksicht beweiset, nicht ein Theater seiner Sprache hieher kommen zu lassen, und also dadurch unsere Erhaltung möglich macht; so ist es die erste Schuldigkeit, ihm in vernehmlicher Sprache und faßlich genauer Mimik verständlich zu werden.[59]

Iffland therefore seeks to combine an appeal to artistic pride with self-interest. His ultimate sanction is the King's wish to receive a report accompanying the budget on the contribution of every member of the company. Though he has evaded the command to produce such a report up to now, the standard of playing may force him to do so. There is a very contemporary ring to Iffland's words. It was always a matter of great concern to him to attain financial security and to have a pension to rely on, to enjoy the advantages in other words of other members of the *Bürgertum*. He always linked this argument to artistic concerns, such as the need for stability for individuals and companies to develop. Goethe too, with a much more modest ensemble and budget, strove to give a measure of job security (by, for example, issuing contracts for three years and discouraging *Gastspiele* for fear of poaching) so that there was a possibility of developing a unified style.

The Berlin theatre was not closed by the French, nor was the company replaced by a French one. It was forced to relinquish its German title of *Nationaltheater*, becoming 'La société dramatique et lyrique Allemande de S. M. le Roi', and all play bills had to be printed in French as well as in German. Iffland's ability to adapt to the new situation and modify the repertoire to the tastes of the new sections of the audience doubtless helped the theatre survive, in spite of also losing its royal subsidy. Whereas in 1803 176 operas and *Singspiele* were given, in 1807 it was 229. In 1803 19 ballets were performed, in 1807 the number was 59. In 1808 181 operas and *Singspiele* were given, 51 ballets and 53 pantomime-ballets. There was also a huge increase in the number of (often short) comedies and farces from 75 in 1803 to 180 in 1807 and 153 in 1808. The number of tragedies reduces from 40 in 1803 to 16 in 1807 and 1808. The popularity of

---

59   'Circular', p. 121.

French composers such as Dalayrac, Méhul and Grétry was already established in Berlin. Iffland supplemented the comic repertoire with a number of translations he made himself of short comedies by Picard, at that time popular in Paris, publishing them under the title *Beiträge für die Deutsche Schaubühne: In Übersetzungen und Bearbeitungen ausländischer Schauspiele*.[60] The number of performances of Molière increased. In the much reduced tragic repertoire Schiller's *Phädra* proved a useful item, as did *Die Braut von Messina*, as it had no political resonance, unlike *Die Jungfrau von Orleans*, which was not played at all during the French occupation. The fact that Schiller and Lessing (*Emilia Galotti*) were still played suggests that Iffland took what opportunity he had to preserve some drama of literary stature rather than abandoning it altogether.

The theatre could of course easily become a rallying point for patriotic feeling. In a famous incident Iffland himself was placed under house arrest for two days for appearing in the theatre with flowers pinned to his coat on Queen Luise's birthday, thus prompting applause from the audience. The official announcement blamed him for not seeking permission. When it came to the King's birthday on 3 August permission was sought to mark the occasion: 'Es wurde [...] von der Direction die Oper Armide vorgeschlagen, als welche zu Allusionen und excedirenden Empfindungen ganz und gar nicht Veranlaßung geben kann.'[61] Gluck's opera was not in fact given. *Oedip zu Colonos. Ein lyrisches Drama in Drey Aufzügen* by Sacchini was chosen, presumably being equally free from the danger of political resonances. Though Iffland was known for his devotion to the royal family, he clearly saw the risk involved to his whole enterprise of not staying within the proper bounds. In one respect the French occupying force came to his aid. A notice was published warning that any audience member caught whistling in or at the performance would be sent to the commandant.[62]

---

60   5 vols (Berlin: Braunes, 1807–12).
61   Brandenburgisches Landeshauparchiv, Rep. 30 Berlin A (Polizeidirektorium Berlin), Nr. 440/1, Bl. 117, 3 July 1808.
62   A copy is preserved in the Brandenburgisches Landeshauptarchiv, Rep. 30 Berlin A, Nr. 440/1.

The King did not return to Berlin until December 1809, a year after the withdrawal of the French occupying forces. In a letter to his sister Louise, Iffland recounts being called to the royal box on 25 December after a performance of his short comedy *Der Verein*, where the King told him:

> Ich habe Sie stets für einen großen Künstler und wohldenkenden Mann gehalten; Sie haben sich in meiner Abwesenheit auf jede Weise als treuer Patriot bewiesen. Heute Abend geben Sie mir abermals einen Beweiß davon, der mir an das Herz greift.[63]

This royal recognition was clearly very important to Iffland. The King distinguished him with the *Roter Adlerorden dritter Klasse*, the first time such a decoration had been awarded to an actor. In 1811 it was decided to consolidate theatre, opera (including the remnants of the old Italian opera) and ballet into one organization called the *Königliche Schauspiele*, of which Iffland was made the first director.

During his Berlin time Iffland continued his strenuous programme of *Gastspiele*, no doubt in part because they were a lucrative supplement to his income and he was always struggling with debts. He was often absent from Berlin for about three months a year. As during his later Mannheim days, offers were made to him by other theatres, for example by Stuttgart in 1802[64] and, more temptingly, by Vienna in 1808/09, at the time of the French occupation. A move there would mean the possibility, as had happened in 1796, of stipulating the clearing of his debts as a condition. The negotiations with Vienna were protracted and resulted in an extremely generous offer, detailed in a letter by Iffland to Friedrich Ludwig Schmidt, actor, playwright and later director at the Hamburg theatre. The strong likelihood of the move makes Iffland ponder its pros and cons:

> Es ist gewiß nicht angenehm, auf der Brandstätte vormaliger Palläste umherzuwandeln in einer ausgestorbenen Glückseligkeit zu seufzen und auch wohl zu

---

63   Geiger 1, p. 221.
64   See the letters printed in Geiger 2, pp. 147–50.

weinen. Doch scheint es mir auf der andern Seite unverantwortlich, bloß um des Geldes und mehrerer Gemächlichkeit willen, aus der Reihe heraus zu treten.[65]

The move did not proceed, according to Geiger because Friedrich Wilhelm III was unhappy about it and according to Hajdecki because the Viennese authorities had received a report from Berlin alluding to Iffland's homosexuality and involvement in Freemasonry.[66]

The collapse of the negotiations with Vienna meant that Iffland was responsible for trying to retrieve something of what was lost during the French occupation. In 1803 the number of performances of tragedy was 55.[67] Whereas in 1807 and 1808 only 16 tragedies were given each year (57 and 68 Schauspiele in these years), in 1809 the number rose to 34 and in 1810 to 45. For the first six months of 1811 it is 27. So we see evidence of Iffland trying as soon as possible to bring back more serious drama. Of the performances of tragedy in 1809 23 were of Schiller and in 1810 the number was 24. Die Jungfrau von Orleans, which, as mentioned above, had not been performed during the occupation possibly for reasons of economy as well as because of its patriotic resonances, made a triumphant return. New serious drama that was also stageworthy was extremely hard to find, one indication of which may have been the revival of Gotter's Mariane and Leisewitz's Julius von Tarent, both plays written and premièred in the 1770s. Shakespeare (Hamlet, Macbeth and King Lear), Goethe (Egmont), Voltaire (for example, Goethe's translation of Mahomet) and Racine were also played.

What the recovery after the occupation did not bring was a revival of the number of performances of Iffland's own plays. In 1806 he was put on 14 times as compared with 68 performances of Kotzebue. In 1809 he was put on 4 times and in 1810 9 times. A similar

---

65   Letter dated 10 March 1809 to Friedrich Ludwig Schmidt, Stiftung Archiv der Akademie der Künste, Sammlung Merbach, Rep. 100 Mf. A. 5. 28. 52–69.

66   Alexander Hajdecki, 'Iffland und sein Wiener Engagement zum Theaterdirektor im Jahre 1809. Eine archivalische Literaturstudie', Erdgeist 3/2 (1908), 41–45. The Viennese court received a report from a correspondent in Berlin: 'man versicherte mir, er sei der Sodomie ergeben' (p. 44). He also mentions claims that Iffland was connected to Freemasons in Berlin but does not confirm them.

67   The figures here are taken from the Datenbank Berliner Nationaltheater.

decline is evident from the Weimar statistics. The peak years for Iffland in Weimar were those around 1800, but the subsequent decline was rapid, with 2 performances in 1809 and only one in 1810. This may well have been a matter of disappointment to Iffland. He continued to write as many plays in Berlin as he had in Mannheim, but few found favour with audiences in the way *Die Jäger* or *Die Hagestolzen* had done. He was, of course, less versatile than Kotzebue. But disappointed or not, he was a businessman, and if his plays were not drawing audiences they had to go from the repertoire.

After the death of Schiller Iffland continued to keep a close eye on the Weimar theatre (he corresponded regularly with Franz Kirms, Goethe's financial deputy at the theatre) and returned for *Gastspiele* in 1810 and 1812.[68] Two works of Goethe premièred in Iffland's last years were *Torquato Tasso* (1811), presented 'nach dem von dem Dichter eingereichten Manuskript' and played altogether 77 times by the 1880s,[69] and the early pastoral *Die Laune des Verliebten* (1813), which remained in the repertoire up to the middle of the nineteenth century. Through Kirms Iffland approached Goethe in 1810 to supply a stage adaptation of his *Faust*, the first part of which had appeared in 1808.[70] Goethe refused, but in 1812 he sold Iffland his stage adaptation of Shakespeare's *Romeo and Juliet*, based on the Schlegel blank verse translation, for the immense sum of 600 Talers.[71] The play went on to be very successful but Goethe's version was dropped in 1817. Other Shakespeare plays added to the repertoire in those final years were *Coriolanus* in Daniel Falk's adaptation and *Othello* in Heinrich Voss's translation, to which Schiller had contributed shortly before his death, though the former was played only twice and the latter only four times.[72]

---

68 A number are published; see, for example, Geiger, 'Schauspielerbriefe'.
69 See Schäffer and Hartmann, p. 84. The Weimar première was in 1807.
70 See Wahle, p. xxiv.
71 See Goethe's letter to Kirms of 22 February 1812. He promised Iffland exclusive rights to the manuscript and undertook not to publish the text for three years (WA IV, 22, 288–89).
72 See Schäffer and Hartmann, p. 14 and p. 64.

Iffland's punishing schedule in Berlin and his constant *Gast-spiele*, always involving his playing multiple roles within a very short time, finally began to take their toll and from 1813 he succumbed more and more frequently to illness. The fact that he was increasingly unable to combine effectively all his activities, particularly after the creation of the *Königliche Schauspiele* in 1811, is attested by a letter cited by Teichmann in his very restrained summing up of the former's regimen: 'Er ist ein sehr großer Schauspieler in komischen und ernst sentimentalischen Rollen; überall aber wo Kraft erfordert wird, sowohl auf den Brettern als bei der Direction, zeigt sich seine natürliche Schwäche.'[73] From 1813 dates Iffland's somewhat embittered response to a directive from the Prussian minister Hardenberg, impressing on him the need to exercise strict economy, dismiss all superfluous personnel and ensure that he was responding to audience demand in what was put on.[74] Such a missive to a man of Iffland's experience and to one whose efforts had ensured that the Berlin National Theatre was, along with Vienna and Hamburg, a leading stage in the German-speaking world, must have been provoking. It is not clear whether his draft response was ever sent, but it offers a final statement in defence of his policy regarding the repertoire:

'Stücke im Geschmack des Publikums geben.'
Wer ist Publikum in Berlin? Haude und Spener[75] oder einzelne Theecotterien, mißvergnügte Autoren, *parleurs* am Dessert oder das Publikum im Theater? Wenige wollen Goethe, mehrere Schiller, viele den Rochus Pumpernickel.[76] Viele preisen Mozart, wenige besuchen ihn; die 'Vestalin' wird geliebt, wenig besucht.[77] […]

---

73   Teichmann, pp. 103–04. He does not divulge the name of the letter-writer, but calls him someone 'der die gründlichste Kenntniß und das gediegenste Urtheil über Theater und Theaterwesen besaß' (p. 103).
74   See Wilhelm Altmann, 'Ifflands Rechtfertigung seiner Theaterverwaltung vom 27. Juli 1813', in *Archiv für Theatergeschichte*, vol. 1, ed. by Hans Devrient (Berlin: Fleischel, 1904), pp. 86–94 (p. 87).
75   Proprietors of the two leading Berlin newspapers.
76   A musical medley (Quodlibet) by Seyfried and Stegmayer.
77   *La Vestale*, opera by Spontini.

Der Direktor hat also für das Publikum zu sorgen, was Berlin enthält; er muß streben, diesem mannigfach zu sein, und das Repertoir beweist, daß er das ist. Er darf nicht auf den Salon, nicht auf den einzelnen Mißvergnügten, nicht auf den überreizten schönen Geist, nicht auf den gelangweilten Abonnenten, der jeden Tag ein neues Stück sehen möchte, nicht auf den parteisüchtigen Gelehrten hinsehen: er muß alle im Blicke haben, von allen sich beurteilen, von allen sich mißverstehen lassen.[78]

His last stage appearance was in January 1814. He died of a pulmonary illness on 22 September 1814.

---

78   Altmann, pp. 88–89.

Conclusion

From the 1770s and into the 1780s the expansion of theatre, popular taste and financial constraints created an environment that seemed to guarantee the lasting success of family drama on the German stage. Tragedy, in particular high tragedy, seemed to have no future in performance. Schiller's extraordinary combination of poetic imagination, intellectual energy and sure instinct for stage drama enabled his later plays to buck the trend of popular contemporary theatre (and indeed set new trends themselves) and be successful with a broad audience rather than only with a literary elite. Iffland's policy of making Schiller's later plays the centrepiece of his repertoire and hence his role in the formation of a national repertoire is his enduring, though often overlooked, legacy to the German theatre.

By focusing on the repertoire, this study has, however, attempted to illuminate more than the detail of the intriguing symbiosis that developed between these two men. It has aimed to reveal something of the dynamics of the evolution of German theatre over a crucial forty-year period, namely the interdependence of dramatic texts, performance, changing literary and popular tastes and economic, and to a lesser extent political, conditions. During those forty years, during which revolution and wars added to the problems the German states had to contend with, theatre in Germany remained a precarious enterprise, with stages flourishing and collapsing, leading innovation for a time and then stagnating. But during this period there is no doubt that theatre made immense progress towards establishing its importance in the public mind as a cultural institution. In addition, the acting profession started to gain the respectability that Iffland had constantly striven for. One of the legacies of eighteenth-century particularism in the nineteenth century was that theatre traditions were built up in towns and cities (many of them former capitals) throughout Germany. The rise of nationalism in the nineteenth century, however baleful some of its consequences ultimately were, undoubtedly played its part in boosting the position of theatre as a manifestation of German cultural aspirations and sense of, or hope for, a shared identity. The extraordinary prestige of Goethe and Schiller as cultural icons within this process, and after unification in 1871 in particular, consolidated the position of Schiller's dramas as expressions of the nation.

By highlighting Iffland I have not wished to diminish Goethe's role in Schiller's return to the theatre. He was undoubtedly vital to the emergence of his friend's later plays and to their staging; without him and the Weimar Court Theatre, though Schiller would certainly have found his way back to tragic drama, he might not have returned to the practical world of theatre. The knowledge that Goethe shared his literary aims, including his aspirations for German theatre, and the process of discussing his work with him were essential to his later creativity. But Weimar had only a small provincial theatre, despite its renown through Goethe's involvement with it. Iffland was Schiller's most important link with the wider theatrical world.

After Schiller's death, as mentioned at the end of Chapter 7, Iffland maintained his connection with Weimar. After Iffland's death, though Goethe's interest in the theatre was diminishing sharply, the Weimar–Berlin connection was, if anything, strengthened. Iffland's position was filled not by another professional man of the theatre but by the more usual aristocratic *Intendant*. Carl Reichsgraf von Brühl (1772–1837) remained in charge until 1829. He was acquainted with and strongly admired Goethe, whose idea of theatre as an institution reflecting literary and artistic aspirations he shared. In keeping with the literary emphasis he brought to his task, Brühl made it a priority to put on new productions of the plays of Schiller, Goethe and Shakespeare that had been introduced by Iffland. He increased the repertoire of Shakespeare plays and introduced Calderón, a dramatist favoured in Weimar who had not been taken up by Iffland. The most striking indication that Brühl wanted to follow Goethe's lead in style as well as in repertoire was his engagement in 1815 of two leading members of the Weimar ensemble, Pius Alexander Wolff and his wife Amalie, formerly Amalie Malcolmi (whose first notable success was as Johanna in the Weimar première of *Die Jungfrau von Orleans*). Wolff, who was also engaged as a *Regisseur*, was thus perfectly placed to move the Berlin ensemble in the direction of the Weimar style, though in practice this was very hard to achieve where existing styles and the repertoire were so diverse.

While Schiller's plays helped create, and in Weimar were show-pieces of, the Weimar style, elsewhere, as in Berlin, they were capable of a life of their own, of being adapted to the more realistic style of other theatres and to the demands of a more heterogeneous audience than the one found in Weimar. While Oellers, whose study of Schiller reception includes a compact survey of theatre performance up to 1832, points out that the Berlin productions attracted audiences there and at other theatres by the offer of spectacle, it is striking that even such a challenging play as *Die Braut von Messina* was not infrequently performed well into the 1820s.[1] What is also remarkable about the statistics for the period up to the 1830s is that every play of Schiller's was in the repertoire, even if *Fiesko* was the least often performed. At the same time, it would be misleading to suggest that his plays dominated every stage. Rather they provided the core of a classical repertoire that could maintain its hold over audiences. Some precise figures will make that clear.

After Schiller's death and from the end of the French occupation and into Brühl's time Berlin continued to offer a substantial number of Schiller performances each year: 23 in 1809, 24 in 1810, 21 in 1813, 30 in 1814, 26 in 1815, 26 in 1816.[2] Elsewhere (and obviously many theatres played only three or four times a week) the numbers are lower. Mannheim, for example averaged about 7 performances per year during those years. In Weimar itself there is a decline from 1815 onwards, another indication of Goethe's withdrawal from the theatre. Stuttgart was late to stage some of the plays because King Friedrich disliked them, while the director of the Munich theatre, the playwright Joseph Marius Babo, was not enamoured of Schiller until *Die Jung-frau von Orleans* was premièred in 1812 and was very successful.[3]

---

1   Norbert Oellers, *Schiller. Geschichte seiner Wirkung bis zu Goethes Tod* (Bonn: Bouvier, 1967), pp. 327–30). For a survey of theatre reception up to 1832 see pp. 324–42.

2   Information for 1811 and 1812 in the Sammlung Oscar Fambach and the Daten-bank Berliner Nationaltheater is incomplete.

3   Oellers, pp. 335–37.

At Hamburg, by contrast, Schiller was played some 15 to 20 times a year between 1805 and 1815.[4] The following table[5] gives an indication of the performance figures at a range of theatres for the immediate post-Iffland period and into the 1820s:

	1818	1822	1827	1830
Berlin	14	16	18	13
Weimar	3	3	6	5
Mannheim	7	3	6	5
Leipzig	14	14	8	−*
Dresden	7	7	8	6
Frankfurt	16	12	4	11
Stuttgart	12	11	5	7
Hamburg	10	16	15	8
Vienna	16	6	20	11

*statistics not available

Again, the totals vary in part according to the number of nights the theatre was regularly open. The modest numbers of performances at the theatres with which Schiller was most closely associated, Weimar and Mannheim, are striking by contrast with Frankfurt, Leipzig and Berlin. Though there is a slight decline in 1830, the figures indicate that by this point Schiller is firmly established, even if he does not dominate the repertoire. Frank's statistics in Appendix 1 for Frankfurt in the 1830s give 64 performances over 10 years (1830–39). Looking further into the future, Stahl's give 394 performances at Mannheim between 1839 and 1889, an average of 9.5 per year, putting Schiller in second place for this period after Shakespeare.

---

4   Oellers, p. 333.
5   The information is drawn from the Sammlung Oscar Fambach, the Datenbank Berliner Nationaltheater and from Bernhard Frank, *Die erste Frankfurter Theater AG (1792–1842) in ihrer Entwicklung von der 'Nationalbühne' zur 'Volksbühne'. Ein Beitrag zur Erforschung von Schauspiel-Stil und Regie des 19. Jahrhunderts,* Studien zur Frankfurter Geschichte, 2 (Frankfurt am Main: Kramer, 1967) pp. 64–65. The statistics for Vienna are in Oellers, p. 340.

The wider impact of Schiller's stage success had two major results: the opening up of the stage to German verse drama and the rise in popularity of Shakespeare. If Schiller was played regularly, if not very frequently, Goethe's verse dramas and Lessing's *Nathan der Weise* also came to be played regularly, if even less frequently, while Schiller's adaptations of *Egmont, Iphigenie auf Tauris* and *Nathan der Weise* played their part in the renewed accessibility of these works for the stage. *Torquato Tasso* was not premièred until 1807[6] but thereafter enjoyed productions at many theatres. While Schiller epigones such as Collin began to flourish early in the nineteenth century, major verse dramatists such as Kleist, Grillparzer and Hebbel also emerged. The fact that they could be widely performed at all is testimony to Schiller's lasting impact not only on verse speaking in the theatre but on the perception of verse drama as viable on stage.

The breakthrough to verse speaking also smoothed the way for the acceptance of Shakespeare on stage in verse and therefore, slowly, in something like accurate translations rather than in the heavily adapted versions familiar from the late eighteenth until well into the nineteenth century. The translations begun by August Wilhelm Schlegel, edited by Ludwig Tieck and then completed by Wolf von Baudissin and Dorothea Tieck were first published as a complete edition between 1825 and 1833. A second edition then appeared in 1839–40 and from then on these were the translations that dominated on the stage. It is one of the remarkable facts of Iffland's career that, whatever the background politics of relations with the Romantics may have been, he was the first director to stage *Hamlet* in blank verse. That a theatre world had been created in which verse speaking was an indispensable ability prepared the way for the huge cult of Shakespeare that flourished in the middle and later nineteenth century. Even today Shakespeare is by far the most performed single dramatist on the German stage, but Schiller, who wrote far fewer plays, is often in second place. Now that any piety towards him as a *Klassiker* has long since ceased, he, along with Goethe, Kleist and Lessing, still presents a challenge that directors willingly take up.

---

6   On 16 February in Weimar.

Appendix

A The most frequently performed playwrights at the Mannheim National Theatre (1779–1929)

(based on E.L. Stahl, *Das Mannheimer Nationaltheater. Ein Jahrhundert deutscher Theaterkultur im Reich* (Mannheim: Bensheimer, 1929), pp. 404–05)

1779–1839

Kotzebue	1487	Schröder	197
Iffland	418	Goethe	192
Schiller	276	Ziegler	184
Jünger	210	Weissenthurn	153
Shakespeare	200	Beck	134

1839–1889

Shakespeare	408	Scribe	200
Schiller	394	Angely	109
Benedix	357	Görner	98
Birch-Pfeiffer	228	Putlitz	97
Goethe	201	Gutzkow	91

1889–1929

Schiller	668	Hauptmann	190
Shakespeare	554	Blumenthal	180
Goethe	233	Lessing	180
Sudermann	210	Hebbel	164
Schönthan	204	Strindberg	136

265

B   Comparative performance numbers for the Frankfurt National Theatre (1820–40)

(based on Bernhard Frank, *Die erste Frankfurter Theater AG (1792–1842) in ihrer Entwicklung von der 'Nationalbühne' zur 'Volksbühne'. Ein Beitrag zur Erforschung von Schauspiel-Stil und Regie des 19. Jahrhunderts*, Studien zur Frankfurter Geschichte, 2 (Frankfurt am Main: Kramer, 1967), pp. 64–65).

	Schiller	Shake-speare	Goethe	Lessing	Kotzebue	Iffland
1820	10	1	5	1	58	5
1821	11	3	1	4	51	5
1822	12	4	1	–	44	11
1823	14	5	–	2	33	5
1824	17	4	2	–	22	5
1825	12	–	2	–	27	9
1826	8	1	–	–	41	11
1827	4	–	2	–	46	8
1828	7	8	2	4	44	6
1829	4	8	5	3	31	4
1830	11	5	8	4	16	3
1831	9	7	4	1	13	6
1832	10	6	6	–	33	4
1833	5	4	6	3	18	3
1834	8	4	12	4	17	6
1835	6	9	3	3	31	4
1836	5	2	4	–	9	2
1837	3	3	4	1	13	3
1838	12	4	4	2	7	1
1839	7	5	4	2	11	4
1840	8	5	2	–	14	6

The highest total of performances of Iffland's plays in any single year is 29 (1797) and of Kotzebue's 79 (1816).

C Hoftheater Coburg and Gotha (1827–1918)

(based on Andrea Heinz, *Quantitive Spielplanforschung. Neue Möglichkeiten der Theatergeschichtsschreibung am Beispiel des Hoftheaters zu Coburg und Gotha (1827–1918)*, Jenaer Germanistische Forschungen, Neue Folge, 4 (Heidelberg: Winter, 1999), pp. 405–407).

Most frequently performed dramas with number of performances

1	*Robert und Bertram* (Raeder)	69
2	*Wilhelm Tell* (Schiller)	62
3	*Preciosa* (Wolff)	61
4	*Kabale und Liebe* (Schiller)	56
5	*Aschenbrödel* (Görner)	55
6	*Krieg im Frieden* (Moser & Schönthan)	55
7	*Don Karlos* (Schiller)	54
8	*Maria Stuart* (Schiller)	54
9	*Die Räuber* (Schiller)	50
10	*Dorf und Stadt* (Birch-Pfeiffer)	49
	Die Journalisten (Freytag)	49

Most frequently performed authors/composers (with no. of works)

1	Richard Wagner	675 (10)
2	Friedrich Schiller	486 (17)
3	François Auber	407 (19)
4	Gustav von Moser	395 (42)
5	Albert Lortzing	382 (7)
6	Wolfgang Amadeus Mozart	378 (8)
7	Giacomo Meyerbeer	364 (5)
8	Charlotte Birch-Pfeiffer	336 (35)
9	Roderich Benedix	328 (27)
10	Carl Maria von Weber	323 (7)

Shakespeare is 15th on the list with 232 performances of 18 works. Goethe is 18th with 219 performances of 13 works. The large number of works of Schiller includes translations and adaptations.

Glossary

Gastspiel
The term used for a series of performances by an actor (or musician) at a theatre to which he/she is not regularly attached.

Intendant
The name given to the person, usually a member of the court aristocracy, with responsibility for a court theatre. The *Intendant* normally had little or no involvement in the practical or artistic aspects of the theatre but had a supervisory and financial role. Dalberg at Mannheim and Goethe in Weimar were thus exceptions to the rule.

Kulissen
Pairs of mobile wings, painted with the required set and positioned at either side of the stage, stretching to the back in such a way as to create an impression of depth and a realistic perspective. *Kulissen* often slotted into rollers and could be withdrawn and replaced quickly to effect the transformation of the set.

Musiktheater
A general term to cover all types of theatrical entertainment with a musical component, usually sung. In the eighteenth and early nineteenth century such entertainments encompassed the *durchkomponiert* opera as well as the play that incorporated a number of songs (sometimes designated *Schauspiel mit Gesang*).

Prinzipal
The theatrical entrepreneur, usually also an actor, who was at the head of a travelling company and ran it on a commercial basis.

Regisseur

The name given to the member of an acting company whose responsibility it was to rehearse the plays. By contrast with modern rehearsal procedures and the modern implications of the term *director*, in the Schiller–Iffland period rehearsals were often minimal and the *Regisseur*'s task was chiefly to arrange rehearsals and at them to make sure that the cast was aware of exits and entrances.

Rollenfach

The collective name for the various types of role an actor could specialize in. Members of companies were engaged with these specialisms in mind such as young romantic leads or character roles such as fathers, mothers, servants, soldiers.

Wanderbühne

The term denoting both an individual travelling company (also *Wandertruppe*) and travelling companies collectively.

Bibliography

Primary sources: Archives

Brandenburgisches Landeshauptarchiv, Potsdam: Pr. Br. Rep. 30 Berlin A Polizeidirektorium (440/1, 441)
Deutsches Literaturarchiv, Marbach: Handschriftenabteilung, Iffland-Sammlung
Goethe- und Schiller-Archiv, Weimar: Iffland-Bestand
Preußisches Geheimes Staatsarchiv PK, Berlin-Dahlem (GStA PK): I. HA Rep. 36: Geheimer Rat Hof- unf Güterverwaltung
Sammlung Oscar Fambach, University of Bonn
Stiftung Archiv der Akademie der Künste, Berlin: Sammlung Merbach
Thüringisches Hauptstaatsarchiv, Weimar: Generalintendanz des DNT Weimar and Sammlung Pasqué

Primary printed sources

Iffland

Devrient, Otto (ed.), *Briefe von A.W. Iffland und F.L. Schröder an den Schauspieler Werdy* (Frankfurt am Main: Rommel, 1881)
Duncker, Carl (ed.), *Iffland in seinen Schriften als Künstler, Lehrer und Director der Berliner Bühne* (Berlin: Duncker & Humblot, 1859)
Geiger, Ludwig (ed.), A.W. Ifflands Briefe an seine Schwester Louise und andere Verwandte 1772–1814, Schriften der Gesellschaft für Theatergeschichte, 5 (Berlin: Gesellschaft für Theatergeschichte, 1904)
—— *A.W. Ifflands Briefe, meist an seine Schwester, nebst andern Aktenstücken und einem ungedruckten Drama*, Schriften der Gesellschaft für Theatergeschichte, 6 (Berlin: Gesellschaft für Theatergeschichte, 1905)
—— 'Schauspielerbriefe. 23 Briefe A.W. Ifflands und zwar 21 an Goethe und Kirms, je 1 an H.A.O. Reichard und G. Forster. 2 Briefe von Frie-

derike Unzelmann-Bethmann an Goethe', *Goethe-Jahrbuch* 26 (1905), 51–92

Iffland, August Wilhelm, *Albert von Thurneisen. Ein bürgerliches Trauerspiel in vier Aufzügen* (Mannheim: Schwan, 1781)

—— *Albert von Thurneisen. Ein bürgerliches Trauerspiel in vier Aufzügen*, ed. by Alexander Košenina (Hanover: Wehrhahn Verlag, 1998)

—— *Almanach für Theater und Theaterfreunde* (Berlin: Oehmigke jun., 1807)

—— *Almanach fürs Theater 1811* (Berlin: Saalfeld, 1811)

—— *Almanach fürs Theater 1812* (Berlin: Duncker & Humblot, 1812)

—— *Beiträge für die Deutsche Schaubühne: In Übersetzungen und Bearbeitungen ausländischer Schauspiele*, 5 vols (Berlin: Braunes, 1807–12)

—— *Bewußtseyn. Ein Schauspiel in fünf Aufzügen* (Berlin: Decker, 1787)

—— *Elise von Valberg. Ein Schauspiel in funf Aufzügen* (Leipzig: Göschen, 1792)

—— *Fragmente über Menschendarstellung auf den deutschen Bühnen. Erste Sammlung* (Gotha: Ettinger, 1785)

—— *Die Hagestolzen. Ein Lustspiel* (Leipzig: Göschen, 1793)

—— *Die Jäger. Ein ländliches Sittengemälde in fünf Aufzügen* (Berlin: Decker, 1785)

—— *Die Jäger. Ein ländliches Sittengemälde in fünf Aufzügen*, ed. by Jörg Mathes (Stuttgart: Reclam, 1976)

—— *Die Kokarden. Ein Trauerspiel in fünf Aufzügen* (Leipzig: Göschen, 1791)

—— *Der Komet. Eine Posse in einem Aufzug*, ed. by Claude. D. Conter and Johannes Birgfeld (Hanover: Wehrhahn Verlag, 2006)

—— *Die Mündel. Ein Schauspiel in fünf Aufzügen* (Berlin: Decker, 1785)

—— *Meine theatralische Laufbahn. Mit Anmerkungen und einer Zeittafel von Oscar Fambach* (Stuttgart: Reclam, 1976)

—— *Reue versöhnt. Ein Schauspiel in fünf Aufzügen* (Berlin: Decker, 1789)

—— *Theater*, 24 vols (Vienna: Klang, 1843)

—— 'Briefe über die Schauspielkunst', *Rheinische Beiträge zur Gelehrsamkeit*, 1781/1, 65–69; 1781/11, 364–73; 1781/12, 451–56; 1782/1, 50–59

—— *Über Schauspieler und Schauspielkunst. Ausgewählte Abhandlungen von August Wilhelm Iffland und Johann Gottfried Seume* (Dresden: Verlag der Kunst, 1954), pp. 23–34

—— *Verbrechen aus Ehrsucht. Ein ernsthaftes Familiengemälde in fünf Aufzügen* (Mannheim: Schwan, 1784)

Minor, Jakob, *Aus dem Schiller-Archiv. Ungedrucktes und Unbekanntes zu Schillers Leben und Schriften* (Weimar: Böhlau, 1890)

Schiller, Friedrich, *Schillers Don Karlos. Edition der ursprünglichen Fassung und entstehungsgeschichtlicher Kommentar*, ed. by Paul Böckmann (Stuttgart: Klett, 1974)

—— *Schillers Kabale und Liebe. Das Mannheimer Soufflierbuch*, ed. by Herbert Kraft (Mannheim: Bibliographisches Institut, 1963)

—— *Schillers Räuber. Urtext des Mannheimer Soufflierbuches*, ed. by Herbert Stubenrauch and Günter Schulz (Mannheim: Bibliographisches Institut, 1959)

—— *Schillers Werke. Nationalausgabe*, ed. by Julius Petersen and others, 42 vols (Weimar: Hermann Böhlaus Nachfolger, 1943–)

—— *Schiller, Werke und Briefe*, ed. by Otto Dann and others, 12 vols (Frankfurt am Main: Deutscher Klassiker Verlag, 1988–2004)

—— *Schiller, Werke und Briefe. Berliner Ausgabe*, ed. by Jochen Golz and others (Berlin: Aufbau Verlag, 2005)

Other primary sources (including repertoires)

Alth, Minna von (ed. for the Österreichischer Bundestheaterverband), *Burgtheater 1776–1976. Aufführungen und Besetzungen von zweihundert Jahren*, 2 vols (Vienna: Ueberreuter, 1979)

Annalen des Theaters, ed. by Christian August Bertram, 20 vols (Berlin: Maurer, 1788–1797)

Anon. (Reinhold, Carl), *Saat von Göthe gesäet dem Tage der Garben zu reifen. Ein Handbuch für Aesthetiker und junge Schauspieler* (Weimar and Leipzig: n.p., 1808)

Böttiger, Karl August, *Entwickelung des Ifflandischen Spiels in vierzehn Darstellungen auf dem Weimarischen Hoftheater im Aprillmonath 1796* (Leipzig: Göschen, 1796)

—— *Literarische Zustände und Zeitgenossen. Begegnungen und Gespräche im klassischen Weimar*, ed. by Klaus Gerlach and René Sternke, 3rd edn (Berlin: Aufbau Verlag, 1998)

Burkhardt, Carl August Hugo, *Das Repertoire des Weimarischen Hoftheaters unter Goethes Leitung, 1791–1817*, Theatergeschichtliche Forschungen, 1 (Leipzig: Voss, 1891)

Briefwechsel des Herzogs-Großherzogs Carl August mit Goethe, ed. by Hans Wahl, 3 vols (Berlin: Mittler, 1915)

Ekhof, Conrad, 'Ungedruckte Briefe Conrad Ekhofs. Aus der Handschrift veröffentlicht und erläutert von Professor Ludwig Geiger', *Bühne und Welt*, 7 (1905), 657–64

Eichendorff, Joseph von, *Sämtliche Werke des Freiherrn Joseph von Eichendorff*, ed. by Wilhelm Kosch and August Sauer, 22 vols (Regensburg: Habbel, 1908–86)

Fambach, Oscar, *Das Repertorium des Hof- und Nationaltheaters in Mannheim 1804–1832* (Bonn: Bouvier, 1980)

—— *Das Repertorium des Stadttheaters zu Leipzig 1817–1828* (Bonn: Bouvier, 1980)

—— *Das Repertorium des Königlichen Theaters und der italienischen Oper zu Dresden 1814–1832. Mit einem Vorwort und 4 Registern* (Bonn: Bouvier, 1985)

Forster, Georg, *Georg Forsters Werke. Sämtliche Schriften, Tagebücher, Briefe*, ed. by the Akademie der Wissenschaften der DDR and the Berlin–Brandenburgische Akademie der Wissenschaften (Berlin: Akademie-Verlag, 1958–)

Genast, Eduard, *Aus dem Tagebuch eines alten Schauspielers*, 4 vols, (Leipzig: Voigt & Günther, 1862–66)

Gerlach, Klaus, Datenbank Berliner Nationaltheater, Berliner Klassik (research project of the Berlin-Brandenburgische Akademie der Wissenschaften), http://zopeman.bbaw.de/BK/theater

Goethe, Johann Wolfgang von, *Goethes Werke. Herausgegeben im Auftrag der Großherzogin Sophie von Sachsen*. Four divisions, 143 vols (Weimar: Böhlau, 1887–1919)

—— *Johann Wolfgang Goethe. Sämtliche Werke. Briefe, Tagebücher und Gespräche*, ed. by Hendrik Birus and others, two divisions, 40 vols (Frankfurt am Main: Deutscher Klassiker Verlag, 1987–99)

—— *Johann Wolfgang Goethe. Sämtliche Werke nach Epochen seines Schaffens. Münchner Ausgabe*, ed. by Karl Richter in collaboration with Herbert Göpfert and others. 21 vols in 30 (Munich: Hanser, 1985–99)

Gotter, Friedrich Wilhelm, *Gedichte*, 3 vols (Gotha: Ettinger, 1788)

—— *Der schwarze Mann. Eine Posse in zwey Akten*, ed. by Michael Rüppel, Vergessene Texte des 18. Jahrhunderts, 7 (Hanover: Revonnah Verlag, 1996)

Gottsched, Johann Christoph, *Die Deutsche Schaubühne. Faksimiledruck der Ausgabe von 1741–1742*, ed. by Horst Steinmetz, 6 vols (Stuttgart: Metzler, 1972)

Grumach, Ernst and Renate, *Goethe. Begegnungen und Gespräche*, 6 vols (Berlin: de Gruyter, 1965–)

Hahn, Karl-Heinz and others (eds), *Briefe an Goethe. Gesamtausgabe in Regestform,* 7 vols (Weimar: Böhlau, 1980–2004)

Herz, Henriette, *Henriette Herz in Erinnerungen, Briefen und Zeugnissen*, ed. by Rainer Schmitz (Leipzig and Weimar: Kiepenheuer, 1984)

Hiller, Johann Adam, *Autobiographie, Briefe und Nekrologe,* ed. by Mark Lehmstedt (Leipzig: Lehmstedt, 2004)

Hoven, Friedrich Wilhelm von, *Biographie des Doktor Friedrich Willhelm von Hoven, Königl. Bayer'schen Obermedizinrats* (Nuremberg: Schrag, 1840), later reprinted as *Lebenserinnerungen,* ed. by Hans-Günter Thalheim and Evelyn Laufer (Berlin: Rütten & Loeng, 1984)

Jördens, Karl Heinrich, *Lexikon deutscher Dichter und Prosaisten*, vol. 2 (Leipzig: Weidmann, 1807)

La Roche, Sophie, *Briefe über Mannheim* (Zurich: Orell, Gessner & Füssli, 1791)

Lecke, Bodo (ed.), *Dichter über ihre Dichtungen. Friedrich Schiller*, 2 vols (Munich: Heimeran, 1970)

Lessing, Gotthold Ephraim, *Das Theater des Herrn Diderot*, 2 vols (Leipzig: Voss, 1760)

——*Gotthold Ephraim Lessings Werke und Briefe*, ed. by Wilfried Barner and others, 12 vols (Frankfurt am Main: Deutscher Klassiker Verlag, 1985–)

Litzmann, Berthold, *Schröder und Gotter. Eine Episode aus der deutschen Theatergeschichte*, (Hamburg and Leipzig: Voss, 1887)

Martersteig, Max, *Die Protokolle des Mannheimer Nationaltheaters unter Dalberg aus den Jahren 1781 bis 1789* (Mannheim: Bensheimer, 1890)

Reinwald, Christophine, 'Schillers Jugendjahre. Eine Skizze von Christophine Reinwald geb. Schiller. Mitgetheilt von Robert Boxberger, *Archiv für Litteraturgeschichte*, 1 (Leipzig: Teubner, 1870), pp. 452–60

Schäffer, C. and C. Hartmann, *Die Königlichen Theater in Berlin. Statistischer Rückblick auf die künstlerische Thätigkeit und die Personal-Verhältnisse während des Zeitraums vom 5. December 1786 bis 31. December 1885* (Berlin: Berliner Verlags-Comtoir AG, 1886)

Schlegel, August Wilhelm, *Kritische Schriften und Briefe*, ed. by Edgar Lohner, 7 vols (Stuttgart: Kohlhammer, 1962–74)

Schmidt, Friedrich Ludwig, *Denkwürdigkeiten*, ed. by Hermann Uhde, 2nd edn, 2 vols (Stuttgart: Cotta, 1878)

Stengel, Stephan von, *Denkwürdigkeiten*, ed. by Günther Ebersold (Mannheim: Palatium Verlag, 1993)

Streicher, Andreas, *Schillers Flucht*. New edition by Paul Raabe (Stuttgart: Steinkopf, 1959)

Tieck, Ludwig, *Ludwig Tieck's Schriften*, 28 vols (Berlin: Reimer, 1828)

—— *Schriften*, ed. by Manfred Frank and others, 12 vols (Frankfurt am Main: Deutscher Klassiker Verlag, 1985–)

Trierweiler, *Tagebuch der Mannheimer Schaubühne*, 2 vols (Mannheim: Schwan, 1786, 1787)

Walter, Friedrich, *Archiv und Bibliothek des Großh. Hof- und Nationaltheaters in Mannheim 1779–1839*, 2 vols (Leipzig: Hirzel, 1899)

Wolzogen, Caroline von, *Literarischer Nachlaß der Frau Caroline von Wolzogen*, ed. by D.R. Hase, 2 vols (Leipzig: Breitkopf & Härtel, 1848/49)

Varnhagen von Ense, Karl, *Denkwürdigkeiten des eigenen Lebens*, ed. by Joachim Kühn, 2 vols (Berlin: Wegweiser Verlag, 1922)

Zeitung für die elegante Welt, ed. by Karl von Spazier (Berlin: Janke, 1801–42)

Secondary sources

Alafberg, Fritz, *Wolfgang Heribert von Dalberg als Bühnenleiter und als Dramatiker* (Berlin: Ebering, 1907)

Altmann, Wilhelm, 'Ifflands Rechtfertigung seiner Theaterverwaltung vom. 27. Juli 1813', in *Archiv für Theatergeschichte*, vol. 1, ed. by Hans Devrient (Berlin: Fleischel, 1904), pp. 86–94

Bauman, Thomas, *North German Opera in the Age of Goethe* (Cambridge: CUP, 1985)

Bellmann, Günther, *Schauspielhausgeschichten. 250 Jahre Theater und Musik auf dem Berliner Gendarmenmarkt* (Berlin: Links, 1993)

Bender, Wolfgang (ed.), *Schauspielkunst im 18. Jahrhundert. Grundlagen, Praxis, Autoren* (Stuttgart: Steiner, 1992)

—— Siegfried Bushuven and Michael Huesmann, *Theaterperiodika des 18. Jahrhunderts. Bibliographie und inhaltliche Erschließung deutschsprachiger Theaterzeitschriften, Theaterkalender und Theatertaschenbücher*, Teil 1: 1750–1780, 2 vols, Teil 2: 1781–1790, 3 vols, (Munich, New Providence, London: Saur, 1994)

Bienert, Michael, *Schiller in Berlin oder Das rege Leben einer großen Stadt*, Marbacher Magazin, 106 (Marbach am Neckar: Deutsche Schillergesellschaft, 2004)

Binneberg, Kurt, 'A.W. Ifflands Gothaer Jahre. Kritische Anmerkungen zu seiner Autobiographie', in *Sammeln und Sichten. Festschrift für Oscar Fambach zum 80. Geburtstag*, ed. by Joachim Krause, Norbert Oellers and Karl Konrad Polheim (Bonn: Bouvier, 1982), pp. 158–82

—— 'Zwischen Schwärmerei und Realismus. Die beiden Textfassungen von A.W. Ifflands Drama *Die Jäger*', in *Textkritik und Interpretation. Festschrift für Karl Konrad Polheim zum 60. Geburtstag,* ed. by Heimo Reinitzer (Frankfurt am Main, Berne: Lang, 1987), pp. 161–75

Blanning, Timothy C.W., *Reform and Revolution in Mainz 1743–1803* (Cambridge: CUP, 1974)

Brachvogel, Albert E., *Geschichte des Berliner Theaters*, 2 vols (Berlin: Janke, 1877, 1878)

Brandt, George W. and Wiebke Hogendoorn, *German and Dutch Theatre 1600–1848* (Cambridge: CUP, 1992)

Braun, Julius W., *Schiller und Goethe im Urtheil ihrer Zeitgenossen. Zeitungskritiken, Berichte und Notizen*, 3 vols (Leipzig: Schlicke, 1882)

Brauneck, Manfred, *Die Welt als Bühne. Geschichte des europäischen Theaters* (Stuttgart, Weimar: Metzler, 1996)

Brown, Jane K., 'Drama and Theatrical Practice in Weimar Classicism', in *The Literature of Weimar Classicism*, ed. by Simon Richter, The Camden House History of German Literature, 7 (Rochester, NY: Camden House, 2005), pp. 133–64

Bruford, Walter H., *Germany in the Eighteenth Century* (Cambridge: CUP, 1935)

—— *Theatre, Drama and Audience in Goethe's Germany* (London: Routledge and Kegan Paul, 1950)

—— *Culture and Society in Classical Weimar* (Cambridge: CUP, 1962)

Buchwald, Reinhard, 'Herzog Karl Eugen gründet ein Nationaltheater' in *Gestaltung Umgestaltung. Festschrift Hermann August Korff*, ed. by Joachim Müller (Leipzig: Koehler & Amelang, 1957), pp. 76–91

Carlson, Marvin, *Goethe and the Weimar Theatre* (Ithaca and London: Cornell University Press, 1978)

Daniel, Ute, *Hoftheater: Zur Geschichte des Theaters und der Höfe im 18. und im 19. Jahrhundert* (Stuttgart: Klett-Cotta, 1995)

Daunicht, Richard, 'Von Doebbelin zu Iffland. Das Berliner Nationaltheater, 1786 bis 1814', *Theater der Zeit*, 11 (1956), 7–16

Devrient, Eduard, *Geschichte der deutschen Schauspielkunst*, new extended edition by Willy Stuhlfeld (Berlin: Eigenbrödler, 1929)

Devrient, Hans, *Johann Friedrich Schönemann und seine Schauspielergesell-schaft*, Theatergeschichtliche Forschungen, 11 (Hamburg and Leipzig: Voss, 1895)

Dewhurst, Kenneth and Nigel Reeves, *Friedrich Schiller. Medicine, Psychology and Literature* (Oxford: Sandford, 1978)

Doebber, Adolph, *Lauchstädt und Weimar. Eine theatergeschichtliche Studie* (Berlin: Mittler, 1908)

Eloesser, Arthur, *Das bürgerliche Drama. Seine Geschichte im 18. und 19. Jahrhundert* (Berlin: Hertz, 1898).

Fetting, Hugo, *Conrad Ekhof. Ein Schauspieler des achtzehnten Jahrhunderts*, (Berlin: Henschelverlag, 1954)

—— 'Das Repertoire des Berliner Königlichen Nationaltheaters unter der Leitung von August Wilhelm Iffland (1796–1814) bei Berücksichtigung der künstlerischen Prinzipien und kulturpolitischen Wirkungsfaktoren', unpublished dissertation, University of Greifswald, 1977

Fischer-Dieskau, Dietrich, *Goethe als Intendant* (Munich: DTV, 2006)

Fischer-Lichte, Erika, *Kurze Geschichte des deutschen Theaters* (Tübingen and Basel: UTB, 1993)

Flemming, Willi, *Goethe und das Theater seiner Zeit* (Stuttgart: Kohlhammer, 1968)

Frank, Bernhard, *Die erste Frankfurter Theater AG (1792–1842) in ihrer Entwicklung von der 'Nationalbühne' zur 'Volksbühne'. Ein Beitrag zur Erforschung von Schauspiel-Stil und Regie des 19. Jahrhunderts*, Studien zur Frankfurter Geschichte, 2 (Frankfurt am Main: Kramer, 1967)

Frantzke, Thomas, *Goethes Schauspiele mit Gesang und Singspiele 1773–82* (Frankfurt am Main and Berne: Lang, 1998)

Freydank, Ruth, '"Es ist Ihr Triumph, nicht meiner …" Ifflands Berliner Schiller-Inszenierungen', *Theater der Zeit*, 5 (1987), 22–25

—— *Theater in Berlin* (Berlin: Henschelverlag, 1988)

Frick, Werner, 'Klassische Präsenzen. Die Weimarer Dramatik und das Berliner Nationaltheater unter Iffland und Graf Brühl', in *Wechselwirkungen. Kunst und Wissenschaft in Berlin und Weimar im Zeichen Goethes*, ed. by Ernst Osterkamp (Berne, Berlin, Frankfurt am Main: Lang, 2003), pp. 231–66

Gall, Lothar, *Bürgertum in Deutschland* (Berlin: Siedler, 1989)

Genée, Rudolph, *Hundert Jahre des Königlichen Schauspiels in Berlin 1786–1886* (Berlin: Hofmann, 1886)

Glaser, Horst, *Das bürgerliche Rührstück, Analekten zum Zusammenhang von Sentimentalität mit Autorität in der trivialen Dramatik Schröders,*

278

Ifflands, Kotzebues und anderer Autoren am Ende des 18. Jahrhunderts (Stuttgart: Metzler, 1969)

Golz, Anita and Jochen, '"Ernst ist das Leben, heiter sey die Kunst": Goethe als Redakteur des "Wallenstein"-Prologs', in *Im Vorfeld der Literatur. Vom Wert archivalischer Überlieferung für das Verständnis von Literatur und ihrer Geschichte*, ed. by Karl-Heinz Hahn (Weimar: Böhlau, 1991), pp. 17–29

Hajdecki, Alexander, 'Iffland und sein Wiener Engagement zum Theaterdirektor im Jahre 1809. Eine archivalische Literaturstudie', *Erdgeist* 3/2 (1908), 41–45

Hartmann, Horst, 'Das Mannheimer Theater am Ausgang des 18. Jahrhunderts', in *Theaterinstitution und Kulturtransfer II*, ed. by Anke Detken and others (Tübingen: Narr, 1998), pp. 123–34

Hartmann, Tina, *Goethes Musiktheater. Singspiele, Opern, Festspiele, 'Faust'* (Tübingen: Niemeyer, 2004)

Heinz, Andrea, *Quantitive Spielplanforschung. Neue Möglichkeiten der Theatergeschichtsschreibung am Beispiel des Hoftheaters zu Coburg und Gotha (1827–1918)*, Jenaer Germanistische Forschungen, Neue Folge, 4 (Heidelberg: Winter, 1999)

Herrmann, Wilhelm, *Thaliens liebster Sohn. Iffland und Mannheim* (Mannheim: Gesellschaft der Freunde des Mannheimer Nationaltheater e.V., 1960)

——'August Wilhelm Iffland und die Leininger Fürsten', *Mitteilungen des historischen Vereins der Pfalz*, 65 (1967), 208–29

—— *Hoftheater – Volkstheater – Nationaltheater* (Frankfurt am Main, Berne: Lang, 1999)

Hoecker, Gustav, *August Wilhelm Iffland, der Menschendarsteller, Dichter und Bühnenleiter* (Glogau: Flemming, n.d.)

Holstein, Hugo, 'Zu Schillers Reise nach Berlin', *Studien zur vergleichenden Literaturgeschichte* 4/4 (1904), 471–75

Homering, Liselotte and Karin Welck (eds), *Mannheim und sein Nationaltheater. Menschen – Geschichte(n) – Perspektiven* (Mannheim: Palatium Verlag/ Reiss-Museum, 1998)

Howald, Ernst, '*Elise von Valberg*. Zur Aesthetik des Rührstücks', in *Philosophischer Eros im Wandel der Zeit* (Munich, Vienna: Oldenbourg, 1965), pp. 233–41

Huber, Peter, 'Goethes praktische Theaterarbeit' in *Goethe Handbuch*, vol. 2, *Dramen*, ed. by Theo Buck (Stuttgart: Metzler, 1996), pp. 23–30

Kindermann, Heinz, *Theatergeschichte Europas*, vols 4 and 5 (Salzburg: Otto Müller, 1961, 1962)

Klingenberg, Karl-Heinz, *Iffland und Kotzebue als Dramatiker* (Weimar: Arion Verlag, 1962)

Knudsen, Hans, 'Die Hamburger Uraufführung des *Don Karlos* und ihre Darsteller', *Die Scene*, 8, Hefte 10–12 (1918), 134–37

Koffka, Wilhelm K., *Iffland und Dalberg. Geschichte der classischen Theaterzeit Mannheims* (Leipzig: Weber, 1865)

Kopelke, Wolfdietrich, *Was wir bringen. Das Weimarische Hoftheater unter Goethe* (Bonn: Dümmler, 1987)

Kosch, Wilhelm, *Theater und Dramen des 19. Jahrhunderts* (Leipzig: Dyk, 1913)

Košenina, Alexander, *Anthropologie und Schauspielkunst. Studien zur 'eloquentia corporis' im 18. Jahrhundert*, Theatron, 11 (Tübingen: Niemeyer, 1995)

Krämer, Jörg, *Deutschsprachiges Musiktheater im späten 18. Jahrhundert. Typologie, Dramaturgie und Anthropologie einer populären Gattung*, 2 vols (Tübingen: Niemeyer, 1998)

Krause, Markus, *Das Trivialdrama der Goethezeit 1780–1805. Produktion und Rezeption* (Bonn: Bouvier, 1982)

Krauss, Rudolph, *Das Stuttgarter Hoftheater von den ältesten Zeiten bis zur Gegenwart* (Stuttgart: Metzler, 1908)

Krebs, Roland, *L'Idée de 'Théâtre National' dans l'Allemagne des Lumières. Théorie et Réalisations*, Wolfenbüttler Forschungen, 28 (Wiesbaden: Harrassowitz, 1985)

Krükl, Karl, *Leben und Werk des elsässischen Schriftstellers Anton von Klein. Ein Beitrag zur Geschichte der Aufklärung in der Pfalz* (Strassburg: Oleire, 1901)

Kunze, Walter, *Goethes Theaterleitung im Urteil der Zeitgenossen* (Munich: Wolf, 1942)

Lampe, Karl, *Studien über Iffland als Dramatiker mit besonderer Berücksichtigung der ersten Dramen* (Celle: Ströher, 1899)

Langer, Suzanne K., *Feeling and Form. A Theory of Art developed from 'Philosophy in a New Key'* (London: Routledge and Kegan Paul, 1953)

Laube, Heinrich, *Das norddeutsche Theater. Ein neuer Beitrag zur deutschen Theatergeschichte* (Leipzig: Weber, 1872)

Linder, Jutta, *Ästhetische Erziehung. Goethe und das Weimarer Hoftheater* (Bonn: Bouvier, 1990)

Ludwigsburger Schlossfestspiele (ed.), *Das Ludwigsburger Schloßtheater. Kultur und Geschichte eines Hoftheaters* (Stuttgart: DRW-Verlag, 1998)

Marquard, Marion, 'Zur Bedeutung der Singspiele von Weisse und Hiller für den französisch–sächsischen Kulturtransfer im 18. Jahrhundert', *Cahiers d'Etudes Germaniques*, 28 (1995), 95–108

Martens, Wolfgang, 'Der Literat als Demagoge. Zum Thema der poetischen Gefährlichkeit des Schriftstellers um 1790, entwickelt am Beispiel von Ifflands Antirevolutionsdrama *Die Kokarden*', in *Presse und Geschichte. Beiträge zur historischen Kommunikationsforschung I* (Munich: Verlag Dokumentation, 1977), pp. 100–36

Martersteig, Max, *Das deutsche Theater im 19. Jahrhundert. Eine kulturgeschichtliche Darstellung* (Leipzig: Breitkopf & Härtel, 1904)

Matthes, Isabel, *'Der allgemeinen Vereinigung gewidmet': Öffentlicher Theaterbau in Deutschland zwischen Aufklärung und Vormärz* (Tübingen: Niemeyer, 1995).

Maurer-Schmook, Sibylle, *Deutsches Theater im 18. Jahrhundert* (Tübingen: Niemeyer, 1982)

Meyer, Herbert, 'Schiller und der Theaterdichter Flickwort. Betrachtungen zu einem unbekannten Brief Gotters', *Mannheimer Hefte*, 1961/ Heft 1, 14–22

Michelsen, Peter, 'Die große Bühne' in Michelsen, *Der Bruch mit der Vaterwelt. Studien zu Schillers 'Räubern'*, Beihefte zum *Euphorion*, 16 (Heidelberg: Winter, 1979), pp. 9–63.

Mönch, Cornelia, *Abschrecken und Mitleiden. Das deutsche bürgerliche Trauerspiel im 18. Jahrhundert. Versuch einer Typologie* (Tübingen: Niemeyer, 1993)

Mortier, Roland, *Diderot en Allemagne (1750–1850)* (Paris: Presses Universitaires de France, 1954), translated as *Diderot in Deutschland* (Stuttgart: Metzler, 1972)

Niehaus, Michael, 'Voreilige Reden, zurückgehaltene Worte. Familienkommunikation bei Iffland', in *Das Unterhaltungsstück um 1800. Literaturhistorische Konfigurationen – Signaturen der Moderne*, ed. by Johannes Birgfeld and Claude D. Conter (Hanover: Wehrhahn Verlag, 2006), pp.121–43

Niggl, Günter, *Geschichte der deutschen Autobiographie im 18. Jahrhundert. Theoretische Grundlegung und literarische Entfaltung* (Stuttgart: Metzler, 1977)

Oellers, Norbert, *Schiller. Geschichte seiner Wirkung bis zu Goethes Tod* (Bonn: Bouvier, 1967)

——'Die Heiterkeit der Kunst. Goethe variiert Schiller', in *Edition als Wissenschaft. Festschrift für Hans Zeller*, ed. by Gunter Martens and

Winfried Woesler, Beihefte zu *Editio*, 2 (Tübingen: Niemeyer, 1991), pp. 92–103

Orel, Alfred, *Goethe als Operndirektor* (Bregenz: Russ, 1949)

Pargner, Birgit, *Zwischen Tränen und Kommerz. Das Rührtheater Charlotte Birch-Pfeiffers (1800–1868) in seiner künstlerischen und kommerziellen Verwertung* (Bielfeld: Aisthesis, 1999)

Pasqué, Ernst, *Goethes Theaterleitung in Weimar. In Episoden und Urkunden*, 2 vols (Leipzig: Weber, 1863)

Paulin, Roger, *The Critical Reception of Shakespeare in Germany 1682– 1914. Native Literature and Foreign Genius* (Hildesheim, Zurich, New York: Olms, 2003)

Petersen, Julius, *Schiller und die Bühne. Ein Beitrag zur Litteratur- und Theatergeschichte der klassischen Zeit* (Berlin: Mayer & Müller, 1904)

—— 'Schiller und das Weimarer Theater', *Jahrbuch der Goethe-Gesellschaft*, 8 (1921), 179–95

—— (ed.), *Schillers 'Piccolomini' auf dem Kgl. National-Theater zu Berlin. Ifflands Regiebuch der Erstaufführung am 18. 2. 1799* (Berlin: Gesellschaft für Theatergeschichte, 1941)

Pichler, Anton, *Chronik des Großherzoglichen Hof- und Nationaltheaters in Mannheim* (Mannheim: Bensheimer, 1879)

Pinatel, Joseph, *Le drame bourgeois en Allemagne au XVIIIme siècle* (Lyon: Bosc et Riou, 1938)

Pugh, David, *Dialectic of Love: Platonism in Schiller's Aesthetics* (Montreal and Kingston, Ont.: McGill–Queen's University Press, 1996)

Reichard, Georg, *August Wilhelm Schlegels 'Ion'. Das Schauspiel und die Aufführungen unter der Leitung von Goethe und Iffland* (Bonn: Bouvier, 1987)

Reus Klaus-Dieter (ed.), *Faszination der Bühne: Barockes Welttheater in Bayreuth, Barocke Bühnentechnik in Europa. Eine Dokumentation der Ausstellung des Grundkurses Theatergeschichte am Gymnasium Christian-Ernestinum* (Bayreuth: Gymnasium Christian-Ernestinum, 1999)

Riedel, Wolfgang, *Die Anthropologie des jungen Schiller* (Würzburg: Königshausen & Neumann, 1985)

Rippere, Victoria, *Schiller and 'Alienation'* (Frankfurt am Main, Berne, Las Vegas: Lang, 1981).

Rudloff-Hille, Gertrud, *Schiller auf der deutschen Bühne seiner Zeit* (Weimar and Berlin: Aufbau Verlag, 1969)

Salehi, Sigrid, *August Wilhelm Ifflands dramatisches Werk. Versuch einer Neubewertung* (Frankfurt am Main, Berne: Lang, 1990)

Satori-Neumann, Bruno, *Die Frühzeit des Weimarischen Hoftheaters unter Goethes Leitung (1791 bis 1798)*, Schriften der Gesellschaft für Theatergeschichte, 31 (Berlin: Elsner, 1922)

Schings, Hans-Jürgen, *Die Brüder des Marquis Posa. Schiller und der Geheimbund der Illuminaten* (Tübingen: Niemeyer 1996)

Schlösser, Rudolf, *Friedrich Wilhelm Gotter. Sein Leben und seine Werke. Ein Beitrag zur Geschichte der Bühne und Bühnendichtung im 18. Jahrhundert*, Theatergeschichtliche Forschungen, 10 (Hamburg and Leipzig: Voss, 1894)

—— *Vom Hamburger Nationaltheater zur Gothaer Hofbühne 1767–1779*, Theatergeschichtliche Forschungen, 13 (Hamburg and Leipzig: Voss, 1895)

Schmidt, Otto, 'Die Uraufführung der *Räuber* – ein theatergeschichtliches Ereignis', in *Schillers Räuber. Urtext des Mannheimer Soufflierbuches*, ed. by Herbert Stubenrauch and Günter Schulz (Mannheim: Bibliographisches Institut, 1959), pp. 151–80

Schmitt, Peter, *Schauspieler und Theaterbetrieb. Studien zur Sozialgeschichte des Schauspielerstandes im deutschsprachigen Raum 1700–1900*, Theatron, 5 (Tübingen: Niemeyer, 1990)

Schmieden, Alfred, *Die bühnegerechten Einrichtungen der Schillerschen Dramen für das Königliche Nationaltheater zu Berlin. Erster Teil. 'Wilhelm Tell'* (Berlin: Fleischel, 1906)

Schneider, Louis, 'Iffland als Direktor des Berliner National-Theaters', *Almanach für Freunde der Schauspielkunst* (Berlin: Duncker & Humblot, 1852–54), Part 1, 1852, pp. 76–109, Part 2 1853, pp. 71–92, Part 3 1854, pp. 126–78

Schrickel, Leonhard, *Geschichte des Weimarer Theaters von seinen Anfängen bis heute* (Weimar: Pause, 1928)

Schulz, Günter, 'Zwei Schiller-Autographen', in *Jahrbuch der Deutschen Schiller-Gesellschaft*, 3 (1959), 19–33

Schusky, Renate, *Das deutsche Singspiel im 18. Jahrhundert. Quellen und Zeugnisse zu Ästhetik und Rezeption* (Bonn: Bouvier, 1980)

Sengle, Friedrich, 'Goethes Nachspiel zu Ifflands Hagestolzen (1815), in *Zwischen Aufklärung und Restauration. Sozialer Wandel in der deutschen Literatur (1700–1848)*, ed. by Wolfgang Frühwald and Alberto Martino (Tübingen: Niemeyer, 1989), pp. 307–16

Sharpe, Lesley, 'Schiller and Goethe's *Egmont*', *Modern Language Review*, 77 (1982), 629–45

——'Schiller and Goethe's *Iphigenie*', *Publications of the English Goethe Society*, 54 (1984), 101–22

283

—— 'Voltaire's *Mahomet* and the Repertoire of the Weimar Court Theatre' in *Nachdenklicher Leichtsinn. Aufsätze zu Goethe und Goetherezeption*, ed. by Heike Bartel and Brian Keith-Smith (Lewiston, N.Y. and Lampeter: Mellen, 2000), pp. 155–67

—— 'Schiller and the Mannheim National Theatre', *Modern Language Review*, 100 (2005), 121–37

—— 'Schillers *Egmont*-Bearbeitung im theatralischen Kontext', *Goethe-Jahrbuch*, 112 (2005), 137–46

Sheehan, James, *German History 1770–1866*, The Oxford History of Modern Europe (Oxford: OUP, 1989)

Sichardt, Gisela, *Das Weimarer Liebhabertheater unter Goethes Leitung* (Weimar: Arion Verlag, 1957)

Siedhoff, Sigrid, *Der Dramaturg Schiller. 'Egmont'. Goethes Text – Schillers Bearbeitung* (Bonn: Bouvier, 1983)

Sittard, Joseph, *Zur Geschichte der Musik und des Theaters am Württembergischen Hof*, 2 vols (Stuttgart: Kohlhammer, 1890)

Sørensen, Bengt Algot, *Herrschaft und Zärtlichkeit. Der Patriarchalismus und das Drama im 18. Jahrhundert* (Munich: Beck, 1984)

Stahl, Ernst Leopold, *Das Mannheimer Nationaltheater. Ein Jahrhundert deutscher Theaterkultur im Reich* (Mannheim: Bensheimer, 1929)

—— *Das europäische Mannheim: die Wege zum deutschen Nationaltheater* (Mannheim: Hakenkreuzbanner-Verlag, 1940)

Steiner, Gerhard, '"Unmittelbare Gegenwart der beseelten Natur". Georg Forster und der Schauspieler Iffland', in *Der Weltumsegler und seine Freunde*, ed. by Detlef Rasmussen (Tübingen: Narr, 1988), 101–15

Stubenrauch, Herbert, *'Mein Klima ist das Theater': Schiller und Mannheim. Sonderausgabe zum 150. Todestag Friedrich Schillers* (Mannheim: Südwest-Werbung, 1955)

—— 'Musikus Miller im Turm. Schillers unbekannte Bühnenbearbeitung von *Kabale und Liebe*', *Weimarer Beiträge*, 1 (1955), 233–45

—— *Wolfgang Heribert von Dalberg. Lebensskizze und Lebenszeugnisse. Nationaltheater Mannheim: Bühnenblätter für die Spielzeit 1956/57* (Mannheim: Südwest-Werbung, 1957)

—— 'Schillers Fall – Zur Chronologie eines undatierten Schillerbriefes', *Jahrbuch der Deutschen Schillergesellschaft*, 1 (1957), 142–56

—— 'Schiller und die Schauspieler. Ein unveröffentlichter Brief Ifflands vom 19. Januar 1785', *Jahrbuch der Deutschen Schillergesellschaft*, 2 (1958), 43–59

Stümcke, Heinrich, *Iffland und das Berliner Königliche Nationaltheater. Gedenkrede gehalten in der Festsitzung der Gesellschaft für Theatergeschichte* (Leipzig: Wigand, 1909)

Teichmann, Johann Valentin, *Literarischer Nachlaß*, ed. by Franz Dingelstedt (Stuttgart: Cotta, 1863)

Uhde, Hermann, 'August Wilhelm Iffland' in *Westermanns Illustrierte Monatshefte* 26 (1869), 586–99

Uhland, Robert, *Geschichte der Hohen Karlsschule in Stuttgart* (Stuttgart: Kohlhammer, 1953)

Wahle, Julius, *Das Weimarer Hoftheater unter Goethes Leitung. Aus neuen Quellen bearbeitet* (Weimar: Verlag der Goethe-Gesellschaft, 1892)

Wahnrau, Gerhard, *Berlin, Stadt der Theater* (Berlin: Henschelverlag, 1957)

Waldura, Markus, 'Die Singspiele', in Theo Buck (ed.), *Goethe Handbuch*, vol. 2, *Dramen*, pp. 173–94

Walter, Friedrich, *Geschichte des Theaters und der Musik am Kurpfälzischen Hofe* (Leipzig: Breitkopf & Härtel, 1898)

Weichberger, Alexander, *Goethe und das Komödienhaus in Weimar 1779–1825*, Theatergeschichtliche Forschungen, 39 (Leipzig: Voss, 1928)

Weil, Rudolf, *Das Berliner Theaterpublikum unter A. W. Ifflands Direktion (1796 bis 1814). Ein Beitrag zur Methodologie der Theaterwissenschaft* (Berlin: Verlag der Gesellschaft für Theatergeschichte, 1932)

Wieczorck, Alfried (ed.), *Lebenslust und Frömmigkeit: Kurfürst Carl Theodor (1724–1799) zwischen Barock und Aufklärung*, 2 vols (Regensburg: Pustet, 1999)

—— and Liselotte Homering (eds), *SchillerZeit in Mannheim* (Mannheim: Reiss-Engelhorn-Museen; Mainz: von Zabern, 2005)

Wierlacher, Alois, 'August Wilhelm Iffland' in *Deutsche Dichter des 18. Jahrhunderts*, ed. by Benno von Wiese (Berlin: Schmidt, 1977), pp. 911–30

Wilkinson, E.M., 'Schiller's Concept of *Schein* in the Light of Recent Aesthetics', *German Quarterly*, 4 (1955), 219–27

Williams, Simon, *German Actors of the Eighteenth and Nineteenth Centuries. Idealism, Romanticism and Realism* (Westport, Conn. and London: Greenwood, 1985)

—— *Shakespeare on the German Stage*, vol. 1: 1586–1914 (Cambridge: CUP, 1990)

Wilpert, Gero von, *Schiller-Chronik* (Stuttgart: Kröner, 1958)

Yates, W.E., *Theatre in Vienna. A Critical History 1776–1995* (Cambridge: CUP, 1996)

Index

295

Das teutſche Comödienhaus.   *La Comédie allemande.*

Das Mannheimer Nationaltheater in der urſprünglichen Geſtaltung
durch Lorenzo Quaglio (1778)

Stich von Klauber   Schloßmuſeum Mannheim

1. The Mannheim National Theatre 1778.

2. Title page of A.W. Iffland's *Dramatische Werke* with portrait.

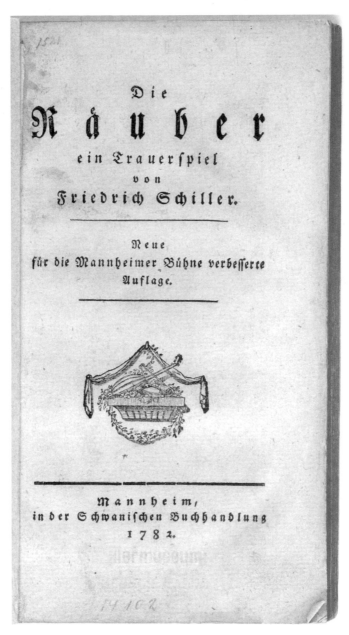

3. Title page of *Die Räuber ein Trauerspiel*.

Ich werde unfinnig, ich laufe davon!
II^r A. 3te fe.

4. 'Ich werde unsinnig, ich laufe davon!'
(*Die Räuber. Ein Schauspiel*, Act 2, Scene 3).

Das Hoftheater in Weimar nach dem Umbau durch Thouret.
1798—1825.

5. The Weimar Court Theatre after its reconstruction by Thouret.

6. *Wallensteins Lager.*

7. 'Mich, mich verrät man!': Iffland as Wallenstein.

Maria Stuart
in dem Trauerspiel gleiches Nahmens

8. Friederike Bethmann-Unzelmann as Maria Stuart.

9. The coronation procession from the Berlin production of
Die Jungfrau von Orléans.

10. *Die Braut von Messina.*

Britische und Irische Studien zur deutschen Sprache und Literatur

Nr. 23 Fred Whalley: The Elusive Transcendent. The Role of Religion in the Plays of Frank Wedekind, 2002. 204 S.

Nr. 24 Philip Ward: Hofmannsthal and Greek Myth: Expression and Performance, 2002. 295 S.

Nr. 25 Florian Krobb and Jeff Morrison (eds.): Poetry Project. Irish Germanists Interpret German Verse, 2003. 276 S.

Nr. 26 Andreas Kramer, Eric Robertson and Robert Vilain: A Bibliography of Yvan Goll. 2006. 377 S.

Nr. 27 Peter Hutchinson (ed.): Landmarks in German Drama, 2002. 244 S.

Nr. 28 W. E. Yates, Allyson Fiddler and John Warren (eds.): From Perinet to Jelinek. Viennese Theatre in its Political and Intellectual Context, 2001. 290 S.

Nr. 29 Hannah Burdekin: The Ambivalent Author. Five German Writers and their Jewish Characters, 1848–1914, 2002. 338 S.

Nr. 30 Elizabeth M. Wilkinson and L. A. Willoughby: Models of Wholeness. Some Attitudes to Language, Art and Life in the Age of Goethe. Edited by Jeremy Adler, Martin Swales and Ann Weaver, 2002. 271 S.

Nr. 31 Martin Kane (ed.): Legacies and Identity. East and West German Literary Responses to Unification, 2002. 209 S.

Nr. 32 Peter Hutchinson and Reinhard K. Zachau (eds.): Stefan Heym: Socialist – Dissenter – Jew; Stefan Heym: Sozialist – Dissident – Jude, 2003. 220 S.

Nr. 33 Peter Hutchinson (ed.): Landmarks in German Short Prose, 2003. 208 S.

Nr. 34 Matthew Philpotts: The Margins of Dictatorship: Assent and Dissent in the Work of Günter Eich and Bertolt Brecht, 2003. 377 S.

Nr. 35 Peter Hutchinson (ed.): Landmarks in German Comedy. 2006. 245 S.

Nr. 36 Eleoma Joshua: Friedrich Leopold Graf zu Stolberg and the German Romantics, 2005. 206 S.

Nr. 37 Janet Stewart and Simon Ward: Blueprints for No-Man's Land, 2005. 228 S.

Nr. 38 Paul E. Kerry (ed.): Friedrich Schiller. Playwright, Poet, Philosopher, Historian, 2007. 343 S.

Nr. 39 Hilary Brown (ed.): Landmarks in German Women's Writing, 2007. 213 S.

Nr. 40 Ruth Whittle & Debbie Pinfold: Voices of Rebellion: Political Writing by Malwida von Meysenbug, Fanny Lewald, Johanna Kinkel and Louise Aston, 2005. 208 S.

Nr. 41 John Warren and Ulrike Zitzlsperger (eds): Vienna Meets Berlin: Cultural Interaction 1918–1933, 2005. 298 S.

Nr. 42 Lesley Sharpe: A National Repertoire: Schiller, Iffland and the German Stage, 2007. 306 S.

Nr. 43 Frazer Clark: 'Zeitgeist and Zerrbild: Word, Image and Idea in German Satire 1800–1848, 2006. 297 S.

Nr. 44 Barbara Burns: 'The Prose Fiction of Louise von François (1817–1893), 2006. 151 S.